Contents

Secrets of
Performing
Confidence

For Actors, Musicians, Performers,
Presenters and Public Speakers

Andrew Evans

A & C Black • London

This book is for my son, Adam

First published 2003
by A & C Black Publishers Limited
37 Soho Square, London W1D 3QZ
www.acblack.com

ISBN 0-7136-6288-3

© Andrew John Evans 2003

A CIP catalogue record for this book is available from
the British Library.

A & C Black uses paper produced with elemental chlorine-free
pulp, harvested from managed sustainable forests.

Typeset in 10 on 11.5pt Photina
Printed and bound in Great Britain by
Creative Print and Design (Wales), Ebbw Vale

Introduction

It is frustrating to feel that we could do better, particularly in an increasingly competitive performing environment. Most of us know that we have untapped potential inside us, and can even realise it in rehearsal or in occasional peak performances. Most of us also know that under pressure and in front of critical professionals and audiences, self-doubt can degrade our performances and at times leave us in a state of despair as we feel we have performed well below our best.

This is why psychologists who specialise in performers, like those who work with top sportspeople, 'psych people up' for performances and events. It is these skills that we all need when we face audiences, and this book intends to run through the methods and theory that have helped many performers to achieve success in recent years.

The material and methods in this book have been developed over fifteen years of working with performers – mainly performing artists and people in the media – and also lawyers, computer programmers, senior executives and a whole range of people who have to stand up in front of colleagues and the public and perform effectively and with expertise.

Seeing individual performers for personal consultations over a time scale of several months, as I have done, has offered the opportunity to try new things out and see how they actually work in practice at various events, and then talk about them afterwards. This experience has provided a repertoire of helpful mental skills that appear to work for a wide range of people. Such tried and tested techniques form the basis of this book. What has worked has been continued and refined; what has not proved helpful has been discarded. The goal from the outset has been to give performers the tools and the understanding to cure themselves of the typical stresses and anxieties of the profession, so that they acquire the confidence of knowing that they can deal with the inner demons.

We already have a huge advantage in understanding the human being – we are one. With a little guidance, the way our minds and bodies work can become clearer to us, and we can make educated decisions as to how to handle situations, rather than leaving things to chance and good luck. As many sportspeople have joked 'It's funny – the more I practise, the luckier I get.'

I have had the privilege of playing a central part in the main UK clinics specialising in performing artists over the past fifteen years – Arts Psychology Consultants, the ISSTIP clinics, BPAMT, and the careers

1

section of the Dancers Career Development Trust. This book is built on a considerable amount of unique data in the Arts Psychology Consultants databank, drawn from over 500 performing artists, and covering personality traits, career values and preferences, team skills and various problems and their outcomes. In addition we have data from the other clinics in the UK. Problems such as stage fright figured prominently, and I have seen and treated over 120 cases of this.

Increasingly, burnout is becoming a problem, and because of competition in the business there are inevitably those who resettle in other jobs – often with great success – and who require a period of career counselling and general support during the period of transition. Dancers, of course, go through transition as an inevitable part of their career profile, and I have had the pleasure of seeing over sixty of our leading dancers in conjunction with this resettlement.

I believe that we can attribute success in the performing arts to four main factors: image, talent, hard work and attitude. Image, though important, is largely outside the scope of this book. Talent and creativity are covered in chapters one and ten, and work, preparation and practice in chapter four. Attitude is maybe the factor that is least understood and can be most improved. It covers not only personality, motivation and confidence (chapters one to three), but also some taught skills like career management, assertiveness and negotiating ability which are vital in today's competitive world. This elusive quality which we might call 'resourcefulness' also covers self-management, strategic thinking, self-promotion and dealing successfully with stressors and performance nerves, so that auditions and competitions can really advance one's career. There is an element of luck in achieving success, but performers frequently underestimate the importance of making the right moves, feeling well prepared, and being in the right place at the right time. There is, therefore, plenty of information throughout the book to help sharpen these skills.

This book is aimed at all performers and takes into account several recent developments in treating typical problems like stage fright. At this point, fifteen years after I first started dealing with performing artists, the theory and practice has moved on considerably, offering performers access to really modern and effective treatment plans. These are offered here in a self-help form and in language which is non-technical and easy to understand. The emphasis is on simplicity, effectiveness and practical solutions. Performers are busy people and want solutions that work as fast as possible. Hopefully they will find what they need in this book.

Andy Evans, 2003

CHAPTER 1

The Performer's Personality

Who is the performer? For the purposes of this book we will take the performer as being primarily an actor, a musician, a singer, a dancer or an entertainer (comedian, magician, etc.), and as such a member of Equity or the Musician's Union. Sections in the book on preparing for events and dealing with stage fright are also relevant to public speakers, business people who give conference papers and presentations, and those who have to talk on the media, such as radio and TV presenters.

What sort of character is the performer? We can get a good idea of the 'typical' personalities of performers by putting together data from personality tests, and as we will see there is a distinct 'performer's personality' which, as the folklore surrounding show people might suggest, is some way different from the average. Although individuals will vary considerably, such data helps us identify common personality types, traits, work preferences and values of performers, providing us with further insights into their motivations.

The data in this chapter comes from 298 performers, clients of Arts Psychology Consultants, who filled in questionnaires over the fourteen years from 1988 to 2002. Mostly these were clients who were considering career changes and so were given career analyses. There were also 56 dancers in transition, mostly from the major companies and including some well-known soloists, who were referred by the Dancer's Career Development Trust. Lastly there was a sample of 98 performers who took part in a two-year scheme devised by Arts Psychology Consultants to retrain unemployed people in the arts as part of the Government's 'Restart' programme (see page 240 for full data).

The breakdown of performers is shown below – note that the unemployed performers were a mixture of 3 dancers who had finished dancing through injury, 29 actors and 66 musicians, of which 7 were classical and 59 popular, including 2 jazz musicians. This confirms the widely held belief that actors and rock musicians are the most likely to be unemployed for long periods. The rock musicians were band members or individuals caught in the poverty trap with no contract, agent or regular

	Dance	Drama	Music (Class)	Music (Popular)	Total	(Music Total)	(Unemp. Performers)
Subjects:	56	56	98	88	299	186	98
Percentages:	19	19	33	29	100	62	33

gigs, and whose occasional work was hardly sufficient to cover the out-lay on instruments, equipment and travelling expenses. Their classical and jazz brethren are more fortunate, and earn more as a result of frequent freelance work; the handful that were long-term unemployed included people getting over injuries or emotional problems.

Personality types

The Myers-Briggs Type Indicator (MBTI)®

The idea of personality 'types' comes from psychoanalyst Carl Jung. A later version of his basic theories, the Myers-Briggs Type Indicator (MBTI), is widely used. It proposes that there are sixteen different types of personality in our population. None of these types is 'good or bad', they are simply all different, and a successful performer can be any of them. The MBTI personality type is built up of four different personality dimensions or 'indices': Extraversion-Introversion, Sensing-Intuitive, Thinking-Feeling, Judging-Perceiving. Within each index we all tend to have a natural preference for one trait or 'function' rather than its opposite, such as for 'Feeling' rather than 'Thinking'. We make use of the stronger or more typical function more often, by relying on feelings to make a decision, for example. We do not, however, use the preferred function exclusively, in much the same way as a right-handed person will continue to use the left hand for certain tasks, such as holding a fork.

Typical results for performers

The MBTI gives both type of preference and the clarity of each preference. Since the scores are averaged out, the clarity of preference will be less extreme than in individual cases. The data in Figure 1.1 shows the scores for our sample.

Extravert (E)–Introvert (I)

The first index describes how we orient ourselves towards life: extraverts tend to focus outwards into the world, introverts inwards into thoughts and feelings.

Extraverts like variety and action, and are sometimes impatient with long, slow jobs. They tend to act quickly, and sometimes without thinking. They are good at greeting people and take an interest in who they are and how they do their jobs. They like having people around them in the working environment, and like talking on the telephone rather than writing. When they learn a new task, they enjoy talking it through with someone as a good way of picking it up.

Introverts are interested in the ideas behind things. They like a quiet atmosphere for concentration, and dislike being interrupted by

Figure 1.1 MBTI preferences for performers

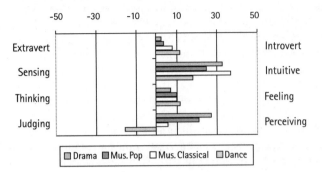

the telephone when working. They are quite happy working alone for long periods, sometimes on a single project. They would just as soon communicate in writing, and like reading through the instructions for a new task as a way of mastering it, rather than talking it over with someone. They like to think before acting, and sometimes consider things rather than actually doing them. They can find themselves lost in their thoughts, and sometimes fail to notice others or have difficulty in remembering names and faces.

There may well be two distinct parts of the performer's psyche – the sociable one that responds to audiences, fellow performers and new acquaintances, and the introverted one that creates alone and has an inner focus of concentration while rehearsing or improvising. Dancers and classical musicians are the most introverted of our group, though it is worth noting that on the 16PF (*see* page 15) all performers score as more extraverted because that index gives more weight to social skills which all performers – as entertainers who regularly face the public – have to some degree. Performers are more extraverted as a whole than people involved in other creative professions, such as artists. These tendencies may reflect lifestyles and typical working habits: composers, writers and painters lead a largely solitary existence.

Sensing (S)–Intuitive (N)
The second index describes how we gather information about the world: sensing types trust actual information gathered through the senses (what they see around them, hear, feel, taste, etc.); their possessions and environment are therefore important to them. Intuitive types speculate on hidden meanings behind what is immediately apparent, and so are less sensitive to their environment and more concerned with abstract possibilities.

Sensing types focus on reality and the here-and-now, enjoying the uniqueness of each event. They like applying what they have learned to a problem and think established ways of doing things are often right. They tend to work steadily, with a realistic idea of how long things will take, and like to reach conclusions step by step. They like it when things are simple, concise and easy to follow. They believe facts are important, and can be good at precise work. They may not put much faith in 'inspiration', thinking that 'imaginative' people tend to exaggerate rather than see the obvious.

Intuitive types like to focus on how things could be improved, and enjoy challenges, possibilities and learning new things. They tend to follow inspirations and hunches, and tend to leap to conclusions quickly, even if this means getting the facts a bit wrong. They do not like doing the same thing repeatedly or having to take time for details or precision when they want to get at the larger picture. They often work in bursts of energy with slack periods in between, and can be quite enthusiastic about starting new tasks. They constantly question why things are as they are, and tend to make things more complex than some think necessary.

The artistic personality as a whole is heavily biased towards the imaginative, which Jung calls 'intuitive'. All performers are considerably more imaginative than the average person, and this proneness to fantasy may account for the difficulty some have in establishing realistic and objective goals for their careers. The exception to this is ballet dancers, about a third of whom are realistic and share the same 'physical' type of personality as sportspeople (*see* page 172).

Thinking (T)–Feeling (F)
The third index reflects how we make decisions. Thinking types decide 'with the head' by using objective reasoning, while feeling types decide 'with the heart', weighing up feelings and inner hunches until a path forward is clear.

Thinking types believe they are logical, can put things in their right order, have a talent for analysing people and situations, and can speculate on the outcomes of various choices. They are attracted to principles and often respond to people's ideas rather than their feelings. They hate injustice, and like to be treated fairly. Where the situation warrants, they can be firm or tough-minded with other people, even to the point of hurting people's feelings without realising it.

Feeling types believe in people: their values, their feelings and what makes them happy. They like harmony and will work to make it happen. They dislike having to tell people unpleasant things and so try to get around it or make it less hurtful. They tend to be sympathetic to people and try to please them where possible. In return, they feel good when others praise or compliment them. They put people before principles, and think of choices in life in terms of the effect they will have on people.

Both dance and music are non-verbal art forms, so artistic decisions and thoughts use some degree of right brain activity (*see* page 26).

'Feel' in music and dance is vital, as are such completely non-verbal phenomena as keeping a beat. As Duke Ellington said, 'It don't mean a thing if it ain't got that swing.' Acting is verbal and so more is carried out in the left brain speech area (*see* page 26), although much is done through movement and gesture and the way the face is handled in close-up. Actors do appear to be more thinking than their non-verbal counterparts on the MBTI.

Judging (J)–Perceiving (P)

The fourth index shows how we tend to deal with the meanings and events of our lives. The judging type has a preference for decision-making, and will do this through either thinking or feeling, as indicated above. The perceptive type has a stronger response to the actual information-gathering process, and will do this through either sensing or intuition, as indicated above. It is as if judging types are happier with 'answers', while perceptive types remain curious about the actual questions life continually poses.

Judging types work best when they can plan things from the outset and then follow that plan. They enjoy getting things settled and finished so they can move on to other matters. They need only the basic essentials to start work, and then schedule projects so that each step gets done on time, using lists as agendas for action. They dislike having plans interrupted or rescheduled by others once they have been made. They tend to be satisfied once they have made up their mind over something, and tend to decide things more quickly than others who seem to labour over various choices.

Perceiving types believe in keeping an open mind, adapting well to changing situations and leaving things open for last-minute changes. They like to know all about a new job, and find making decisions difficult when they feel the need for more information. They tend to postpone unpleasant jobs, and while periodically making lists of things to do, they tend not to finish things on the list. They can make a start on a lot of projects and find it hard to finish them all, but get a lot done when under pressure from a deadline.

As one would suspect from their rigorous practice, rehearsal and concert routines, dancers and classical musicians tend to have more of a tolerance for structure and planning functions than their fellow performers. Planning has obvious uses in preparation but can leave any performer more nervous if the performance requires spontaneity or things unexpectedly go wrong. For jazz musicians, an improvisatory mind is particularly important since music is being created 'on the fly'. Actors and popular musicians tend to have a more 'take it as it comes' approach to life, and are more likely to be unemployed – in the case of actors four-fifths are unemployed at any given time. Our sample reflects this, since over half were not working at the time of testing and included long-term unemployed.

The quality of openness and willingness to follow the flow of inspiration may be important in contributing to peak experiences where we perform unusually well 'as if by some sort of magic'. This kind of peak experience tends to be easier without a score, so orchestral musicians are at a disadvantage, though such experiences are not unknown.

The drawback of spontaneity, however, may be inadequate organisation when this is needed. Unemployed performers do not show a lack of talent as much as a lack of planning, which seems the highest single factor indicating why they make less of their careers than the middle range of professionals (see Chapter 8). At the very top level of talent there is a swing back to the spontaneous attitude, but here talent may be unstoppable, or recognised and exploited by others. Planning may favour careers while openness may favour performance – both are part of success.

Conclusions

Artists are the ideas people, with a future focus, whose strength is creativity. They are attracted to projects and are good at initiating ideas. They may be poor at carrying these through unless they have the self-discipline to finish tasks, and are prone to work in binges or at the last minute. They are often 'Perceiving' (spontaneous) as opposed to 'Judging' (planning) and prefer to leave options open for lateral thinking. This improvising tendency is found in the highest creatives (judged by peers), but risks a lack of organisation, procrastination, and inability to decide what they want to do. Some may have multiple skills and be unable to choose which to pursue, so that they may end up doing nothing.

As such they are weak at living in the present, observing reality, and following step-by-step routines. Since two-thirds or more of the population are good at realistic thinking, they are considered absent-minded and impractical by the person in the street. They may equally be resented for their imagination and flow of ideas, and this can cause perpetual friction in their lives. They may think they are not appreciated for their imaginative virtues, and simply criticised for their realistic weaknesses. Since they are furthest removed from the company worker who has a fixed daily routine, they may receive most criticism from that quarter, and may reciprocate by criticising company workers as having boring lives.

The non-verbal performers often have a 'feeling' focus, less so actors, photographers and film people. This puts them into the same personality categories as counsellors and psychologists. On paper they seem to have the same inherent personality skills that make good counsellors, and should certainly have the intuition to pick up the feelings of others.

Personality traits

The Cattell 16 Personality Factor Questionnaire (16PF)

When we start to go beyond basic preferences, such as extraversion or introversion, we enter the world of personality traits. Nobody has yet established how many traits are either 'fundamental' or mutually exclusive: some favour five or seven, some sixteen, others many more. And while there is broad agreement on many of the traits, no theory is exactly the same as another.

One of the widely accepted definitions of personality traits is that of Raymond Cattell, which is used in his 16PF. In order to work out scores for each trait, a sophisticated questionnaire is required, but the following descriptions of each trait should give you an idea of how your own personality compares with the average for performers. As in the MBTI, each trait has two opposite poles, such as 'Cool–Warm'. Scores closer to either pole (small or large scores) show distinct characteristics of the trait in question. Middle scores (around 5.5) show a balance of both tendencies, neither being very marked. The averaged-out scores shown here are less extreme for each trait than those of actual individuals, but show a similar diversity in direction and strength of tendency.

Figure 1.2 Typical personality traits of performers

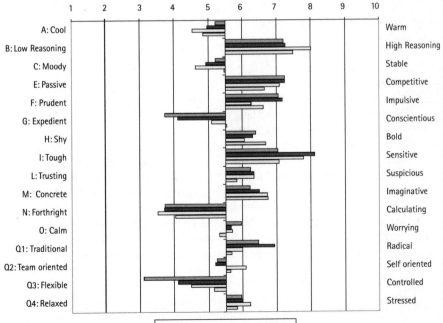

16PF Factors for performers

A. Cool–warm

Cool – Detached and emotionally reserved. Critical and at times uncompromising. Attracted to ideas or things rather than people, and able to work alone happily.

Warm – Good-natured, warm-hearted and easy-going with people. Ready to participate, co-operate and adapt to others. Generous, and able to compromise and take criticism.

Performers tend to be slightly detached, partly because they are self-critical. Such critical detachment is very marked in scientists and academics, and is considered a component of creativity. Classical musicians are the most self-critical and also score highest for interest in science and technology.

B. Lower/higher reasoning ability

Unlike the other traits, this is based on a short reasoning test, the results of which give a broad measure of intelligence. Higher scores correspond to a more abstract ability to reason.

Because the 16PF contains only thirteen verbal reasoning questions, it has been criticised for being neither wholly reliable nor wholly culture-fair. True scores as assessed on more robust tests may be as much as two points higher, but nevertheless the scores on this factor show that all performers – including dancers in the major companies – are much higher than average in intelligence, with classical musicians again the highest.

C. Moody–Stable

Moody – Affected by feelings and mood swings and prone to frustration, anxiety, sleeplessness or hypochondria. May get upset easily.
Stable – Calm, mature and able to cope with reality. Able to keep inner conflicts and emotions under control.

Performers in general are emotional people subject to mood swings, and at bad times in their personal and professional lives they are also subject to depression and feelings of hopelessness. Moodiness is more marked than the average, with musicians scoring highest, but since this factor is fairly situation-dependent, it can vary over time within the same personality. High stability scores are associated with meditation, which seems to have a beneficial effect on mood swings. Dancers are the most stable, scoring the same as the population average.

E. Passive–Competitive

Passive – Mild-natured and able to accommodate or conform to the wishes of others. May bottle up inner aggressions or show them as correctness or fussiness.

Competitive – Self-assertive, preferring to put ideas into practice and have things one's own way. Outer forcefulness may disguise some inner insecurities.

The majority of performers are competitive, and some extremely so. Popular musicians and actors are the most competitive, possibly because they have to fight much harder for work and are at higher risk of unemployment. But while this brings advantages in self-promotion, the more passive performer can be surprisingly effective (and rich). Lack of ego can bring sensitivity to other performers and a general 'feel-good factor', and performers who have the ability to make their colleagues feel as if they can do no wrong – like drummers Martin Ditcham (Chris Rea) and Billy Hart (Herbie Hancock) – are greatly in demand for tour and studio work.

F. Prudent–Impulsive
Prudent – Restrained and cautious. Perceived as serious and dependable.
Impulsive – Enthusiastic, responsive and happy-go-lucky. Needs variety.
Performers are impulsive and more risk-taking than average – hardly surprising in a risky profession where it is crucial to take advantage of lucky breaks. Again, popular musicians and actors score the highest, and interestingly they are more likely to rate excitement as a high job value. This is partly because they are more extravert and so more 'stimulus hungry'.

G. Expedient–Conscientious
Expedient – Disregardful of social standards or obligations, particularly where they conflict with one's own norms or inner beliefs.
Conscientious – Persevering, responsible, aware of social duties and respectful of ethical norms. At times may take a strict or moralistic view of other people's actions.

Performers are generally expedient and free-thinking, content to make their own rules and reluctant to follow social norms. Since many already feel rejected by the more traditional parts of society, this is hardly surprising. Yet again, popular musicians and actors are the most rebellious. Classical musicians are more conscientious, and this may partly result from their need to conform to strict practice routines and their higher social status. Dancers are the most conscientious, equalling the population average.

H. Shy–Bold
Shy – Timid, reticent and sensitive to threats. Cautious of revealing one's real self to larger groups, preferring the comfort of small groups or personal contact.
Bold – Venturesome, uninhibited and responsive to challenge, seeing the occasional risk as part of living life to the full.

Many performers score as introverted on the Myers-Briggs but are not socially shy, since they are frequently in front of the public, used to teamwork and possess a range of social skills, including in many cases a sharp sense of humour, a spontaneous sense of fun and an ability to charm others. Interestingly, dancers are the least socially shy, even though they are the most introverted on the MBTI.

I. Tough–Sensitive

Tough – Effective, practical and down-to-earth, with a logical and no-nonsense approach to reality. May undervalue experimental aspects of art and culture as fanciful or pretentious.

Sensitive – Tender-minded, refined and sensitive to culture and inner feelings. Perceived by more practical people as self-indulgent, dependent or over-protected.

Clearly performers need to be high on sensitivity to do justice to the poetry and complexities of their medium. Such sensitivity does, though, expose them to the criticism of others and the emotional impact of their world. Musicians are the most sensitive, and popular musicians score very high on this, showing a very vulnerable and easily bruised ego.

L. Trusting–Suspicious

Trusting – Adaptable, tolerant, easy to get on with and ready to forget difficulties and ill feelings.

Suspicious – Prone to anxious insecurity and feelings of mistrust or resentment. Tending to control this insecurity in stubborn, demanding or opinionated behaviour.

Performers are not particularly trusting people, and while in some this may be a long-standing trait, in others it may be a reaction to the competitive and back-stabbing aspects of the performing arts and the unfortunate presence within the profession of individuals capable of depriving artists of large sums of money, as many high-profile court cases have demonstrated. Predictably musicians are highest on this, as the amount of litigation suggests.

M. Material–Imaginative

Material – Careful, conventional and concerned with the details of practical reality. May undervalue imagination and inner fantasies in oneself and others.

Imaginative – Self-motivated, wrapped up in inner urgencies and spec-ulations, and drawn to the larger picture. Careless or bohemian over practical constraints and details.

As with sensitivity, it is a given that performers need to be imaginative. In fact the trio of high sensitivity, high suspicion and high imagination is typical of artistic profiles. To a certain extent these factors feed each other – high sensitivity throws up a range of melodramatic mental scenarios where the artist fears being taken advantage of or suffering bad things. This may also explain why some artists are renowned hypochondriacs.

N. Forthright–Shrewd

Forthright – Natural, unpretentious, at times naïve, approaching people and events with an open warmth. Tending to see the best in people, but not always to perceive their negative qualities.

Shrewd – Diplomatic and calculating, with a penetrating and unsentimental approach to people and problems. Perceived as streetwise and hard to fool.

The performer's lack of trust in others and tendency to be exploited is compounded by a lack of guile and a habit of saying exactly what is in the mind. The lack of shrewdness on this, the 'Machiavelli' factor, exposes artists to all manner of treachery and politics, but leaves little artifice to fight back with since they fiercely defend their right to truth and self-expression.

O. Calm–Worrying

Calm – Self-assured about one's capacity to deal with people and events. May sometimes be over-confident, overlooking feedback from others.

Worrying – Prone to high expectations of oneself and to worrying over difficulties. May be self-reproaching and harbour exaggerated feelings of inadequacy.

Performers tend to worry at times – it is in the nature of the profession – but they are generally less prone to feelings of guilt since they are familiar with defending and justifying their views. Actors are the biggest worriers and dancers the least.

Q1. Traditional–Radical

Traditional – Conservative, preferring established ideas and approaches to experimental innovations. Tolerant of traditional difficulties.

Radical – Liberal, free-thinking and able to devise creative new approaches to traditional problems. Distrustful of tradition for its own sake.

Artists by their very function are concerned with reassessing the aspects of life to which their imagination and creativity have given them unique access and sensitivity. If art never left the confines of tradition it would stagnate and atrophy. Not all performers are strongly radical, but radicalism is needed to advance the quality and nature of the performing arts. Actors and popular musicians are the most radical, as they are the most free-thinking. Both groups tend to experiment more and do more new work than dancers and classical musicians.

Q2. Team-oriented–Self-oriented

Team-oriented – A 'joiner', valuing the spirit of group activity and the support of others in following a course of action.

Self-oriented – Resourceful, able to work alone, preferring to rely on own decisions rather than those of others.

Performing is a mixture of individual and team activity, so one would expect both aspects to be present in the performing profile, depending on the subject. Classical musicians and dancers are the most independent and self-sufficient.

Q3. Flexible–controlled

Flexible – Careless of conventional social protocol, preferring to follow inner urges and impulsive feelings. Tolerant of ambiguity and disorder, but may suffer from too little self-control.

Controlled – In control of feelings and actions. Precise, and aware of self-image. Favouring planning over spontaneity.

Artists are creatures of inspiration, and so one would expect a more flexible response. In particular there is little of the controlled self-image associated with this factor. In the sense that creativity is order out of chaos, there must be some familiarity with the chaotic and random as well as the ability to create system and form out of it. This tolerance for ambiguity contributes to performers' generally sharp sense of humour. Low scores on this are frequently seen in individuals, and as with 'Perceiving' on the MBTI there is a danger that too little self-control can adversely affect career advancement. Dancers and classical musicians have the most self-control, while actors are particularly weak on this: extended periods of unemployment possibly make it hard for them to structure their thoughts and activities.

Q4. Relaxed–Stressed

Relaxed – Leisurely, unfrustrated and unwilling to sacrifice personal well-being for stress and tension. Tending to calm down easily and not let things dwell on the nerves.

Stressed – Easily irritated and frustrated by things large and small, taking time to calm down when upset. Prone to constant 'workaholic' activity, and may need to relax more.

High levels of stress are seen in some individuals, particularly those with responsibility for putting on shows (one ten-scoring theatre producer despaired that 'everything has to be done yesterday at the latest'). On the other hand, many performers are fairly easy-going and live contentedly in their actual and daydream worlds, protected from burnout by doing activities which give them great pleasure and satisfaction. The most stressed are actors, probably due to underwork stress rather than overwork stress, and classical musicians who usually have heavy schedules of playing, rehearsing and instrumental teaching and are most likely to suffer from the effects of long-term stage fright.

Second order factors

The sixteen traits shown above can be used to derive further second order factors or 'major traits'.

Figure 1.3   16PF Second Order Factors for performers

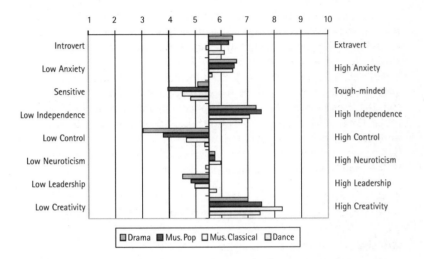

As in the above, very high or low scores show strong tendencies, while middle scores (around 5.5) show a balance. Second order factors are combinations of some of the sixteen primary traits. They show performers as slightly extravert, prone to anxiety and sensitive-minded, with high independence and lower than average control over themselves. They do not appear to be fundamentally neurotic – it is more true to say that they are sensitive and prone to anxious reactions, something not helped by the insecure nature of the profession. Leadership is around average, and of course creativity is high or very high.

The full picture is of an intelligent personality, dominant in the factors influencing creativity – sensitivity, imagination, competitiveness, radicalism, critical detachment and self-sufficiency. While performers are somewhat detached and critical towards their work and working colleagues, they also have a more impulsive social side showing boldness, risk-taking and competitiveness. While musicians all show independence of judgement, actors and popular musicians are more team-spirited than classical musicians and dancers. They are also more expedient and non-conformist, and less conscientious than their classical counterparts.

Performers are not neurotic as such but are prone to some degree of stress, guilt and worry. Where anxiety shows up most is in terms of mood swings and feelings of insecurity. The particular sensitivity to both self-criticism and criticism from others is one of the most typical and damaging sources of anxiety. This is not helped by a personality which is naturally sensitive, responds with feelings, and is particularly affected by the ups and downs of the profession.

Forthrightness is very marked – artistic expression in itself relies on truth and integrity. You can cheat others in the profession but it is hard to cheat one's own muse. The downside of a competitive environment is the vulnerability of having such a naïve and trusting nature, which tends to see the good in people and lacks the cynical penetration to deal shrewdly with business matters.

One useful coping mechanism performers have – in particular jazz and rock musicians (many of whom become comedians) – is a sharp sense of humour. Aside from its capacity to create good social bonds and relax the atmosphere, this also shows an underlying tolerance for ambiguity and even a relish for experiencing it. Performers are thereby less prone to the frustrations felt by more inflexible people when their wishes do not fall into the frameworks they set for them.

Team roles

Belbin

A large number of organisations were analysed by R. Meredith Belbin to determine the most common roles people played in them. Eight typical roles were obtained: five 'production' roles and three hierarchical ones. The original names are rather quaint: Plant (creative), Resourcer-Investigator (researcher), Shaper (the trouble-shooter or negotiator), Monitor-Evaluator (strategy, quality control) and Completer-Finisher (finishes work, something of a perfectionist). Finally, Chair (the elected

Figure 1.4 A diamond model for creativity, from divergent to convergent ideas

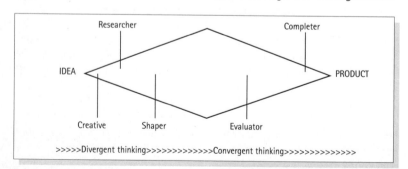

Figure 1.5 Belbin team roles for performers (from 16PF)

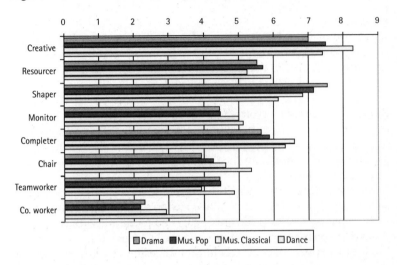

leader), Team Worker (as the name implies) and Company Worker (the lowliest position, dependable and carries out instructions).

If we see the process as a production line, with the idea at one end and the product at the other, then performers' scores are very close to those of creatives in general. They score highest in the first stages of creativity which require divergent or 'lateral' thinking and where the challenge is greater – innovating, research and problem-solving. They are weaker on more convergent thinking like strategy, since they tend to be impulsive and risk-taking rather than sober and cautious. When it comes to completing work all performers can be critical and painstaking, even perfectionist, with classical musicians scoring the highest and unemployed performers the lowest.

In terms of hierarchical roles, performers make adequate chairpeople and team workers but generally poor employees, particularly in roles where they have to carry out orders with little control over the choice and direction of their activities. Dancers are the best chairpeople and team workers, and can even take orders to a large extent – a reflection of the very organised environment in which they are brought up and work. The more original and rebellious the performer, the lower the company worker score, and even minus scores are technically possible when derived from the 16PF. There is a clear preference for projects rather than routines, and this is confirmed by the preferred job values.

Occupational interests

Holland

The world of work has been divided into different occupational categories in many ways. The method used by John Holland is widely used and respected. Within these various occupational categories, people in the performing arts tend to be employed in the following activities:

Realistic interests – typically involve manual and trade skills, tools, machines or working with animals. Within music they involve looking after and transporting equipment, such as the job of the 'roadie' during rock tours and concerts. In the theatre and ballet they involve sets and stage management.

Investigative interests – tend to be found within the fields of science and technology. Applications within music technology and film include studio work, computers, editing, cameras, lights and sound and electronics.

Artistic interests – span the arts and media in general.

Social interests – include teaching, counselling, and the health and helping professions. Performers are naturally drawn to them because they frequently teach, do a lot of teamwork, and take a lively interest in people and the 'meaning of life'.

Enterprising interests – typically to do with business, sales and management. Performers are generally self-employed businesses in themselves, and so need certain business and promotional qualities to do well in the profession. Some later go into sales or management within the business.

Conventional interests – tend to be administrative, and are generally avoided by performers because of the office environment and predictable routines involved, though some do work administratively in arts management, agencies, broadcasting or record companies.

Figure 1.6 Occupational interest scores for performers

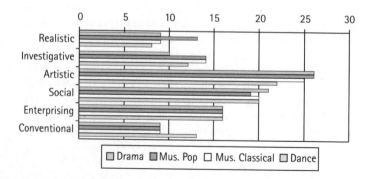

The data in Figure 1.6 reveals that performers show a clear preference for the arts and for many aspects of working with people, such as teaching, counselling and the helping professions. This double interest is consistent across performers, and reflects their 'Feeling' preference. It is even possible to say that the performer and the teacher, counsellor or psychologist are fundamentally the same person, and this is borne out by strong tendencies towards social and helping activities, such as the charity work done by events such as Live Aid and many individual celebrities. For some reason dancers are lowest on artistic interests and highest on social ones – maybe because at transition they are already adjusting their ideas to other interests. They are discussed further in Chapter 8 in the section on Transition.

Besides these two dominating interests there is a lesser but still appreciable interest in technology and scientific ideas. This is particularly the case with classical musicians for some reason, despite the fact that popular musicians come into more regular contact with studio technology and need to use and understand a whole range of stage equipment.

There is also an interest in enterprising, business or project skills, which correspond to performers' creative potential and their generally self-employed status. Many performers have difficulties with invasive sales techniques, which go against their genuineness and social ethics, but they can be very effective persuaders if they develop the requisite skills and attitudes. Even dancers, who worry inordinately about their inability to express themselves in words, can be effective persuaders, and have some of the most impressive physical presence and body language of all.

Where performers are generally poor is in repetitive administrative tasks. Popular musicians score highest on practical hand skills, and have more practice in maintaining or putting together their equipment.

Job values

In any career our job values indicate what we need to be present in order for us to feel happy and fulfilled. If our work contains a large measure of preferred values we should find it naturally interesting and congenial.

Preferred values for performers are predictably creativity and artistic work, followed by variety and communication. These closely match the lifestyle of the performer, so some degree of lasting satisfaction should be expected. Social and emotional values like friendship at work and contact with others are also high, and should be found in the camaraderie typical of the profession. Independence and time freedom are also high, once again underlining the performing artist's dislike of an imposed routine and a preference for self-directed activities.

Figure 1.7 Job value list

A predictable routine	Fast pace	Pressure
Artistic work	Friendship at work	Recognition
A well-known organisation	Helping others	Responsibility
Challenge	Ideal workplace	Security
Chance of promotion	Independence	Status and respect
Communication	Learning new things	Taking risks
Community work	Making decisions	Teamwork
Competition	Money	Time freedom
Contact with others	Peace	Variety
Creativity	Persuading people	Working alone
Excitement	Physical challenge	
Expertise	Precision work	

Figure 1.8 Performers' most and least liked job values

All performers	Dancers	Actors	Musicians, classical	Musicians, popular
Creativity 93	Creativity 19	Creativity 19	Creativity 24	Creativity 31
Artistic work 65	Communication 15	Artistic work 13	Artistic work 20	Artistic work 19
Communication 50	Artistic work 13	Communication 11	Friendship at work 12	Communication 14
Variety 41	Money 13	Excitement 10	Variety 12	Friendship at work 13
Friendship at work 38	Challenge 12	Independence 9	Communication 10	Money 13
Learning new things 32	Variety 10	Recognition 8	Time freedom 10	Time freedom 11
Money 32	Friendship at work 9	Variety 8	Learning new things 9	Variety 11
Challenge 30	Learning new things 8	Challenge 6	Excitement 8	Learning new things 9
Recognition 30	Contact with others 7	Learning new things 6	Expertise 8	Expertise 7
Time freedom 28	Recognition 7	Contact with others 4	Recognition 8	Recognition 7

Most preferred values – numbers show how many times they were rated in top 3

All performers	Dancers	Actors	Musicians, classical	Musicians, popular
A predictable routine 117	A predictable routine 25	A predictable routine 18	A predictable routine 33	A predictable routine 41
Physical challenge 63	Community work 19	A well-known organi-sation 13	Physical challenge 29	Competition 18
A well-known organi-sation 55	A well-known organi-sation 15	Competition 11	Persuading people 19	A well-known organi-zation 16
Competition 54	Working alone 15	Precision work 11	Competition 15	Physical challenge 16
Persuading people 50	Persuading people 13	Working alone 8	Fast pace 12	Persuading people 14
Working alone 44	Taking risks 12	Physical challenge 7	Pressure 12	Pressure 13
Community work 39	Physical challenge 11	Community work 6	A well-known organi-zation 11	Working alone 11
Pressure 38	Competition 10	Fast pace 6	Working alone 10	Fast pace 7
Fast pace 32	Precision work 8	Peace 5	Community work 9	Responsibility 7
Taking risks 26	Pressure 8	Pressure 5	Taking risks 7	Community work 5

Least preferred values – numbers show how many times they were rated in top 3

Challenge and learning new things are both high, and these values should be guarded into middle age to ensure that burnout does not creep up on the hardened professional, for instance in jazz bands, orchestras and opera pits which can repeat the same repertoire year in and year out. Among some parts of the performing profession, like popular musicians, there is more emphasis on expertise, recognition, money and good working conditions – maybe a testament to their sensitivity to their perceived status and the legacy of years spent going up and down the M1 in Ford Transit vans.

Low values are largely the opposite of these, but are not always that easy to eliminate from the performer's life. A predictable routine is universally disliked and is lowest by some margin. Performers get around this in different ways – musicians dep out (put in a deputy for) their regular jobs to take on interesting new opportunities or one-off gigs they want to do, while actors try to get time off TV soaps to do theatre work. Dancers in the major companies and actors in long runs are the worst sufferers from a predictable routine, though their job security is some consolation. Pressure situations are generally disliked – physical effort, fast pace, persuading people and competition. This last is ironic for a group of people scoring very high on competitiveness as a trait. Clearly they don't appreciate the competition of others for the choice jobs in the business. It is also interesting that while performers have social values, they dislike large organisations and are reluctant to take responsibility for helping within the community beyond their occasional charity performances. Again their independent personality makes them better loners than leaders.

Knowing yourself

Your natural character type is typically your most relaxed way of doing things, so using it to identify key talents can help build up a positive self-image. It also helps to be conscious of vulnerabilities like lack of shrewdness and a difficulty in trusting others. At times we all talk and act on the assumption that it would be nice if others were like ourselves, as when Professor Higgins says in *My Fair Lady* – 'Why can't a woman be more like a man?' While performers have much common ground, they are also different in some ways from each other and can be very different from the characteristics of the general population.

Differences are not the same as weaknesses, and Professor Higgins is a typical example of the logical man who thinks the feeling-centred woman is stupid or unable to make 'proper' decisions. This is of course untrue – general artistic and interpretive abilities (and indeed general life abilities) are not quite the same as logic, and instinctive decisions that come from the emotions may not only be right, they may sometimes be the only ones possible in a non-verbal medium such as music or dance. Conversations and transactions between opposite types may effectively be parallel monologues, like the hospital manager who says, 'We have to lose ten beds,' and the nurse who replies, 'That's impossible, there are people in them.' Both are true to type, and compromise may require a conceptual leap into another view of the world.

If you are able to make such 'leaps' into the inner world of other people, you can gain valuable insights, as method actors are particularly trained in doing. Personalities come in all shapes and sizes, and you are not handicapped because you do not have certain 'key' traits – all traits have positive uses, and people with one type of trait may complement those with others. In addition, you only have *tendencies* towards preferred traits – you actually use all of them at some time.

Different personalities cope with life in different ways, and knowing your own range of 'coping' strategies gives you an idea of how you deal with life events. Humour and generosity have been shown in surveys to be top of the list of effective coping mechanisms, and the typical performer who has these qualities is already using some very effective personal skills.

Where does performing talent come from?

The majority of the research into inherited versus acquired talent has been carried out with musicians, much of it at Keele University under Professor John Sloboda. Such research shows that musical ability runs in families and is more prevalent where both parents and all grandparents are musical. Not all the members of such families need to be musicians themselves, but several are likely to have potential musical ability in the sense of being able to sing in tune, remember melodies easily, hear musical intervals and rhythms and understand the notes in harmonies.

Yet despite the influence of a favourable musical background, studies show that several highly talented musicians have come from humble homes where there was little musical activity, and there is up to a 25 per cent chance that a child will be musical even if neither parent is apparently so. It is equally true that a number of children of musical parents show little musical motivation or talent.

It is also difficult to determine whether musical ability is determined by genes or a musical upbringing, because the home environment will already have played a role by the time musical ability is apparent. It may be partly an innate talent, and partly a skill that is enhanced by a favourable milieu and effective teaching and practice. Professor Sloboda makes a strong case for the acquisition of musical skills through repetition and practice, but at the highest levels of musicality, technique –

while important – may be less critical than the profundity of the musical imagination, and this in turn introduces a variety of other personality traits, such as sensitivity, intelligence and originality.

Identifying your musical map

The term 'musical map' can be used to define the systems by which you can locate notes, rhythms, intervals and instrumental sounds within the total musical experience you hear in your head, i.e. how your 'map' sounds.

Exercise: Imagine a piece of music that you know particularly well and try to establish the following.

- *What do you hear? How many individual musical lines or harmonies – melody and bass or inside parts as well? All instruments or just a characteristic 'timbre', e.g. woodwind, brass, strings?*
- *How much do you hear? How good is your recognition of harmony and melody? Can you hear unusual melody lines with unusual intervals? Can you reproduce in your mind difficult harmonic shifts or only fairly straightforward ones?*
- *How strong and accurate is your sense of rhythm? Do you hear music without a precise beat, or do you hear a precise beat which tends to stay in time?*
- *What do you remember? How far 'into' a piece can you hear? Can you hear a whole song or a short piece? Can you hear a whole movement of a classical piece? Do you hear just the 'main bits' and not the linking passages that may be much less distinctive, or can you hear everything?*
- *What do you dream? Do you often dream music or only rarely? Can you remember any of it on waking? Are you able to write it down or play it? Do you recognise actual melodies and harmonies, or is it just a general effect?*

Between them, these questions cover auditory and rhythmic ability and the strength of musical imagery available to each person. Some of these capacities may be inherited, such as 'auditiveness' rather than predisposition to visual images, or the sort of 'note-perfect' memory that exceptional musicians such as Mozart possessed. Modern research shows that many musical abilities, however, can be learned and improved with practice and familiarity. This includes pitching notes either 'perfectly' or in relation to each other, and a variety of performing and compositional skills.

Perfect pitch

Perfect pitch is a way of locating notes on your musical map by hearing their 'absolute' pitch, which can easily be checked for accuracy against a tuning fork or piano. Musicians with perfect pitch are greatly envied by those without it, who can feel quite unjustifiably inferior. Though not the only way of pitching notes, it has distinct advantages. Experiments with pianists who were asked to learn pieces on a dummy silent keyboard showed that those who had perfect pitch were better able to 'hear' the notes and so memorise the pieces more easily.

There are also times when perfect pitch is a problem. In a playing situation where there is conflict about pitch, as when other players are sharp or flat, this can cause discomfort, anger and frustration. Once absolute pitch is identifiable it can become over-sensitive. This is particularly true of violinists and instruments where pitching notes is crucial. The pitch may even become more important than the music.

Relative pitch

Improvising or jazz musicians are particularly good at hearing melody and harmony. They often know hundreds of different chord progressions from memory, and can imagine in their head or sing out loud innumerable improvisations over common 32-bar progressions. From a very early age – maybe the first time they try playing the piano and locating notes on the keyboard – they are used to hearing the relationship of one note to its surrounding ones. They quickly become good at identifying intervals, and so can follow quite complex melodic lines in their head by relating all the notes to each other by means of their pitch within the melodic context.

Using this system, the pitch heard in the head may be quite different from its 'actual' value – C may be G, for instance. But even in transposed form, the melody is just as accurate and the harmony just as correct. In the same dummy keyboard experiments with pianists, improvising musicians also did well through being able to hear and remember the moving harmonic and melodic context of the pieces.

If you do not have perfect pitch, you can improve your musical map by practising other ways of locating notes in your memory. You can improve your ability to link notes and chords to each other by improvising either on an instrument, by humming or whistling, or silently in your head. Start with easy sequences or 'changes' as they are called in jazz, and build up to more challenging ones. In jazz terms this would mean going from a blues to John Coltrane's 'Giant Steps'. Where you encounter difficulty in shifting from one chord to another, rehearse it until you can do it. Doing this away from instruments is a good way of filling in idle moments in queues or on journeys, and has the added virtue of rehearsing purely mental solutions to chord changes. This results in a fresher and more original approach without the clichés that come from well-practised phrases, and imagined solutions can later be practised on the instrument. Classical musicians can rehearse awkward leaps and intervals in the same way.

Musicality and artistic talent

The question of what musicality is has been discussed for centuries, and the answer is likely to remain more in the realms of taste and aesthetics than in scientific fact. For example, who is the more musical out of the following?

- An orchestral violinist with a good technique but mediocre aural ability, who cannot improvise or play without music.
- A master drummer from Africa who knows nothing of Western music.
- A well-known music critic who does not play an instrument.
- The world's best piano tuner.

Without agreeing what musicality is, it would be hard to choose between the above. All have elements of musicality, but these are different in each case. The violinist has performing ability, the drummer has creativity, the critic has taste and the tuner has aural ability. Between them, these elements cover most of what we loosely understand to be 'musicality'. 'Musical ability' may be easier to understand as a collection of different aptitudes. These include:

- tonal memory – identifying and remembering notes
- pitch – identifying notes and intervals
- rhythm – identifying and playing different rhythms
- harmony – identifying and using chords
- melody – distinguishing and using phrases.

Such things as aural ability are easy to test, and this would also be true of the elements of dance and technical aspects of acting, such as realistic accents. Taste is virtually impossible to quantify. Creativity can be measured in some way, while performing ability is constantly disputed by critics. Different people give different weight to factors like technical ability, interpretation, originality and style, and such disagreement is notorious among the juries of international competitions, where technique and the ability to carry out all the dates that result from winning may predominate over charisma and the capacity to please an audience.

One good way of finding your own style is totally free improvisation, rather than variations on a structure. Allowing ideas to come freely into your head, then trying them out helps contrast your own style with external influences, and is a way of getting closer to your inner ideals. It is a way of cleaning out the influences of favourite heroes and establishing what sounds are really going round in your head. These may be quite surprising, and include unexpected influences. Doing this helps you go back to and start stylistically from first principles, finding what comes spontaneously to mind when you are not trying to imitate or perform any particular style.

Music and the brain

The dominant side of your brain partly depends on whether you are right-handed or left-handed. The right hemisphere of the brain controls the left side of the body and vice versa. In right-handers the dominant left brain controls the dominant right hand. In left-handers some of the dominant left-hemisphere functions, like speech, can develop in the right hemisphere. The left side of the brain is called the dominant or major hemisphere because it deals with language and calculations and so tends to be the analytical or problem-solving side. The right side of the brain or minor hemisphere usually has only elementary language function but superior spatial and pattern sense. For this reason it is associated with non-verbal mental imagery like colour and design, and spatial visualisations like perspective and shapes. Research suggests that the right brain plays a particular part in artistic or musical expression as well as being more closely linked to emotions and dreams.

Experiments with musicians suggest that the right side of the brain tends to respond to the overall emotional and auditive effect of music and is used more by those with little understanding of theory and little professional music training. The left side of the brain tends to be used in a more advanced way to analyse music, and is thus used more by professional musicians. This is quite interesting, since it suggests that professional musicians develop a critical left brain activity which is progressively overlaid on their more primitive responses to sounds. While this has the obvious function of monitoring the quality of music-making, it may sometimes be an advantage to disable such analysis and to let a more emotive way of listening to sounds take over. It is likely that this happens in music therapy sessions or free improvisations, where participants are left free to explore sounds uncritically rather than being expected to make any musical sense. Musicians who try this experience a 'spatial' feeling which accesses all sorts of emotions and visualisations, and may recall childlike responses associated with a good deal of innocent pleasure.

Other effects of disabling the critical left brain function can be achieved by drugs, which inhibit accurate judgement. Deprived of a critical analysis of its form, music will then tend to become a pleasant soundscape where each element has an enhanced emotional appeal: the reediness of a clarinet, the crash of a fortissimo, the hypnotic rhythm of the drums. This way of hearing music can appear better at the time because it is new and intense, but it is effectively a distorted reproduction in which particular elements are brought forward and others pushed back. In the long run, if music were heard without structure, no effort would be made to create the masterpieces we know today.

Talent in dancers, actors and entertainers

Dancers have very special physical criteria – their bodies need to conform to certain shapes, heights and functions, and many talented dancers give up for purely physical reasons. There is disagreement on some aspects, such as height – Balanchine loved tall dancers and this school survives still in New York. Weight, however, needs to be strictly controlled. Grace of body movement is more innate, and some dancers are naturally gifted in this way.

Comedians need to be naturally funny, and according to comedy-magician Jerry Sadowitz need a further two years' training in the 'school of hard knocks' to build up an act and be able to successfully deal with audiences. Magicians need years of practice, since their work is almost entirely sleight of hand, and many begin as children. According to Jerry, most of them stay that way emotionally, since they substitute trickery for a more mature adjustment to adult life.

Acting requires a certain look, but whether that gets you work is anybody's guess, as expressed by actor Paul Clemens (McClelland, 1985): 'It's so difficult for a young actor in Hollywood today – you're on your own. When you go up for a role you're either too young, too fat or too thin, unless somebody already has you in mind. Just getting the interviews for roles is tough – as is making sure that the agent doesn't lose sight of you. Frustration is your constant companion in Hollywood.'

Few actors would disagree with this. Their technical education is often very extensive and includes skills like accents, horse riding, sword fighting, dancing, singing and performing a range of stunts. But at the end of the day, getting parts is more a case of luck than in any other part of the profession.

CHAPTER 2

Motivation

Motivation is the dynamo behind all healthy, self-activated action, goal-setting and career planning. Maximum motivation comes from total commitment. Unfortunately, human beings are complex and mostly there is a mixture of positive and negative motivation, and at times confusion about which path to take or how to deal with the frustration of our desires remaining unfulfilled.

When we talk of motivation towards a performing career we also have the additional problem of the public image of the arts and artists, which can be either negative or positive. To some this is seen as the most glorious and wonderful thing in life, offering the adulation of the masses and the promise of great fame and riches. This is the dream that fuelled the ambitions of all those stage mothers that propelled their own inner ambitions and the lives of their offspring towards the gates of Hollywood during the golden era, and which continues unabated to this day.

To others the performing arts are the worst possible career, full of uncertainty, inner agony and offering the prospect of penniless days in the company of life's drifters. And if classical musicians are partly cushioned from the worst criticisms by virtue of the obvious technical expertise they possess and the higher social circles they inhabit, there is little to protect dancers or rock musicians from negative attitudes. As one rocker put it, 'Most people regard musicians as one step up the social ladder from rapists and muggers, and it's this alienation from the non-musician that I believe creates most of the problems. The public judge a musician only by the money he earns. If he's rich, he's a great man. If he's poor, he's a time-wasting parasite who should get a "real" job. Even despite the purely economic fact that Elton John has probably paid more tax than Wigan and brought in more foreign earnings than British Steel, it is not a "real" job' (Wills and Cooper, 1988).

The reality of a typical performing career is neither fame nor ruin, but this polarisation still exists in the public mind and influences parental and school attitudes to the child who shows early interest in performing. The child internalises such attitudes and can carry them around for the rest of their life. All these factors influence motivation in different ways.

Early motivation

Positive motivation in early years frequently comes from a quasi-magical introduction to a future art form. A film director describes the thrill of going with his father to a film set, where there were colourful backgrounds, charismatic actors in period costume and a bewildering variety of cranes, cameras, gantries and other previously unheard of things, all bathed in a frenzy of bright light and activity. Saxist Wayne Shorter describes how he saw a shiny sax in a shop window and begged his father to get him one – it just looked so wonderful to the eyes of a child. Many dancers are intoxicated as children by the whole world of dance – the physical movement, the grace, the costumes, the sets and the music. These early memories may be the strongest motivation behind a future career. In the best of cases they go together with genuine interest and talent. In the worst cases they may propel into performing careers children who later find they lack the talent or staying power to become a success, and this causes tears and heartache as their magical desires conflict with the exigencies of the profession.

Early rewards for performing may be critical or uncritical. Both create problems. As any artist knows, feedback needs to be realistic to be of any value. The talentless child may be made a huge fuss of for pirouetting in front of friends and neighbours; the talented child may be told off repeatedly for no real reason. A concert pianist recalls how as a child he could never satisfy his father, who had been denied a chance to take up a scholarship to study the piano at music college by his own father, a singer who had callously frittered away the money on his own self-aggrandisement. The bitterness caused by this huge disappointment had made the father critical of his son's mistakes, grudging of the fact that he had overtaken him in technique and musicianship by his early teens, and envious of the son's career opportunity of becoming a concert pianist – something he had once so fervently wished for himself.

Nobody should underestimate the importance and destructive quality of grudges and jealousies within families, particularly when it concerns the relative talents of the family members. The long list of casualties includes John Wilkes Booth, who achieved notoriety by assassinating Abraham Lincoln. He was a failed actor who had lived in the shadow of his more successful brothers Edwin and Junius. According to Lane (1959), although he claimed to be striking a blow for 'the South', his real revenge was directed at his own family: 'It was the furies of jealousy that drove the actor to fire the shot that shook the Western World.' Other family feuds include the much popularised mother-daughter struggles of Joan Crawford, Judy Garland and countless others.

Reinforcement of the child's performing efforts comes from actual rewards like applause ('clever is when people clap their hands'), appearing in school productions and winning competitions. It also comes from the art form itself – the magic of music, the romance of make-up and costume, the compelling feel of bodily rhythms. Such direct reinforcement is a fairly uncomplicated stimulation of motivation. What is much more complex is parents as role models and siblings as rivals. What is even more volatile in terms of motivation is the things said by significant others about the child's talent and activities.

Spells and curses

To a child, performing is an enchanted world of sound, rhythm and feeling that makes all sorts of good things happen – love, closeness, excitement, rewards, applause – just as magic makes wonderful things happen in stories. The power of this enchanted world is intense for the young child. And so is the power of words said during this early period. A child can and does take words literally at their face value. Helpful expressions may have permanent benefits, harmful expressions can do untold damage. Often parents and other adults say crushing things without realising what they are literally saying, word for word. 'Shut up or I'll chuck you out of the window' may be frightening to the child, yet the parent only remembers saying, 'Can't you make less noise?' The effect of such expressions is magnified by the significance of the person who says them, the mother being the most important of all.

'Spells' and 'curses' are expressions of the populist psychotherapist Eric Berne, who never used Latin words when there was a perfectly good street slang expression for the same thing (to him we owe expressions like 'cashing in stamps', 'strokes' and 'sweatshirt'). A spell denotes a reward or compliment which remains in the memory as a positive motivator. A curse is the opposite – a cynical comment or prediction that things will go badly, which stays in the mind as a de-motivator. Initially such expressions are said by others, but they are soon internalised by children. One has only to eavesdrop on a girl talking to her dolls to find how soon the child picks up parental expressions and attitudes.

Some such expressions remain accessible to the conscious mind, others have to be checked against parents' memories or reconstructed from the results they have had. This is particularly important with curses.

Examples of spells are:
    'You have such a lovely voice'
    'You move so gracefully'

Curses can be simple, as in the following examples:
    'Don't make a noise'
    'Stop showing off'

Curses can also be predictors, and this is often the result of careless comments from parents and teachers:

'You've got a better technique but your sister is the artistic one'

'You're too nervous to be a performer'

'You might make it into rep but never into a major company' (to a member of the Royal Shakespeare Company when in his teens)

Since teachers are prone to a wide variety of predictions, they should bear in mind that on several occasions they have turned out to be completely wrong.

<u>Exercise: Spells and curses:</u>

> *Think back to any particular sayings you remember from earlier life. Were they helpful or harmful? Were they realistic or wrong? Could they benefit from being updated or even discarded completely?*

Ambiguous expressions

An ambiguous expression may be well meant, but carry both positive and negative implications, like the expression 'You look unusually beautiful tonight, Darling'. Another example is the expression 'You will go far', intoned weightily to a young rock musician. He did – and became part of one of Britain's most famous rock bands. The problem came later in life when he wanted to leave the limelight and play more esoteric music for his own personal satisfaction. Nobody had told him where 'far' was. It was as if he was on a train, stuck to the rails and with no destination in sight. He was already famous and had nothing further he needed to prove. He desperately wanted to arrive at the station called 'far' so he could get off and carry on with life. Fortunately he was able to do so once he recognised the ambiguity of the prediction.

Dealing with spells and curses

It seems amazing that we are so emotionally fixated by these early portents, but they do have uncanny powers of ruling our later life. Knowing this, Eric Berne would carry out a deliberately elaborate exorcism of the curses of his clients, which he called 'giving permission'. As with Voodoo and religious exorcisms, the 'magic' (or mumbo jumbo) of the lifting of a curse should be equivalent in gravitas to the laying of the curse in the first instance, to ensure that the subject truly feels liberated.

Other things to remember are that curses say more about the giver than the receiver. 'Turn off that opera, those screechy voices are getting on my nerves', clearly comes from a person who doesn't like opera, and says nothing about others who may find opera the greatest form of human expression. A child who starts to like opera may have to carefully set parental attitudes to one side and agree to differ, assertively if necessary. Spells, by contrast, can be treasured and brought out at moments of crisis. Thoughts like 'My father always believed in me' or 'My gran was so happy when I read to her' can be life-savers in moments of crisis.

Permissions and injunctions

While a spell or curse is typically a comment made regarding a person, a permission or injunction more directly affects what a person can and can't do, and sometimes carries great weight. For example: a successful businessman loved music and was looking forward to music-making later in life. He came into counselling depressed and confused. He had done all the exams up to Grade Eight on his clarinet in the last few years, but claimed to have no motivation to make music. When he discovered the origin of his problem, all was clear – his father had told him in no uncertain terms that 'he could make all the music he wanted when he retired'. Cursed with spending the next four years waiting to retire he decided he'd had enough and bought a saxophone. He joined a local band and left counselling saying he had never had so much fun in his life. And all this as a result of a careless and basically well-meant comment early in life.

Like spells and curses, permissions and injunctions can be ambiguous. Take the phrase 'You have a God-given talent – you should use it wisely'. This gives permission to use it, but an injunction against not using it. What if the person has more than one talent? What if the talent, in reality, is not that great? What do you do with the guilt of letting down God himself by not developing the talent, or the feeling of letting down audiences, or the envy of colleagues or even siblings who were not told they had such a talent? There have been a number of performers who have taken this issue into counselling, some because they were the owners of such a talent and under-achieved because they felt guilty for doing better than their siblings, others who under-achieved because they assumed they had been born without talent. In any case, the concept is elitist and does more harm than good.

Exercise: Permissions and injunctions.

Try to identify any predictions or 'programmes' that might have influenced you. Were they helpful or did they cause you to go down paths that were less than optimal or neglect opportunities? Could they benefit from being updated or even discarded completely?

Personal contracts

Personal contracts are vows made to oneself following life-altering experiences. Examples include:

a) A ten-year-old was mugged in Central Park, and as his robbers ran off he stopped a man walking close by and begged him to run after the youths and get his money back. The man shrugged his shoulders, said, 'There's a lot of it about – there's nothing that can be done' and walked off. The ten-year-old vowed never to rely on adults again, and to do everything needed himself. The ten-year-old was Mino Green, now a professor at Imperial College. Later in life his independence helped him make many original discoveries, though he regrets that he might have been able to trust people more.

b) A twelve-year-old boy went to the headmaster following an edict to the whole school to dismount from their bicycles at the school gates for safety reasons. Seeing that the masters continued to ride up the drive, he pointed out that this could be a safety risk. The response from the headmaster was, 'Boy, you dare to complain about your teachers? Get out of my sight.' The boy vowed never again to accept the word of a teacher without questioning the logic behind it. This again led to original work later in life (as an author), but a strong distrust of educational establishments which cut off some degree of academic opportunities.

c) A second year student became very stressed, was unable to sleep properly and consequently suffered an emotional breakdown. Once recovered she vowed to get eight hours sleep every night whatever the circumstances so she would not have to suffer the distress of a breakdown again. This worked, but left her anxious whenever she felt she had not slept enough, which as a musician on tour occurred with some regularity.

From these examples we can see that the effects of the personal contracts were both good and inappropriate, and they might all have benefited from being revised in later life so they were less categorical and extreme.

Exercise: Personal contracts.

Think back to any vows you made in your life. Were they helpful or did they compromise healthy personal development in some way? Could they benefit from being updated or even discarded completely?

Fear of losing parental love

As a child one may fear that losing a parent's love is the same as losing the parent. Consequently, the parents' likes and dislikes are taken very seriously. By one's teens resistance should be strong enough to ensure the independence of the child, but there may be more problems to deal with. Salvador Dali was one of a number of artists who were actually disinherited or otherwise disowned by a parent, and he found the emotional effects crippling (Gibson, 1996). Continuing into the performing arts without the permission and blessing of parents can be a heavy burden. Sometimes the opposition is obvious and vocal, sometimes unspoken and implicit, and revealed by withering comments like, 'Just remind me, what instrument is it you play?'

There may be a constant emotional undertow saying, 'Maybe they were right – I should have done something else', and in moments of crisis this can surface and cause much soul searching. With stage mothers the opposite can be true – there may be a real, even desperate desire to get off the stage and do something else, but this is postponed for as long as it takes to summon up the strength to dash the parent's (or teacher's) hopes for the offspring. There may be conflicting motivations – the motivation to carry out the parent's wish, for example an over-insistence on classical ballet rather than modern dance, at the same time as a stubborn refusal to follow a career path that has been rammed down one's throat, even if it turns out to be the more preferred option.

When dealing with these feelings, it can help to remember the following.

- People all have different personalities, attitudes, likes and talents – even within families.
- Labels ('the funny one', 'the shy one') may be right or wrong, and children can revise them or cast them off as needed.
- You generally do not lose your parents or their love, but just their approval. Parents, after all, have a right to their tastes and views, too.
- Indifference is sometimes worse than criticism. It is also often misunderstood and taken negatively. Parents can say little but be secretly proud.
- You cannot please people – even parents who share your genes – who do not understand or share your actual personal goals.
- If parents are not supportive, a new support system has to be created from friends, sympathetic relations and one's own partner and children.

There is a further problem – the shifting of parents' attitudes over time, otherwise known as 'the generation gap'. It can be easily overlooked that in the first years of a child's life parents are typically in their twenties and thirties, sociable and fun-loving with a lot of hope and optimism for the future. Their attitudes may well be more positive and flexible and imparted with vividness and enthusiasm. There may be more going out to shows, more music in the house, more dressing up for special occasions. The infant can easily see the parents as involved in culture and the arts and fix early role models in the imagination.

When infant ideas about taking up the enthusiasms of their young parents as a career cement into the desire to go to college to study the performing arts, however, it is typically ten to fifteen years later. Parents, by this time, are more worldly wise, disillusioned or realistic and may fall back on conventional career advice. The result is confusion. A parent seen as loving the theatre may have given up going for years and, as a forty-five-year-old, may rigidly oppose a career on the stage. This fairly typical scenario is best understood with the help of a time chart.

Figure 2.1 A time chart

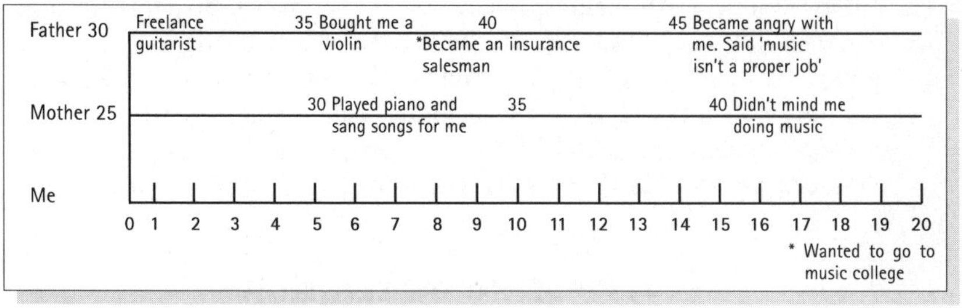

Exercise: Make your own time chart.

Make an age chart using the example in Figure 2.1. Put down the ages of yourself and relevant parents or guardians. Put in their jobs, attitudes and enthusiasms and any critical comments they made. Put down important dates when events happened and when you took up stages of performing. Look at the results and see how time affected the people involved and why they said and did the things they did.

Enthusiasms may fade as life goes on, and the vivid memory of the child becomes 'a far country'. The agonies and indecisions of one generation may even, ironically, be exactly the same as those of the preceding one. This may be lost on the rebellious youth who feels parents 'do not understand'. Generations of the same family may forsake early enthusiasms for sensible careers, passing on to successive children their hidden passions. Five generations of one Indian family were professional accountants and amateur poets. Another irony of the generation gap is that the iconoclasts of yesterday – Stravinsky, Beckett, Nijinsky –

become the establishment figures of today. A further paradox is the whole idea of an academically correct 'Beethoven style' and the like. The 'style' of Beethoven and everyone like him was to overturn academic correctness. Time changes everything.

The internal critic

The whole raft of spells, curses, vows, permissions and injunctions, together with received attitudes and role models, go together to make up the 'internal critic'. A large part of the function of the internal critic is positive, even essential. It retains all the teaching and advice that has helped fashion the core skills of the performer, so is an invaluable feedback loop on what one is doing in the moment. But it does need to be pruned of outdated or unhelpful content, which should be effectively sent in the direction of the recycle bin.

Often the internal critic is heard as a voice, or voices. A useful visualisation exercise is to imagine all these voices as channels on a mixing desk. The operator can then bring up the positive voices in the mix and turn down the negative ones. Obstructive thoughts can also simply be 'blanked' – switched off deliberately in the brain. In fact, the whole system of voices needs to be switched off to undergo Peak Performance experiences and get into 'the Zone'. This is described in more detail in Chapter 5.

Assessing motivation

Choice of form, style and medium

Workshops undertaken with performing artists indicate that the choice of what to concentrate on in one's career is far from straightforward. To assess this, try the following exercise.

Exercise: Art form, style and medium.

Art form: principle field of activity, e.g. dance, music, acting
Style: style within that art form, e.g. classical, modern, folk, jazz
Medium: instrument played, or role, e.g. clarinetist, singer, comedian, character-actor, director, choreographer

- *What was your first art form (as a child or in school)?*
- *What is your most successful art form (gives you the most money and work)?*
- *What is your favourite art form (most enjoyed in terms of sheer pleasure)?*
- *What is your fantasy art form (if you could start again or had the talent and technique)?*

- *What was your first art style (as a child or in school)?*
- *What is your most successful style (gives you the most money and work)?*
- *What is your favourite style (most enjoyed in terms of sheer pleasure)?*
- *What is your fantasy style (if you could start again or had the talent and technique)?*

- *What was your first medium or instrument (as a child or in school)?*
- *What is your most successful medium or instrument (gives you the most money and work)?*
- *What is your favourite medium or instrument (most enjoyed in terms of sheer pleasure)?*
- *What is your fantasy medium or instrument (if you could start again or had the talent and technique)?*

What we typically find with this exercise is that some performers have one single overriding motivation, e.g.

- First instrument: guitar
- Most successful instrument; guitar
- Favourite instrument: guitar
- Fantasy: to play guitar as well as I can

While others have a bewildering range of motivations:

- First art form: dancer (ballet classes until teens, grew too tall)
- Most successful art form: actress
- Favourite art form: singer
- Fantasy art form: to produce a musical with my own text and lyrics

When assessing the first example, there is little to be said apart from 'Good luck!' The second example throws up a number of questions. Was the departure from dance easy or very hard, leaving dashed hopes and a blocking out of anything to do with dance? Is there some dissatisfaction with acting, maybe even reaching the level of burnout? What stopped a successful career as a singer – practical reasons or just lack of self-belief? Is the possibility of producing a musical serious – is the script written and the songs ready to rehearse, and is there enough talent and self-belief to take the project to the point of looking for backers?

Exercise: List your choices of form, style and medium, and then list your thoughts underneath. An example is shown below.

Example – choice of instrument:
First instrument: *Recorder*
Most successful instrument: *Double bass*

Favourite instrument:	*Piano*
Fantasy instrument:	*Saxophone (always wanted to play it...)*
Thoughts:	*I should have played the piano from the outset, but got more work on the bass. To be really happy I should switch back to piano, which is realistic but might take a year or two. The sax will undoubtedly remain a pipe dream...' Carrying on with the bass might mean diminishing motivation unless I did other things like arrange and compose to avoid burnout and give myself fresh challenges.*

Careers can all too often be based on what succeeds in making the most money. But this may not be the best long-term choice if it is going to lead to burnout or if there is a latent skill that could be more successful. Hard choices sometimes need to be made, and some time out for a career self-assessment at key moments in life may be valuable. When it is hard to make decisions, one way of revealing inner feelings is to flip a coin to make a choice, and then assess your immediate reaction to the result – contentment or misgivings. Beware also the logical choice – it may not be the heart's real desire. Too many children are taught ballet when they want to do modern dance, or started on clarinet when they want to play the saxophone. As you become progressively more successful at one thing it becomes harder and harder to change course, and you may face an unnecessarily difficult career choice.

Primary and secondary motivation

Before looking at primary and secondary motivation, take the time to do the following simple exercise.

Exercise: Primary and secondary motivation.

Think of a well-known performer you know something about. Ask the question: 'Why does he or she play music/dance/act/etc.' Write down on a sheet of paper all the possible reasons, trying to list at least six or eight. Do the exercise again, but this time with a well-known sportsperson.

At the end of this exercise, take out the answer 'Because he or she likes it' and list it as column A. This represents the primary motivation. All the rest of the answers are in column B. An example is given below:

a) Because he/she likes it

b) Is good at it
Has talent so shoul
Likes to perform
Meets interesting pe
Money

The concept of primary and secondary motivation comes from sport psychology, where it is an important ingredient of preparing individuals and teams (Bull, 1991). Primary motivation is considered to be the basic urge that drives someone to do an activity – singing, dancing, etc. – and in terms of Freud's Pleasure Principle it can generally be considered to be a strong liking for performing that activity.

Secondary motivation is also indirect, and refers not to the activity itself but to closely associated aspects of it, such as being good at it or deriving money from it. Secondary motivation was not unknown to Freud either – he used the term 'Secondary Benefit' to describe activities like 'being ill' that had an indirect or paradoxical reinforcement. Being ill is not attractive in itself, but the attention and love that it can bring may be desired by a person starved of this.

In talent-centred occupations like the arts one generally assumes a high level of primary motivation, as one does in sport. For an athlete to turn out in all weathers to train assumes a real liking for the physical activity itself, and much the same could be said of dancers and their daily exercises at the barre, or instrumentalists and their daily practice routines.

In business occupations there may be little or no primary motivation – as one Russian succinctly put it, 'Office like office, job like job'. Many such people dread Monday morning, hate the journey in to work, daydream or chat to colleagues throughout the day, and are TGIFed (as the slang for 'thank God it's Friday' nicely puts it) by the end of the week. Their secondary motivations include money, achievement, being good at something – much the same as other occupations but in a different order, and without the balance of a strong primary motivation. The absence of primary motivation – together with the absence of promotion and high levels of expertise – can be one of the elements that distinguish a 'job' from a career. In the arts, because of the level of technical difficulty involved, there are few 'jobs' but many different careers.

Analysing responses

The first thing to look for is how soon the primary motivation is mentioned, which will give a clue as to how strong it is. The second thing to do is to group the secondary motivations (if there are many) into main concepts or categories. It helps to have two or three subjects, for instance two performers and one well-known sportsperson, so as to get a range of responses. The third step is to relate the secondary motivations to the respondent – generally they say more about the respondent than the subject. Take for instance the following example:

Subject – David Beckham.
Question – 'Why does David Beckham play football?'
a) (*Primary*) Not mentioned
b) (*Secondary*) Because he's good at it
  Because there's nothing else he can do that well
  Because he has a talent that he should use
  Because he can earn huge sums of money
  It has enabled him to captain his country at something
  His achievements will be remembered in times to come/after he's gone

The respondent here has focused on achievement and duty, and has overlooked pleasure to a large extent. Such a personality would be likely to be ambitious and driven, but prone to burnout and stress. Compare this with Example 2, again with David Beckham as the subject:

a) (*Primary*) Because he likes it
b) (*Secondary*) He gets to go out with and marry pop stars
  He can mix with interesting showbiz people
  He gets to be on television

Here the respondent has focused on social activities and the attention of others. Such a personality would be likely to have good staying power in terms of primary motivation and continued pleasure, but might achieve less and miss out on career opportunities, and be too concerned with celebrity as an end in itself rather than a consequence of highly developed talent.

The job values of performers give us some information about these motivations – money in their case is lower on the list than artistic work or creativity, and this confirms that performers are driven by primary motivations such as the desire to perform more than by secondary motivations such as money, status and respect.

Different kinds of reward
The particular enjoyment in any art form can vary between one person and another. If we take the example of a violin player, then the main sphere of enjoyment may be in one of the following areas.

a) Social Performing – being part of a group artistic activity and interacting with others, much like team sports. This is typically the thrill of being part of an orchestra, cast or company which is firing on all cylinders and enabling individual members to stretch out and even experiment in the moment. Often there are other associated rewards like deepening of performing friendships and group activities after the show, around rehearsals or on tour.

b) Individual performing – feeling the thrill of creating high-quality art in the flow of doing it. Performers describe the thrill of bringing off difficult moves, the bursts of unexpected inspiration, the satisfaction of mastery of their instrument, the elation of being totally 'inside' a role. On another level the actual movement of sound waves can be its own reward, like a bass guitar player who just loves the intensity of the deep notes throbbing away at the heart of the music. The highest form of satisfaction from this area is the Peak Performance experience.

c) Practising and technical mastery – it is sometimes hard to dissociate the art from the technique, and ideally the motivation is to develop both. There are times when one predominates, and some performers have endless patience in perfecting difficult technical moves in dance or tricky shifts or high speeds in instrumental technique. Performers like Glenn Gould were quite happy to give up playing in public to reach new levels of mastery in private, though their pleasure in actually performing the works they studied clearly remained very strong.

d) Hardware – this applies particularly to instrumentalists, many of whom become very skilled in maintaining and tweaking their instruments, and enjoy some degree of collecting and dealing. Secondary benefits from this can be in the form of creating a need in instrumental colleagues for oboe reeds, rehaired bows and the like, all of which does no harm to one's career. Collecting instruments has even given some players riches far in excess of what they earned through playing. In actors and dancers there can be an intense interest in make-up or costumes, and some carefully collect the costumes of their greatest successes.

These areas are not mutually exclusive, but some tend to predominate over others. In extreme cases the motivation may be in one area only, such as the violinist who loves taking part in music-making in the social context of an orchestra, but has little interest in the instrument or in practising it. Such a restricted area of motivation may have unhappy consequences if too little practice and technical mastery is achieved to enter a good orchestra in the first place.

The opposite is also frustrating. Great artists like conductor Carlos Kleiber or pianist Arturo Benedetti Michelangeli had no great gusto for performing in public and even abandoned it completely at times, though their private study and interest remained intense. And TV and film actors rarely appear in person in theatre productions, though there has been a positive recent trend for even big stars like Nicole Kidman to do so.

Suffice it to say that good motivation in at least one of these areas should remain strong if burnout is to be avoided.

CHAPTER 3

Self-image, Identity and Confidence

Self-esteem

Contrary to the idea that our 'self-confidence', as we call it, is something which can be high or low, it is probably three different parts of our ego, each jostling for control and alternating with the others. We have two secret fantasies which occupy our daydreams – one that we are 'really marvellous', and the other that we are 'really not that good at all'. We are all egomaniacs with inferiority complexes, is a succinct way of putting it.

And then there is reality, the third element, which corresponds to how well we do in practice. This reality level is usually fairly predictable and a lot more stable than we think. If others were to describe our performing ability and typical characteristics it is likely that they would broadly agree on our level of achievement, though they might disagree as to whether they personally liked aspects of our style or not.

The three ego state model in Figure 3.1 helps to explain many of our general human reactions, and can be seen below in relation to our performing self.

How can such irreconcilable fantasies exist alongside each other? Well, in a variety of clever ways:

- In order to sustain the belief that we are really talented, we can somehow contrive to never put our talent to the test. We can do this by making excuses for our instruments, not auditioning or rehearsing, developing strange physical pains, or even giving up performing. Or we can carry on playing with some 'excuse' for not doing well, like being drunk, always arriving late, and so on. We can thus continue to believe that we're secretly marvellous.
- If we don't get the feedback we want from others, we can become rebels and maintain that nobody really understands us – we're marvellous really, it's their fault for not seeing it.
- If others think well of us but we secretly doubt it, we can harbour the inner conviction that we are 'a fraud', and suffer constant guilt and anxiety that one day we'll be found out.

It seems paradoxical that we can have daydreams of being more successful than we are at the same time as worrying that we may be

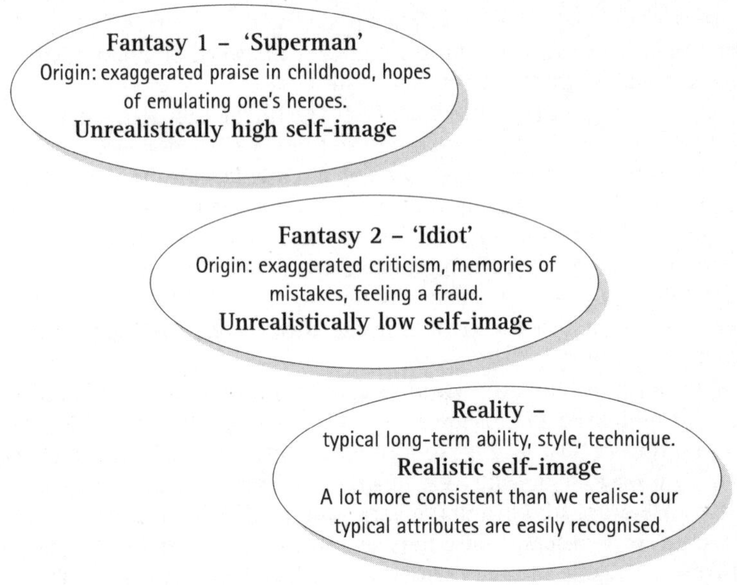

Figure 3.1 The internal world of the performer – the three ego states

exposed as inadequate, but that seems to be the case for many of us. Performers are more concerned with maintaining their inner standards than with any other aspects of the profession, so it is not really surprising that this subject occupies their thoughts.

Life scripts

The way people create superior and inferior fantasies and react to reality demands and positive and negative motivations tends to give them a characteristic 'style' of thought and action. This style determines how they react to life events, and shapes their lives and ambitions. Because this personal program is played out on the stage of life, it can be called a 'life script', a term often used in Transactional Analysis (TA), the creation of psychotherapist and author Eric Berne. TA analyses such life scripts and gives them titles that identify their characteristics, such as 'yes but' or 'if only'. Some typical examples of performers' scripts are given below.

The 'Unfulfilled Greatness' model
The child given too much or indiscriminate praise will at some time encounter some vigorous reality testing when he or she comes up against equally talented performers later in life. The accustomed rewards of a narrow circle of family and friends may evaporate in the

hard world of show business. The child may thus go from feeling 'I'm the greatest', within the limited reality framework of infancy, to the later realisation that 'I'm not the greatest'.

Of course this creates inner conflict. The unconscious, in a narcissistic way, needs and expects more praise than is ever possible in the real world, so the performer may experience a low-level feeling of anxiety, accompanied by the feeling that 'I don't know why I sometimes feel I can succeed and sometimes feel I'm useless'. This is quite normal, and a common train of thought in all spheres of life. The ways out of this dilemma vary. The performer may on the one hand try to raise standards in order to become something like 'the greatest', so that a solution is sought in reality.

On the other hand, the solution may be sought in fantasy. If unreasonably high expectations are set at a primitive age, they are difficult to maintain in reality, leading to feelings of inferiority which are mixed with the original feelings of superiority. This creates a vacillation between the 'grandiose' and the 'inadequate', which is compounded by criticism from others. Praise may be received as either insufficient or unbelievably generous, and criticism may be taken very personally.

If the performer dismisses the criticisms of others as hostile and uncomprehending, and blames audiences and others for not appreciating his or her real talent, it may be possible to preserve an illusion of superiority. In this way the performer may never really improve or indeed come to value the constructive comments of friends and teachers. He may hear his inner voice telling him to play better, and then sabotage it. The result is often isolation and an increasing sense of unreality and paranoia for the 'unappreciated genius'.

How do we deal with this double-bind? By accepting that we all have superior and inferior feelings, the performer can then start to admit the fantasy content and get on with reality, accepting a realistic level of achievement in proportion to his or her goals and talents. It may then become possible to feel real satisfaction for a realistic level of achievement, rather than getting stuck in the fantasy voices of greatness and inadequacy.

This starts the process of positive self-criticism, and improvement from the bottom up, rather than from the top down. The unattainable goal of being 'the best actor in the world', which results in hopelessness, can be replaced by a short-term goal of being, say, 'the best actor in one's street'. If this is attainable then one can move on, set a further attainable goal and reach that. By progressively attaining and then surpassing goals, we start to feel real satisfaction, and base careers on solid talents which are recognised and rewarded by others. Such a person may later say, 'I've been lucky', disguising the real effort that went into attaining these goals. The inner voice may add 'and I think I deserved it, too'.

'If Only' and 'Yes But' scripts

This is a close variation on the 'Unfulfilled Greatness' model. It describes ways of putting off actual achievements by constructing plausible arguments as to why they cannot be carried out. For example:

- If only I could lose a few kilos I could audition for parts
- Yes, I'd like to join a band but first I have to play perfectly.

To avoid having our real talent put on the line and made obvious to ourselves and others, it is hidden by all sorts of mechanisms which stall it. On the face of it illogical, this procedure is actually quite clever and practised by many. It avoids the unpleasant anxiety of having to expose ourselves to reality, possible failure and the judgement of others. It also creates the comforting illusion that while we are not being measured against reality, we are really rather better than we thought, and if our talent is comfortably high we can feel secure. This is like trying to have our cake and eat it. Nobody knows what this 'real hidden talent' is because nobody ever sees it. The actual effect of endlessly postponing our real-life career wastes time and opportunity. In this case the secondary benefit of avoiding criticism has sabotaged the primary benefit of becoming as good as we can within the profession by learning from failures and moving on and up. The antidote, of course, is to make a start somewhere and then judge oneself by one's progress from there.

The 'Rebel' script

Actors and musicians are often associated with rebellious behaviour. This is particularly, but not always, the case with popular and jazz musicians because of their perceived image as radical and against social norms. Rebellion is partly self-defence against aggressive criticism from others, such as 'when are you going to get a proper job?' and accusations of being 'arty' and bad at games at school. Rebelling is a young person's thing, naturally associated with teens and beyond, the time when intense interest in the performing arts is usually developed. It is part of the lifestyle of creative people who experiment with and change the popular state of mass culture at any moment in time. Rebellion contains the act of rebelling, which can be a motivation to express such needs in performance, together with emotions of anger and frustration.

The problem with rebellion is that it alienates people by provoking disapproval and hostility. Performers, being more 'Feeling' than average, need to be loved by at least somebody. This creates a situation in need of some kind of resolution. The 'betrayed' teenager tries to show he is independent of parental approval, and seeks support in like-minded rebels, but this means that he is now dependent on the approval of his peers. The performer may consciously think 'I'm independent of people's reactions', but unconsciously the opposite may in fact be true. He may have exchanged one support mechanism for another.

The perceived loss of parental love and approval normally causes some degree of angry reaction, since anger is itself one of the fundamental stages of loss. Such anger fuels the rebellion. All rebellion, however, needs a cause – just as showing off is dependent on some visible reaction, so the child who rebels against his parents may be depending on some reaction from them. The 'rebel' may consciously maintain that he or she is independent of parental approval, and reinforces this by rejecting establishment or parental values. Inside, however, there may be some degree of yearning for the reinstatement of parental love. Such inner sensitivity can be felt when parents show no interest, do not attend gigs or shows, or constantly suggest other ways of earning a living.

This can all be quite confusing. Rebellious behaviour can lead to fame, scandal and recognition – all types of approval. But the same behaviour can also lead to the inner feeling that the people we most want to please – usually parents – do not love, understand or approve of us. Such was the typical storyline and basic psychology of the Hollywood 'misfit', typified by James Dean and early Marlon Brando films.

As we have seen, 'sabotage' scripts, such as 'Yes But' or 'If Only', have some clear uses. The standpoint of the rebel shares this: the real self need not be shown to anybody or brought to account because there is no need to modify behaviour to make others approve. Freed of the intent to seek approval, the performer can predict that people will not approve, and feels in control of other people's reactions. The performer can then go on to blame others for disapproving of him because they do not understand his real self: nothing is his fault, it is all theirs. The real approval-seeking inner self, meanwhile, need never be shown or brought to account.

The performer may desire to please people, but feel that those same people cannot be pleased. Realistically, the people who matter in his adult career may be quite different from the ones that mattered as a child. Parents, for example, usually have no direct connection with the performer's career. It helps peace of mind to separate those who matter and those who don't. By becoming more emotionally mature, the need for the approval of others is reduced, and the main concern will be in getting on with one's career. Succeeding can be a complex process. It exposes us to other people's evaluations, and it demands the emotional maturity to ignore irrelevant criticism and get by with only the essential approval of those who matter and are close to our aims. With others it is sufficient to 'agree to disagree'.

The 'I'm a Fraud' script

The term 'fraud' is used loosely here – not exactly in the sense of 'imposter'. This script is found particularly in the careers of 'outsiders' or those who are naturally slightly different from the 'norm'. It tends to affect late-starters, foreigners and children who do not follow the same path as their peers. It affects those who do not enter county and national youth orchestras, do not sight-read well or sit grade exams, or who don't go through specialist colleges like White Lodge or the Arts Educational Schools. Since the artist often feels alienated anyway, this produces the effect of being 'a stranger in a strange land'.

Part of the blame for feeling a 'fraud' can be accounted for by the standardisation of arts education. There is an accepted path to follow through training, exams, schools and colleges, companies, orchestras, well-known teachers and master classes. It is easy for those with less conventional paths into the profession – such as actors who did English and Drama at university rather than a drama school – to feel they have missed their main chance and don't know the people who matter. Sometimes these feelings of being a 'fraud' are due to the late development of ability in someone who has abundant intelligence, creativity and talent. Such a person has all it takes to do well, but may still have fixed in his mind the memories of early disasters and being behind his peers in ability. The underlying feeling is that there are fundamental problems that make it difficult to catch up with others in the profession who are thought of as insiders and high achievers.

Sometimes this script is like a 'fear of success'. There is already an expectation of failure so the problem may be with the unknown factor of success, which is seen as the sphere of others more fortunate. What would one do with success? How would one cope? An example of this fear can be seen in a very good singer from abroad who consistently dropped out of competitions in the first round. Her secret fear was that she would win, and that when she had to carry out the inevitable round of appearances she would be revealed as inadequate – a 'fraud', in fact.

The worry is that people will find out that one is in fact quite mediocre. In this way self-doubt is projected on to other people, and the imagination creates the idea that others are constantly thinking, 'Is his/her talent that great or really rather ordinary as we all suspected? Maybe he/she can't perform properly at all'.

While performers themselves may use the word 'fraud' in therapy, this is an extreme exaggeration of what is happening. The basic long-term ability and talent of the performer is quite real – he/she is not a spy or impostor in any sense, and is typically much more able than these negative inner voices may suggest. In fact, many late-starters go on to do well because they have a richness of life experience that transfers positively into their performing and artistic qualities.

The Guilt and Punishment script

Performers grow up in a world where there is constant criticism on all levels – of their talent, lifestyle and achievements. The performer internalises criticism from early years and carries it in the head as the 'internal critic' or censor. This is the 'superego' of psychoanalysis, or the 'critical parent' of Transactional Analysis. The censor mimics parents and authority figures in criticising poor practice and rehearsal, showing off, flirting or having too much fun, and when basic desires for gratification contradict the puritanism of the censor, the result is guilt.

Some of this guilt goes back to simplistic associations made by children:

- the feeling that hands themselves are naughty because they get smacked in childhood. Hands that play an instrument may then be naughty
- play may also be naughty because it is not serious. If it is forbidden by parents, the child may then imagine that 'mummy and daddy don't like me to play'. Practice, in contrast, is serious
- showing off may become an ambivalent, confusing issue. Initially this behaviour may have been greeted with fun and rewards, but later with admonishments to 'stop showing off'. The child may not know whether it is right or wrong to show off, and may become anxious because showing off in public by performing may be 'clever', 'bad' or 'likely to get rewards or anger randomly, or both together'.

Showing off is also 'being looked at'. The child associates this with higher states of excitement – when other people are there and new things happen, or the child is asked to perform in some way. Being looked at later becomes associated with higher adrenalin levels, typical of the 'fight or flight' mechanism (*see* Chapter 6). It is exciting and nerve-racking at the same time. As well as carrying memories of being criticised, showing off becomes simultaneously exciting, naughty and liable to bring punishment. Later in life there are no parents to punish the child, so it may punish itself with stress and feelings of anxiety just to fulfil the familiar and expected consequences.

Such self-punishment is also meant to make the guilt 'go away'. One way of doing this is to sabotage a performance to make sure that one is somehow 'found out'. This is the sort of unconscious saboteur that tells criminals to drop hints as to their identity or guilt. In the performer, this may mean doing quite well, but putting in one small mistake so that the 'critic' can enact its little procedure of crime and punishment. Solo performers such as concert pianists may be quite familiar with this and wonder why such a 'token mistake' is really necessary. One extreme example is of a pianist who made, by his own admission, forty-eight mistakes in the first page, before going on to play the rest of the music well. The signal to the audience was 'Don't expect too much of me'.

Self-punishment may happen in more general ways, by drinking, drug-taking or self-induced vomiting before shows. The aim is to feel that the 'crime' has been properly punished. Part of this ritual can be the excitement of the sin, which becomes mixed with the thrill of the performance and the pre-performance nerves, creating a sinfully self-destructive cocktail. In the case of vomiting or excessive drinking and drug-taking, the physical effects can be quite dangerous and should be stopped with some determination and help.

In a deeper way, the censor can act like an undertow on the whole essence of self-confidence. Even if one's career is going exceptionally well, the censor may still remind the unconscious of past sins and the hostility or indifference of others. In this way, the internal critic sends up danger warnings which bring to light all the old primitive anxieties in otherwise successful performances. Such danger warnings are historical, and should be consciously phased out.

The 'Saboteur' script

Aspects of self-sabotage are described above – deliberate mistakes that tell the audience not to expect too much from the performance. The saboteur script is different from the 'If Only' script in that it actually carries out as many performances as possible, rather than endlessly putting performances and auditions off, but contrives to wreck them in some way. The saboteur can also be the kind of passive aggressive person who contrives to wreck the performances of others. One dancer who had to face this realisation traced it back to her birth order – she was the eldest and ruled the roost until the next child turned out to be not one but twins, which were then shown off to others and made a huge fuss of. She had never forgiven her mother for this shift in allegiance, and took out these hostile feelings on others thereafter, managing – often unconsciously – to spoil things for them. Clearly such behaviour makes one unpopular, and if it can be detected it should be avoided.

Approach-avoidance

Desire to reach a goal may well conflict with doubts and fears which try to avoid that goal. This is called 'approach-avoidance', because the closer you get to the goal, the more it holds you up. This is like snooker players who miss the black ball, footballers who shoot wide at the goalmouth itself, or a partner that fails to turn up at the church on the day of the wedding.

The problem is that desire for a goal remains relatively constant: it is felt both far away and close to the goal. Avoidance, however, may be weak at a distance, where the goal seems mainly attractive, but much stronger close to it, where actual avoidance mechanisms may operate with increasing intensity. An actor may plan to do an audition months ahead, then back out suddenly just before it. This may be for practical reasons, such as lack of preparation, but it may also happen when preparation is quite good.

Dealing with this requires two steps. The first is analysing feelings for and against, taking them realistically into account, and deciding whether the action to be taken is the right one. If it is not, then postpone or abandon it. The second step is then making the decision to go ahead. With professionals, the maximum fear tends to occur at the actual 'agonising over the decision' stage. Once a decision is made, the avoidance fear tends to decrease naturally. This has been proved with professional parachutists, whose fear is greatest at the moment of getting into the aeroplane, after which they know the rest of the drill is inevitable. First timers get most nervous immediately before they jump.

Knowing this helps us cope with the internal 'bargaining' that goes on just before something like an audition. It happens to performers at all levels of competence, including the most talented. Once this period has been successfully put behind us, the commitment to action is positive and the emotions relax as the course of action becomes increasingly clear.

Dealing with life scripts

Life scripts are part of Transactional Analysis, and to understand them it is strongly recommended that you do some further reading. All the books by Eric Berne, its founder, are accessible and easily readable self-help texts. So is *Born to Win* (James and Jongeward, 1978), which is also a good beginner's book. Detailed examples of life scripts are given in Berne's *What Do You Say After You Say Hello*, and illustrations include some fascinating 'scripts' of fairy tales like Cinderella and Little Red Riding Hood. Another master of fairy tales was Bruno Bettelheim, whose book is given in the Recommended Reading section (*see* page 242).

Some things to be borne in mind with scripts are as follows.

- We probably all have elements of these life scripts in our motivational patterns. Since they are commonplace, the presence of some of their aspects is normal and no cause for alarm. They are only worth dealing with when they become exaggerated out of proportion. It is also rather simplistic to suddenly 'discover' that you are one thing or the other and fall into the trap of exaggerating it yourself. Scripts are meant as a guide to natural tendencies, not as a 'diagnosis' of who you are.
- The whole of human existence represents the development of ever more complex forms which have the skills to survive in their environments. The complexities within creative artists contribute to the richness of their talent. Some degree of inner conflict represents the symbolic 'chaos' out of which creativity creates 'order', and may be

a dynamo of internal energy. Dissatisfaction with life is notorious amongst comedians, who can be the most lugubrious people you could ever meet in private. Removing conflict can even adversely affect one's art – John Cleese wondered if therapy made him happier but less funny.

- Even for comedians, there is always the option of talking over some of the 'unconscious' aspects of our inner make-up with a third party, such as a counsellor. If this seems a good course of action, try it. Details of counselling are given in Chapter 11.
- All performers have, understandably, a tendency towards the dramatic. This tendency may be fine for artistic work, but avoid dramatising your own failings as much as possible. Working with a variety of actors, singers, dancers and musicians in counselling overwhelmingly shows that motivation conflicts exist even in those at the very top of the profession. They do not stop us playing or becoming successful.

When we can 'own up' to a realistic image of ourself as others typically see us, we can start making real gains in our careers, rather than forever putting off that wonderful day when 'our talent will be fully revealed to an unsuspecting world'. Fantasy is important to creative artists, such as film-maker Roman Polanski, who said one of the secrets of his art was not knowing where reality ended and fantasy started. In the world of Virtual Reality, imagination has replaced money as a unit of currency. But for the performer, reality is a consistent ability to deliver the goods. And we are not 'as good as our last performance' as some would have us believe – we are as good as a lifetime of study and dedication gives us every right to be.

Developing a sense of scale

Having looked at motivations and barriers to commitment, the next stage is to examine our ambitions and see how they fit with our careers. Matching ambition with reality is the cornerstone of success – it ensures that we get real satisfaction, and it reinforces our self-esteem as we reach our goals. Once we have started to attain the standards we have set for ourselves, it then helps us achieve them consistently.

To differentiate between the real and the unreal, it is essential to develop a proper sense of scale. At the top of the scale, perfection in the arts is not an absolute, unless we are referring to 'perfect intervals' in music which have a mathematical basis. It is a construction of the mind, and has no more validity than 'total imperfection'. It would be extremely difficult to imagine a performance that could not be made worse in any way, and it is equally futile to imagine one that could not be improved upon in some detail. Even mathematicians have difficulty with absolutes – if you have infinity, which is infinite, then can you or can you not have an 'infinity' of infinities?

But if we take out perfection we are in practice left with some sort of scale. In athletics a descending scale of achievement would be: 'world record', 'Olympic record', 'national record', 'local record', etc. There are no such reliable measurements for performances, any more than for emotional states such as love and happiness. Even the idea of 'the highest paid actor' does not reflect definitive attainment, unless you believe that 'the most popular must be the best', as Harold Robbins once remarked when he was the highest paid writer in the world. Titles are equally misleading – the title 'Pianist of the Century' has been given by the press to Richter, Horowitz and Schiff, as well as countless others. And for how long does success have to last – one hit, one year, ten years, a 'lifetime achievement' award, or going down in history as a legend?

Some degree of measurement is possible, such as:

- legendary performance – critics still rave about it
- very satisfying performance – critics loved it
- variable performance – good and bad bits
- technically correct performance, but artistically disappointing
- performance errors noticed by trained professionals
- performance errors noticed by general public
- gross performance errors but piece completed
- performance breaks down completely and is abandoned.

Another way of scaling attainment is to use 'acceptable standards', such as:

- international soloist
- national soloist
- featured performer or principal
- rank and file in leading orchestra, company/choir/band member, corps de ballet
- understudy, extra or dep
- freelance in less well-known company/band/ensemble
- member of semi-professional or amateur group.

We could also scale performers on whether they:

- regularly do recordings or commercial work as a featured performer
- do regular recordings or commercial work as a member of the cast/band
- do recordings or commercial work on an occasional basis
- do not do any recordings or commercial work.

Though unreliable, these sorts of scales do make some sense because there is usually some recognisable 'rite of passage' between one level and another. This is frequently an audition – such as for a major company, for principal or for one of the top desks in an orchestral section – and performers plan carefully as to whether or not to audition at their present level of confidence.

Setting your optimum performance range

The range of performing ability varies between performers. Some, who do a lot of highly paid commercial work, have the reputation of working to tight tolerances, or predictably small ranges of difference. Others have the reputation of being 'inspired or awful'. Consistent performers may be disciplined or conscientious by nature, or they may have become mature and more confident of their mastery. 'Inspired or awful' performers may be highly gifted, but – like Hollywood's legendary hell-raisers – are likely to have problems with such things as:

- self-image: there may be cracks in confidence that sabotage performance
- high-risk 'brinkmanship' tactics: arriving just before the performance starts, drinking alcohol just short of, or indeed beyond, the point where it noticeably worsens standards
- lack of pride in themselves, with a *laissez-faire* approach to getting all aspects of the performance correct. This can result from laziness or confused motivation
- high dependency on others to make things happen, and low performing autonomy
- a truly creative and 'inspirational' personality, which has peaks and troughs of concentration and engagement in the performance.

Raising the top of your range

Matching your inner artistic voice to your outer performance characteristics helps raise the top of your performing range. Performances are not just actual events acted out on stages, they are also virtual performances acted out inside one's mind. They can be thought through in detail even before they are realised. Your maximum possible performance range is partly determined by your capacity to deal with this potential richness and reproduce it in performance or composition. This is an achievable goal and a good means to self-improvement. It has been valued by a number of jazz musicians, such as Charlie Parker, Sonny Rollins and John Coltrane, all of whom worked intensely on their 'inner sounds' until they found the means to reproduce them. Your artistic imagination deserves the greatest respect. For more on this, *see* Chapter 5.

Owning your talent

Another aspect of realising one's potential is 'owning' and admitting one's abilities. This can mean 'buying back' parts of your ego that you may mistakenly have attributed to the inspiration of others. The feeling that others inspire you is commonly experienced when you fall deeply in love with someone and they leave you. You feel that person 'was' the heightened awareness you felt when in love, that the person gave you something you did not have, that the reasons for your enhanced state came from outside yourself and not from your own qualities.

If you analyse this a little, you can see that the inspiration actually came from within yourself. It was you yourself that had the capacity for such an experience, and such experiences are within your own power, ability and emotional scope. Anything you have done at any time has been within your range, and the range of any person may be considerably greater than expected. To get some concept of this, imagine how fast you would run for a bus compared with how fast you would run if chased by a lion.

Our best shot is hard to measure. We do not have the opportunity that athletes have to record their ability in thousandths of a second and record the best times. We have our own measurement – partly external in terms of technique and standard of work, but mainly internal in terms of our self-conceptions. Because of this difficulty in measuring ability, it is important we try to get it right.

Eliminating the 'glass ceiling'

The term 'glass ceiling' has typically been used to describe the invisible attitude barrier that women perceive as blocking their path into management and other traditionally male areas of business. However, its usefulness goes way beyond this. It is, in fact, a particularly good term for describing the ceiling all of us put on our perceived chances in life, our abilities, our social status and how accepted we are by others.

Often people are prevented from enjoying particular aspects of life by their own attitudes and self-imposed psychological restrictions.

- Luxury is avoided by the idea that 'we know good value for money'.
- The benefits of a higher social world are avoided by the idea that 'we know our place in life'.
- The benefit of high earning is avoided by the idea that 'we've never been good at money'.
- Skills that could easily be mastered are avoided by the ideas that 'we're bad at maths, tone deaf, cannot act, write', and so on.

One would assume that those comfortable with fame have a very high glass ceiling, and want to continue life at the top level, but this may not be true in all respects. Famous people still eat in the kitchen, hand over their accounts completely to people they hope they can trust, and shop in supermarkets. Many have to persuade themselves that they can be good at something apart from their primary skill – actors who learn to write plays (Harold Pinter) or sing (Marilyn Monroe); singers who become songwriters (Stevie Wonder) or actors (Frank Sinatra); musicians who learn to produce (Quincy Jones), conduct (Ashkenazy, Rostropovich) or compose (Rachmaninov). Inside many performers lie other parallel skills, and it pays to seriously consider trying some of them.

Just as important is to identify any kind of glass ceiling that stops us getting better. This may mean going further than anyone in the family has, or abandoning 'utilitarian' limits to one's expectations. There is a kind of attitude that prefers a good value product like a new, mass-produced car, and another that seeks out a used model luxury car. In the second case the driver is proving that it is possible, even without great riches, to reach a certain class and excellence; an old Porsche is still a Porsche. The really talented performer may have to break through such a glass ceiling of self-belief on the way to the top. Symbolically, allowing oneself one or two real luxuries shows that the top is not an unreachable phenomenon.

Raising the bottom of your range

Eliminating bad habits and outdated criticisms and learning how to deal with failure help raise the bottom of your performing range, which is usually indicated by things that go wrong. One part of dealing with this is maintaining instruments and equipment in a professionally reliable state, and if necessary carrying appropriate spares. Another part is eliminating unreliable elements of your general conduct such as:

* arriving late for rehearsals or performances, or late enough to make colleagues uncomfortable
* drinking too much or generally being in an 'altered' state of perception which may mean an unpredictable level of performance.

This may be a hard exercise for many who somehow 'hope that it will be alright on the night'. Confidence is *knowing* that it will. Many rely on their ability to pull a good performance out of the bag, but as they take more and more risks there may come a point where there is a serious danger of sabotaging a performance and maybe a career opportunity. This applies especially to drinking, where the amount drunk may gradually increase until one day it becomes almost impossible to perform correctly.

Being superhuman is a fantasy cultivated by alcoholics, possibly because they think, 'If I can do that drunk, then I must really be good – think how well I could do it sober!' Doing it sober may, however, be just a memory. Tempting fate means that you are constantly gambling, sometimes winning small victories which give hope of greater gains. The sting in the tail comes the moment you meet forces stronger than your own. Alcoholics in recovery are the first to testify to this.

Failing safe – the key to succeeding

'If a thing's worth doing, it is worth doing badly,' said writer G.K. Chesterton. And indeed, everything in our lives is vulnerable to failure – equipment, plans, careers, and marriages. People's bodies give out, even rocks wear out. Everything has some kind of 'sell by date'. Yet show business is increasingly a 'success' culture, and the emphasis is on fame and making it to the top. If you judge success as a journey from the bottom up, everything gets better – more work, more income, more acclaim. If you judge everything from the top down, however, then the concept of failure can seem catastrophic. The reality, however, is that careers are full of ups and downs.

Fear of failure can be acute, as in well-known sportspeople. Dr Adrian Taylor notes: 'Fear of failure has been identified as a leading source of stress among many involved in sport, particularly among the younger age groups and those at elite levels. Those who tend to place winning very highly, or who have committed most to succeeding and are also less confident of their own ability, are likely to be the ones who fear failure the most.' (Bull, 1991)

The first step in dealing with failure is to put it into perspective. A 'bad performance' is not a catastrophe – it cannot be compared to a real catastrophe such as an earthquake, war, sudden heart attack, or destructive fire. The second step is to know how to manage failure. When learning to sail a dinghy, you practise capsizing then righting it; in judo, you learn to fall; and regular fire drills are essential in all large buildings. Situations are manageable – even predictable – when you know the routine for dealing with failure. They start to become nerve-racking or dangerous when you have not read the 'how to fail' manual from cover to cover.

It is unfortunate that the idea of 'the pursuit of excellence' proclaimed by some performing arts colleges does not start with a thorough training in how to fail and start again, how to rationalise failure and go forward rather than panicking and being knocked sideways. The same applies to parents who reward cleverness and achievement but who may simply not have the ability to deal with setbacks or failures, or pass on this knowledge to their children.

Do not be afraid of failure – like wrong notes when improvising it can lead you in more constructive directions. The capacity to see failures in scale, to accept them and then go forward to greater things is one of the key qualities of winners – whether in one's art, in sport or in life. Linford Christie won an Olympic gold in his thirties – perseverance pays.

Matching expectations to reality

When stripped of fantasy, reality may look pretty disappointing – getting an imaginative artist to accept the virtues of reality may be like asking a claustrophobic person to enjoy potholing. But reality is a crucial basis from which to improve. Nobody is born playing Hamlet, or even the scale of G – we all need constant reality testing on our way up.

When our expectations match the reality of our work, we achieve maximum harmony. Perhaps the goal of the artist is 'beyond' present reality, but do not underestimate reality itself, even if it seems bland compared to one's fantasies. Part of accepting reality is being true to oneself. Sometimes the performer finds his or her identity through the audience. If audiences laugh unexpectedly at disasters, we have a Tommy Cooper in the making; if they applaud elegance, an Audrey Hepburn; if they go for rebelliousness, a Nigel Kennedy; if they like the grand gesture, a Nureyev. Such shaping is realistic because it is in tune with objective reality. If the performer is happy with that direction, then it is clear that it works.

Difficulties arise when performances and artistic identities have to be shaped to suit others, not just business people like agents, record company executives or producers, but also friends, colleagues and even critics. Expectations set by others can be encouraging but they can equally well be very damaging, as has been seen with spells and curses. Throughout their careers, performers suffer all sorts of constructive and destructive comments, some of which are biased nonsense. Following one's own path and staying in tune with gut feelings and ambitions early in your career is vital to building on the strengths of your own vision – after all, parents, teachers or anyone else cannot perform the part for you on the night.

In the acting profession this can mean paying particular attention to whether roles are suitable or not. It is important to take the jobs that you identify with – it is then easier to learn the lines. Psychology tells us that familiarity with material helps encode it faster and more effectively into memory. The pressure of unemployment forces actors to take jobs that don't suit them, so one consequence is that they have a harder job learning the part. How do you know what suits you? The genre should be sympathetic, and broadly speaking comedy actors may not be expected to do tragedy. Some actors like romantic films and hate Shakespeare and serious drama. Others feel the opposite. One actor can identify completely with the revenge and courage of Hamlet where another will not understand the inherent drama in the part – for the second actor, learning the part will be a nightmare.

Ideally the actor should choose the right parts and then do them well, and it may be necessary to turn down a tempting but unsuitable part. No good scripts arrived for Paul Newman for three years, so he simply didn't work until the right part came along. The alternative can be grim. Peter Sellars fell into the doldrums after a number of shallow films like *Casino Royale*, and it then took him a while to get a big acting role like the lead in *Being There*. The agent is typically no help in choosing parts, since their main motivation is to take a percentage of work done. Often the actor has no 'advisor' as such – only the director once he or she has the job, by which time it may be too late. It's a bad business doing a part badly. It's worse again if you take your frustrations out on the company. You can be talented and unpleasant, untalented and pleasant, but not untalented and unpleasant. Most actors have limitations, even though some actors shift genres with confidence – Al Pacino, for instance, was a remarkably effective Richard III.

It's different for the musician – a violinist has the technique to play all written violin parts, though when we come to improvised styles limitations are more obvious – a bebpop musician cannot automatically play Indian ragas. Free improvisation, in fact, is a way of getting in touch with one's 'true self' – something that both musicians and actors can do.

Perfectionism

Performers constantly strive for high standards, and so the idea of perfectionism seems understandable on the face of it. Surely an attention to detail and a ruthless search for the best way to carry out a technical manoeuvre must be a good thing? In practice, perfectionism may be more of a scourge than a help when it starts to interfere with artistic judgement and the flow of ideas.

I have found by examining my database of personality profiles that the most successful performers I have seen are normal or even low on perfectionism, while those who have dropped out or had psychosomatic problems score extremely high. There is a crucial difference between performing a task perfectly, which is the kind of technical mastery successful performers have, and trying to live up to an 'image' of being perfect, which is where the problems start.

The standards for such perfection may be set by parents, or siblings and peers for whom there is a high degree of envy and obsessive competition, or by artistic role models one strives to emulate (Heifetz for violinists, for instance). The most imaginative artists can even create a nearly-believed-in perfect fantasy version of themselves, incorporating envied physical and mental features of others, which becomes more and more dissociated from their real values and attributes. This is like an identikit collage – this nose, that torso, those eyes, that voice. The idea becomes even more pervasive when plastic surgeons can actually give you your menu of desired features, and show business is becoming flooded with surgical enhancements. In dancers the search for the perfect image can lead to widespread weight disorders and the delusions of anorexia, where the very thin person feels fat and bloated.

There are great dangers in following the chimeric world of images. Successful people generally advance through talent and continuous work rather than perfectionism. They do things while others agonise, sometimes getting up at six in the morning to practise. They market themselves and have meetings with influential people while others day-dream of success.

Maintaining self-confidence

Performers are crucially concerned with their standards of perfor-mance, for obvious reasons. According to a survey of popular musicians carried out by British psychologist and musician Geoff Wills (Wills and Cooper, 1988), the most stressful factor they encountered was 'Feeling you must reach or maintain the standards of musicianship that you set for yourself'. Over half the musicians surveyed claimed to suffer in this way. Musicians, like all performers, strive for high stan-dards, and feel they are inconsistent in reaching them.

This inconsistency is a scourge to any feelings of confidence, and can seem like a roller coaster ride, where you are only 'as good as your last performance'. Reaching the standards you set for yourself is a question of maximising your motivation and matching your ambitions to reality. Maintaining it is a matter of being put off as little as possible by the con-stant variations in performing situations and the ups and downs of a typical career. Maintaining a professionally satisfying standard demands some sort of consistency – being able to rely on a 'constant' source of ability which is always at your disposal.

Creating the 'constant' self

It may not occur to performers to 'create' a part of themselves which can be defined and relied on, yet others will already have done this. All performers are hired for their characteristic qualities on the basis that they are expected to turn in a predictable result. Acquiring a 'constant' self-image is therefore part of reality. The idea of consistency has anoth-er virtue – it neutralises many of the characteristics of anxiety itself, which are typically:

- vague – we 'cannot fight what we do not know'
- internal and subjective, so do not accurately predict reality
- increased by the unpredictability of life events
- vulnerable to the ups and downs of our moods and surroundings.

The 'constant' self is something that can be created and used as a defence against all the external and internal variables to which the per-former usually feels so vulnerable – the variables encountered in performance, and the variable nature of one's own self-esteem.

To identify our 'constant' qualities we can turn them into a list, then contrast this with a list of the 'variable' factors we see as disturbing the consistency of our performances. The constant self is built around:

- ability and technique
- talent, inspiration, artistic qualities and creativity
- self-esteem and inner conviction of worth
- peer rating – feedback of your standards by fellow performers
- career rating – assessment by the standard of work you are offered
- capacity consistently to reproduce something near your ability
- personal qualities and the ability to deal with life events.

Performance variables consist of both internal and external factors. Internal variables measure our own areas of vulnerability, such as:

- variables in own performing state – tiredness, stress, jet-lag, alcohol or drugs, how we react to life events on the day of performance
- variable personal effectiveness – difficulties in coping with life events, susceptibility to career stresses or stage fright, health and general stress.

External variables include specific performance stressors such as venues, acoustics, stage placing, equipment, touring factors and the inability to hear properly. A particular stressor is the presence of critical or disturbing people in the performing environment – colleagues, audiences, partner, friends, family and teachers. These people usually fall into three categories.

- **Disturbing** – negative or critical people. It sometimes requires considerable vigilance to detach yourself from their influence.
- **Neutral** – these people may not give positive feedback, but neither do they give destructive criticism.
- **Inspirational** – these people make life easier for those around them, and are often sought after as fellow performers and indeed friends. The importance of inspirational people is that they allow you to be yourself.

Case history

Here is an illustration of the factors that make up the 'constant' self and 'performance variables'. The musician concerned is a principal player in a professional orchestra who also does freelance work. He suffers from intermittent performance anxiety but has played through many nervous performances with at worst some occasional missed notes. For many years he has played at the top of his profession. The musician's 'constant self' comprises the following.

- Technique – good.
- Sight-reading – good. Prefers to see part sometimes, but can read first time.
- Leadership ability – good. Can do principal parts.
- Musicality – good. Complemented by peers and others.
- Reliability – good. High coping skills, recognised by others.
- Experience – good. Thousands of performances.
- Versatility – good. Clarinets, saxes and flute, plus light music, bands, etc.
- Competitiveness – good. Determined not to be put off.
- Capacity for dealing with crises – good. Can play through feelings of considerable distress.

The variables that this musician needs to guard against are as follows.

- Venue – certain concert halls cause discomfort.
- Conductors and personalities – some work still needs to be done to banish memories of humiliations at the hands of over-critical conductors and to avoid internalising their negativity.
- Rehearsals – there are some bad memories of rehearsals which need to be forgotten.
- Catastrophising – he has a tendency to perfectionism and over-dramatising mistakes. The reality is not nearly as bad as fantasy suggests. Disasters have never occurred, and bad performances have been rare.
- Long struggle to become established – the response to this is, 'You made it in the end. Well done.'
- Perfectionism – there is a need to concentrate more on talent and less on failings. Everyone makes mistakes, and in this case mistakes are rare.
- Lack of pleasure in music-making – too much concentration on duty, control and accuracy has meant some sacrifice of pleasure in the performing situation. In addition, some boredom and lack of motivation may be the result of heavy schedules, repetitive or superficial repertoire and several years in the business. Freshness needs to be brought into music-making by better listening and a more open and relaxed awareness.
- Tiredness and stress – heavy schedules and a family at home have meant frequent rehearsals where concentration has been a struggle. This has contributed to the lack of freshness and to feelings of being below potential, which have been misinterpreted as ability-related performance anxiety. There is a need to get rid of some of the less interesting commitments in order to avoid burnout.

In the example above, the constant qualities of musical ability and professionalism are fairly stable. The environmental factors are more variable, so the subject needs to reaffirm constant ability as a buffer against the ups and downs of the profession. At some moments it is necessary to cope more, at others one can feel naturally confident. Do not over-estimate the power of changing circumstances to unsettle you, but at the same time allow for their existence. If, for example, you simultaneously have to cope with a number of destabilising factors – say, tiredness, stress and relationship problems – then deal with these problems separately on a practical level, and don't confuse them with your performing ability. Where a number of disturbing factors are present, consider damage limitation rather than performing at your best. And if you feel anxious or panicky as a result, don't assume that all future performances could also go badly. This is discussed further in Chapter 7.

Natural life events don't 'destroy' your constant abilities. Your talent and personal effectiveness are always with you. Trust them, and allow them to work in your favour.

Setting performance priorities

In a healthy order of priorities, the profession ('the art') and yourself come before other people and audiences. The priorities for a performer are remarkably similar to those taught in many professions, particularly health care:

- The Profession – loyalty and respect for the art and profession comes first. This represents its standards, ethics, history and personalities, and the simple joy of performing itself. This is an ideal to live up to and a reference when in doubt.
- Yourself – loyalty to your own goals and artistic direction comes second to the ideal of being a professional. This is what keeps your standards high and your heart in the right place. Your priorities towards yourself include mental, physical and artistic self-preservation, and fulfilment of your career plan. You are irreplaceable, and are more important to yourself than audiences who come and go. As Timothy Gallwey says, 'The person should play the game, not the game the person.'
- Other people – other performers, audiences, audition panels, teachers, agents, managers and critics come last. Although they play their part, they should not dominate you or the quality of your work.

The reason for this hierarchy is that the profession represents the most constant set of values, followed by your own values. The most variable and unreliable standards are those represented by other people. A professional is loyal to the art and to himself. An unprofessional performer with no respect for the art and a poor sense of self is of little use to the public or anyone else. It is good for one's career to set boundaries such as not going on stage without professional preparation, not over-using or misusing the body, and not being needlessly intimidated by colleagues, audiences, audition panels, critics and agents.

Positive psyching-up

By reminding yourself of your 'constant' self, you can psych yourself up against external stressors. Rationalisations can help, for instance: 'The audience intimidates me, but when I think about it, I know more about what I'm doing than they do. That's why I'm on the stage and they aren't.' It can also be repeated for audition panels: 'What if some of the audition panel can play better than me? So what? They are not playing – I am.' Other affirmations of personal effectiveness include:

- reminding yourself that genuine catastrophes practically never occur
- reminding yourself that some level of discomfort can be coped with and is not in itself a 'disaster' in the making
- reminding yourself that it is quite possible to 'grow out of' earlier mistakes and inadequacies as these are progressively dealt with in counselling and self-help procedures, and that past mistakes will not materialise like ghosts to haunt performances
- rewarding your progress and telling yourself 'well done' more often
- reminding yourself regularly of the pleasure of your art by allowing yourself to experience real joy in practice or performance. If necessary this may mean, for example, playing favourite music in your free time simply for the pleasure it gives.

Psyching up for particular events should follow the theory of equipotence – the preparation should match the seriousness of the event. Strangely enough, it may not be the high pressure events that go badly. One young soloist found that his Prom debut at the Albert Hall went marvellously well, but he came unstuck in Rhyl while doing a perfectly ordinary provincial tour. It can be a mistake to underestimate the importance of a low-key event – the technical demands may be the same. On the other hand, it can be a mistake to overdramatise an event. The shaky soloist facing a debut concert may have to be continually reminded that the audience are only people, the concert hall is simply bricks and mortar, and there will be plenty of friends and supporters clapping in the first rows. Sometimes it is necessary to psych oneself up, sometimes to psych oneself down. The correct approach is to treat each event as serious but none as awesome.

CHAPTER 4

Preparation, Performing and Public Speaking

Practice and preparation – work and 'superwork'

Exercise:

Think of any time, such as in school or college, when you prepared for something so thoroughly that you were completely certain you would do well and achieve your goal – which you did. If there were many instances of this, think of them all.

It may seem astonishing on the face of it, but some performers have never experienced the certainty of having prepared so thoroughly for something that success is inevitable. Many, many people 'just get by' in life, doing enough to do the job but not enough to really hit the level of their true talent. This fact is so important in careers that some attention needs to be given to the whole phenomenon of working to one's maximum ability. One common reason for under-preparation is that it is 'cool' to be nonchalant about one's talent and 'uncool' to be a relentless swot. In reality it is 'cool' to succeed. One musician who wanted a particular West End job not only bought the score and CD of the show and practised and memorised it over a six-month period, but also took the existing occupant of the job (who was due to retire) out for tea to the Ritz every Sunday until he left. He got the job. Another musician would have assumed that it was sufficient to turn up on the day and sight read well at the auditions.

Superwork is effective in all the performing professions (and in life in general), but it can dramatically improve the career of the actor. Sir Anthony Hopkins is one person who decided that simply learning a part was not good enough. Much more could be achieved by learning the lines so thoroughly that they could be delivered in all kinds of ways and with a variety of different possibilities and inflections. 'Other actors read a part fifty times', he is reputed to have said, 'I read it two hundred times'. This confidence offered him the freedom to experiment and find nuances while knowing that he was technically safe. Other 'technical' actors like Sir Lawrence Olivier prepared elaborately for parts, modelling gestures and physical movements on actual people (as in *Richard III*). Sir Michael Caine is an expert in the tiniest movements and gestures to camera – a technical command that his 'natural' performances can hide. It is no accident that all three figures attained knighthood – they all knew the difference that intense preparation can make to a part. Work at this level is time-consuming and requires dedication, stamina and staying power. Those who make the decision to raise their standards, however, may never go back once they see the nature of the rewards.

Freshness versus preparation

There is a school of thought in acting that says you should come fresh to rehearsals, so the part will be moulded by the director and the interaction with the cast, rather than fixed into a pattern by pre-learning. This has certain obvious advantages, but many disadvantages. The first and most obvious is that learning lines in situations involving others can keep people waiting, and if time is money they can become very annoyed. 'Know your lines and hit the mark' (the mark showed where you were in frame) was a Hollywood given, and in the Golden Era shooting would start at dawn and progress at a rapid pace, stars learning their lines in the evenings before an early bedtime. The traditional 'Rep' culture was equally demanding – you would get your lines on Saturday, learn them on Sunday, and 'block it' (do the moves) on Monday. Act 1 would be rehearsed on Tuesday, Act 2 on Wednesday, Act 3 on Thursday. You would 'run it' on Friday and then 'tech it' (the technical rehearsal, lights, sets, etc.) on Saturday. The programme would thus change every week, and of course the matinees had to be fitted in.

Other valid reasons for knowing lines are the freedom this gives to practise movements and non-verbal aspects of the part, and the opportunity to really get into the part by deep study of the lines. A side effect is that actors who are word perfect at the first rehearsal – as Olivier often was – can be quite intimidating and earn the respect of their peers. Changes in procedure have meant that in recent history the script is rewritten continually by teams of scriptwriters, while bigger stars and especially comedians are given more latitude to change lines and ad-lib, and consequently actors may learn their lines in the taxi getting to the set. Curiously this takes us back in time to earlier days when there was much more improvising, not only in the theatre but also in classical music performances.

Rehearsals may start with the general idea of the text and gradually become more text perfect. Sir Ralph Richardson would learn lines by copying them out, and used different colours of paper to indicate the stages of memorisation, from rough to perfect, as he became progressively more familiar with the lines. As the directors became accustomed to this procedure and the respective colours of paper, this gave him the opportunity to play pranks on them by turning up to the final rehearsal with the paper colour indicating the first rehearsal.

Other changes include much longer technical rehearsals for shows with special effects, like *Chitty Chitty Bang Bang*, and even that is no guarantee that it will work on the night. And the elaborate stunts in action movies mean that the cast simply has to be word perfect to avoid the cost of repeats.

Actors, like many creatives, tend to procrastinate, but there is no benefit in learning lines late. Psychologically, memory works best when material is encoded often and in small quantities. Dyslexic actors, of whom there are a number, including some well-known stars, are obliged to learn their lines early, and find useful strategies such as learning the lines with their cleaning ladies or other people about the house. Ultimately, the justification of learning lines early and thoroughly is, as one actor put it, that 'Only a bad actor is inflexible in a part anyway'.

Using practice to improve self-esteem

Practice is the key not only to good presentation but to self-confidence in general, and those who attempt to do without it are tempting fate. Practice is a particularly 'conscious' time, unlike performing, which may be more fluent and even 'trance-like' in quality. During this period of consciousness it is possible to accomplish several important things:

- Work on technical issues and procedures so they can constantly be produced correctly.
- Develop confidence through going over passages several times correctly, so reinforcing one's self-awareness of having succeeded.
- Practise one or two possible variations on a performance or presentation, so allowing the choice of how to do it on the day to be made spontaneously according to what feels best and fits with the people you are with.
- Work on positive cognitive beliefs, like 'I am good at this' and 'I can do this'.

Eliminating technical problems means practising vulnerable areas deliberately and slowly until they improve to the point where they can be depended on. This means owning up to weaknesses and working on them, and abandoning thoughts such as, 'If it were not for certain aspects of my technique I would be really good.' It has to be assumed that in performance any movements must be automatic, so in practice all details have to be correctly rehearsed. Performance must take place in a state of total readiness, and only in this state can the performer hope for trance-like 'peak' performances where all details are magically correct.

Practise confidence – do not practise stress. At the end of practice periods there should be a good feeling, which becomes cumulative and reinforces self-belief. Practice periods that end in gloom and despondency must be avoided – they have the opposite effect of reinforcing hopelessness. Positive practice is a habit that many professionals, especially older ones, may have fallen out of. This is unwise because practice is needed to keep limbs and mind fluent and to create and maintain an intimate contact with the performing self. Confidence is very effective when built up in the intimate hours of practice and self-communication. Professionals with heavy touring schedules may be tempted to leave out practice due to travelling arrangements, but a number of top professionals – such as guitarist Pat Metheny – make a habit of getting in at least an hour of practice before going on stage. If top people do this, why can't we all?

Pleasure is important during practice, so include something enjoyable in each session. This can be a piece you particularly like, or trying out a new idea. If you are not happy with practising, vary it in any way you like in order to get more pleasure and love out of it. Practise partly like an 'amateur' who does things out of enthusiasm, and within any session include technique, pleasure and adequate breaks. Enjoyable practice avoids the dangers of a bigger problem – repetitive strain injury (RSI). If practice is detached, inhuman and purely mechanical, essential signs of discomfort may be ignored and practice may continue past the threshold of pain. Compulsive repetition, such as desperate last-minute preparation for big events, and mental stresses which then affect the neck and limbs, progressively overload the body and problems can start to occur (Winspur and Wynn-Parry, 1998).

State-induced learning

A known way of enhancing learning is to carry out the process of learning in the state you will be in when you want to retrieve the information. This can be a question of performing mood, or the actual performance location and instrument, in the case of grand pianos. The idea is that a memory stored in a particular circumstance may come to mind better if that circumstance is repeated in performance. In practical terms this may mean doing some learning on stage, or at least learning at the same volume.

In a more theoretical way it raises the question of whether we should 'learn' as we would 'perform', or whether the two processes are better done in different ways. Should we consciously analyse to learn, then forget the analysis when on stage?

Both systems have their proponents. Many recommend that practice be conscious, and performance be unconscious, in that once all the elements are mastered they take place automatically. The Inner Game technique (*see* Chapter 5) proposes that as much learning as possible should be experiential, and based on feelings and insight into the whole experience of performing rather than a constant analysis of detail. It says that 'to play in Self 2 (the natural rather than critical self) you need to practise in Self 2', which accentuates feeling, body learning, intuition and self-directed pleasurable activity. This is also important in that it allows you to make moves instinctively and smoothly – as Chopin recommended for the playing of his *Etudes* – rather than by consciously remembering the technical procedures taught by one's teachers. This gives a stronger sense of one's individual style and helps reach the central essence of the piece. It is possible that optimum learning may do both. This may mean getting the overall feel first, correcting details, then going through the piece in a performing state of mind.

Mastering the elements

The individual elements are the nuts and bolts of performance, and mastering them is made easier by a number of methods that are generally well known to teachers:

- Find the optimum way of expressing a passage – the right speed, loudness and rhythm – then try it either side of the optimum to give you the flexibility of response you need in the moment of performance. Practise 20 per cent faster, to allow you to feel comfortable at the right speed. Do it louder and quieter to gauge where the right level is – this applies both to music and to acting, for instance the volume you choose to express anger, which can vary from a whisper to a roar. Feel secure that you have options you have practised.

- Do not practise mistakes. On first acquaintance with a piece, start slowly and surely, then gradually build up in intensity. The alternative of trying a piece through first to get a general feel for it may help, but only if you can do it without mistakes that later need to be unlearned.

- If you are nervous of forgetting the end of a piece, start memorising it from the end so that it becomes progressively more familiar. Such 'backwards' learning is favoured by some, though it is not a general recommendation.

- Make a point of resolving problems rather than ignoring them. Cowardice in learning results in disaster on the night. Nothing is to be gained by massaging your ego into thinking that it will be 'alright on the night'. Practise around the problem areas, approaching them and leaving them as well as actually getting through them.

- Feel the rhythm of the piece, and the bodily movements that go with that. This applies more with classical music than many players imagine. The lively, dance-like rhythms of composers from Bach to Stravinsky, Chopin to Debussy, should be clear and rhythmic, not merely 'heartfelt' meanderings which reduce a lot of music to nonsense.

- Work out the logic of the piece. Whether this is verbal, dance or music there are clearly understandable logical progressions and an artistic 'argument'. It may also be possible to establish what is the climactic point or essence of the piece, and to rise towards this and then fall away from it.

- Practise effectively by using time-management to prioritise essential learning goals, then moderate and lesser goals. Use 'prime time', when you are fresh and in a good state to memorise, to deal with the most important aspects of learning such as new challenges, problems and passages that need to be learned perfectly.

Strategies differ. While one person preparing for a major competition may use a high-planning, low-risk strategy of rehearsing, another may go for a higher excitement level by performing spontaneously, hoping that technique will follow where the brain leads. Pianist Alfred Cortot would rehearse twenty ways of playing a passage and then play the twenty-first when he went on stage.

Those that want to plan in more detail can work out longer term strategies using calendars and written schedules. This may not be to the taste of everyone, but is one way of meeting deadlines like shows and recitals in such a way as to allow for leisure activity to be fitted in regularly.

Creative people are by disposition natural 'bingers'. They take life as it comes, and when on the crest of an enthusiasm are capable of immense effort, followed by slack periods in-between. Such binges may result in great things, and have meaning and worth up to the point when the mind or body naturally tires. Sometimes inspiration is compelling – writers frequently wake up with ideas and spend the rest of the night gripped in fruitful toil.

When to practise?
The easiest answer to this is 'when you most feel like it'. This has to take into account sociable hours and neighbours, but can vary according to your natural rhythm or your typical schedule. Examples are:

- early morning, for early risers
- midday or early afternoon, for late risers
- an hour or two before going on stage, for soloists or touring professionals who want to be 100 per cent effective on the night
- late at night, for impulsive creatives without neighbours, or musicians with silent keyboards.

The main points are comfort and motivation. Both show that the mind is at its most receptive, and that memorising will be effective. The mind should be fresh and alert, the body relaxed. If it feels stiff, start with some light body exercises or go for a short 'wake-up' walk or jog.

How long to practise?
How long to practise is essentially 'as long as a piece of string', with the following exceptions. Many dancers and classical musicians have been taught a practice schedule that takes them through a whole routine,

such as all the keys, scales, arpeggios and common movements. There may even be different variations of this for different circumstances, such as a short twenty-minute version, a one-hour version and a full two-hour version with breaks in-between. Such a schedule gives security, because it practises the essential rudiments and maintains technique at a constant level.

Such schedules, where choice is involved, should be used at the discretion of the performer rather than out of a compulsive sense of duty, and can be varied to suit other commitments such as learning new pieces and touring. Duty breeds boredom and contempt, while personal motivation allows for positive learning. Motivation is often a question of mood – in a good mood two hours may be too little; in a bad mood twenty minutes may be too much.

Where to practise?

The learning environment should be pleasant at all times wherever possible, because good associations reinforce a positive attitude. Ideally it should be:

- pleasant to be in, with natural light from windows and space in which to teach
- as quiet as possible, using soundproofing to stop sound going out or coming in. This means the student can perform at proper volumes and not feel guilty for making a noise. Where this is impossible, learning aids like practice pads or electronic keyboards with volume controls or headphones may be used as a second-best solution
- firmly sealed off from others – some students are put off by being watched or listened to by other students, family or passers by
- uninterrupted – phones should be put on automatic answering and others told to respect your privacy.

Client-centred teaching

All learning theory shows that learning is faster when positively goal-directed rather than enforced through fear of unpleasant consequences, so a good attitude to teaching is vital. Teachers enhance the learning process by showing humour and pleasant personal contact, and by not being sadistic. Uncontrolled critical comments are very debilitating: the student acquires unpleasant associations which can harm the learning process, feels belittled and useless, loses interest in learning, and experiences unnecessary personal discomfort or distress. This is one of the single most destructive things in the performing arts, and damage done by sadistically over-critical teachers may have to be undone in therapy many years later.

The student should have as much say as possible in the learning process. The teacher has the benefit of objectivity and experience of past students, but may also be subjective and unable to recognise useful ideas suggested by the student. The student starts with the huge disadvantage of having little experience of what methods work, but still has gut reactions and a common-sense idea of the direction in which to go. With these provisions in mind the student should have some say in directing the following.

- **Content** – the student should in part learn what he or she wants to, because the pieces to be learned should be loved and give pleasure.
- **Teacher** – what is right or wonderful for one person may be wrong or boring for another. So it is wise to choose a teacher who is sympathetic and likes what you do.
- **Style** – in the interests of comfort and individuality the student should maintain any useful elements of his or her own style or technique as long as they work well. Changes should lead to progress, not be made for the benefit of the teacher's method. Where a teacher insists on a method, the student needs to look at its results in others before embarking on it, and monitor whether it is a useful change. Changes to embouchure in brass musicians, for example, can give mixed results – with one player they work, with another they cause confusion and are later discarded. Realistically speaking, a teacher may know his own method inside out and be less effective outside it.
- **Musical instrument** – some children are manipulated into playing a second or third choice of instrument, or are given an instrument for 'logical' or economic reasons rather than because they like it (tall people are often given double basses, for example, while children are given recorders). Motivation is clearly strongest when there is the strongest possible bond between musician and instrument, and neither logic nor economics come into what is a bond of love.

A client-centred attitude is also about asking as much as telling. Common questions include:

- how do you think that went – was it how you wanted it?
- which alternative feels better to you?
- where exactly are you experiencing problems?
- what exactly don't you understand?
- what are your career goals? What do you need to learn to realise them?
- how much do you think you have learned at this point – is it more or less than you expected?

The client-centred attitude is, as much as possible, non-judgemental. Common transactions can be rephrased so that they turn the attention away from the person and on to the performance:

'That wasn't very good' can become 'You seemed unhappy about that'.

'Can't you do better than that?' can become 'How do you want to play this?'

The client-centred attitude also makes a point of rewarding positive change and growth:

'That was a lot better – it sounded excellent.'

'I'm pleased with the progress you are making.'

'You really have worked on this, well done!'

Assessing skill and talent

Assessment of skills and aptitudes is a process that psychologists, scientists and statisticians learn to do systematically and objectively. Everyone else tends to do the same thing subjectively, using intuition and personal experience. While assessment of performers by fellow performers has the benefit of inside knowledge, it runs the risk of being biased, inaccurate or of favouring certain elements over the whole picture.

Many great figures of history, such as Einstein and Churchill, were written off as mediocre in school. Their assessors saw them doing one thing in one context and made a subjective reaction. The results were grossly wrong. In the same way, countless performers have been ignored or written off by teachers because they could not do things the teacher wanted, but could do many things the teacher did not value or sympathise with. Consequently, teachers should:

- make a global evaluation of skill, capacity for learning, motivation, personal characteristics such as looks, charisma, leadership and persistence, and potential for creativity. An evaluation based on performing ability alone is not a total picture of useful aptitudes. Many teachers have a sixth sense for the personal qualities that will take performers to the top
- allow for negative side effects of positive qualities. Creative people, for instance, are typically admired for being competitive, imaginative and sensitive, but thought of as a tiresome nuisance for being radical, individualistic and unconventional. There is a well-documented history of creative students being underestimated because of their unorthodox ways of approaching theories and problems
- recommend another teacher if they think they are negatively biased. Counsellors and therapists do this as a matter of course – if there is not sufficient mutual sympathy they may decline to take a client and refer them on. An assessment based on lack of sympathy is starting out badly

- consider objective assessment tools, such as tests of aural skills, to get a fuller view of a student's potential. Some teachers do this as a matter of course.

Peer learning

Experience is an essential part of learning. Besides lessons, practice and individual creativity there is the invaluable process of working with others. This is called 'paying your dues' in the business, and should be done as soon and as much as possible. Without it the performer is like a child with a personal tutor who never goes to school. Such a child has no idea of how to interact socially, how to find a level of activity to which others respond, how to be part of a team or how to deal with problems involving others.

With the advent of plentiful and cheap equipment for home recording, many musicians are turning into socially isolated techies who labour for hours making demos on computers, then attempt to convert them into recording contracts. This is undeniably a creative way of working and one with many rewards, but it may sacrifice the wide range of musical skills that can be learned from interacting with other musicians' approaches. It also ignores the whole process of putting a band together and keeping it together, and the experience of playing to audiences and handling stage equipment. Live music is the 'lifestyle' of the musician, and the language that musicians understand and communicate with.

Improving performances

Staying fresh

However experienced you are, it pays to stay fresh. Those who have been in the business for several years may develop predictable habits which leave them slack or restricted. Variety is one of the very highest job values of performers, so to ensure enough of this:

- listen attentively to what other performers are doing around you
- include new pieces in practice periods
- take on a variety of work
- go back over favourite pieces from time to time to rediscover their qualities
- talk to colleagues about actual performing, not just about money, cars or mutual friends.

Sharing

Many desirable qualities in the musician's life come from sharing. Examples of sharing include the following.

- Talking honestly about difficulties and fears. This is only considered 'forbidden' because it is assumed that colleagues will put about the idea that you are unusable. Those who do talk freely can find that it has surprisingly little effect on the quantity of their work or their reputation, provided that their work is of a reliably high standard.
- Asking others if what you are doing is appropriate and how they would like it performed, and explaining what or how you want them to do something. Be suggestive rather than judgemental, and leave solutions open.
- Amateur or non-paid performances. This is a particularly 'sharing' and voluntary activity, and many say that something special happens when money is not involved, even if there will always be some cynic who says, 'What's the tax on nothing?'

Dealing with performing situations

Pre-performance containment
Containment strategies pre-performance vary with the personality and taste of the performer, the venue and arrangements, and the status of the performer. Whatever the status of the performer, in the moments leading up to the performance, the performer is the star, and this should be clearly understood by all those backstage. Backstage personnel who interrupt the concentration of the performers, overload them with matters that can wait, or simply convey a negative attitude, are being actively annoying. In the case of high status performers, such people may be immediately asked to leave or even be forcibly removed by security personnel.

Depending on the personality and individual taste of the performer, pre-performance containment can include:

- total silence and concentration, with as little distraction as possible
- one or two close and intimate people to chat to, or a supportive backstage team
- physical activity like walking about, with or without other people to chat to.

Stars with dressing rooms often use dressing and make-up routines to calm and stabilise the mood, and to build up a good rapport with the backstage staff, who get to know their foibles and likes.

The audience
- Perceived as: a large mass of critical people who have high expectations and who are looking to pick tiny holes in the performer's technique and presentation.

- In reality: the source of the performer's income. The more numerous they are, the higher the standard of living of the performer. The more they are entertained, the more likely they are to come again.

There is a common view that audiences are by nature critical. This is probably quite far from the truth. Anyone who looks at the audiences for ballets, operas and shows will see a whole host of people, young and old, who are clearly there for an evening out and who want to see a show. In fact, they may be just as critical of themselves as listeners – they may feel that they should be more alert if they are dozing off, and may blame themselves for not being more artistically sophisticated if the performance is less than gripping and seems to go over their heads.

Audiences can also fail to see obvious things. There may be occasions when a number of soloists are depressed because of incidents in their private lives or just general tiredness and burnout. Audiences can see disappointing performances from great artists as a 'failure to give a commitment to the public', when the performer can, in fact, do little better in a depressed mood and has to carry on simply to earn a living. Such are the sad facts of life – artists are not bullet proof and they don't always sound like they do on their records or look like they do in their films.

The audition panel
- Perceived as: a bored and critical collection of professionals who are likely to look for reasons to reject an applicant and pick tiny holes in technique.
- In reality: a group of people whose aim is to find somebody who can perform with the right degree of talent.

Since they have to choose someone, the applicant must persuade the panel that he or she is the one through the usual arts of persuasion: sound and well-prepared arguments, pleasing presentation and proper research into what the panel is looking for. Analysis of how audition panels make decisions reveals that they generally respond to positive all-round quality of interpretation rather than cold and stiff technique and nothing else – we are talking about art, not mathematics. It is hardly surprising that audition panels are affected by the performance – they are there because they love their art, not because they hate you.

Banishing old spells and curses
We have seen how internal criticisms originate in childhood 'spells and curses' cast by parents and other figures of authority. Under the stress of facing auditions and audiences we become more vulnerable to these inner voices. Even worse, audition panels can easily have the emotional effect of bringing back memories of situations where you were 'talked to' or scolded. In the stress of trying to perform at your best the slightest

frown or sign of disinterest may trigger an internal conviction that 'I've done something wrong and they are going to punish me.' Reassure yourself that audition panels are not parental figures with awesome powers.

Failing an audition can be worse: it can trigger the internal conviction that 'I'm really no good – they said I wouldn't make it and they were right.' This also has to be rationalised. The reality will be more like 'They auditioned a number of people and for reasons I don't really know, they chose someone else. There will be more chances to audition, and the circumstances and outcomes will be just as impossible to determine. All I know for certain is that I can try my best.' Disappointment is understandable; morbid fatalism that nothing will ever go right is not.

Auditions and competitions are more likely to take place in front of a panel of actual or perceived teachers, in smaller rooms, in the daytime, and are very conspicuously judged and marked. Thus the association is powerfully with school in general and classroom teaching in particular. To neutralise this it can be very helpful to deliberately change the 'classroom' association to a 'playground' association.

To do this, visualise opening the door not into a classroom, but out of the classroom into the playground. Both images are powerful ones that have been present since the age of five or so. The advantages of the playground scenario are as follows.

- Instead of an older 'authority figure' teacher you have a peer group of your own age.
- It is hard to answer back to a teacher, let alone challenge, negotiate or feel stronger. It is, however, quite possible to challenge, negotiate with, answer back to or be stronger than peers. This radically increases the ability of the audition subject to challenge and feel stronger than the audition panel, which significantly improves self-confidence.
- The ability to challenge is on a continuum with other challenging mental states, e.g. flirting. As well as using this ability externally with the panel, it can be used internally within the performance – challenging and flirting performances come alive and have a dimension lacking in classroom 'didactic' performances.
- Play is fun, and often more exciting than learning.
- Play and games engross the attention, which is what is needed for performance. Classroom activities often allow the mind to wander and daydream, which is exactly what is not wanted in performance. This may be partly due to the physical movement in play and the lack of movement when sitting in a chair.
- Play is noisy and expressive, classroom etiquette is limiting, often requiring silence and deliberate self-control of spontaneous expression.

Auditions are crucial to careers, and contain a number of elements that can be maximised with a little careful preparation. The first is the element of competition. It is tempting when sitting in a waiting room to assess any other candidates present as being better looking, more confident, better known. Negative feelings at this point are absolutely no help, so a resolute rationalising should replace them. Anything can happen at auditions – other candidates can be more nervous than yourself and make more mistakes, they can be wrong for the part or job, and they can even be right for it and turn it down. Second-guessing is no help, and at this stage pre-performance containment is the most important.

Auditions are fairly short, so as with pre-performance containment there is the question of what to do with adrenalin. Adrenalin is covered in more detail in Chapter 6, but for audition purposes the choice while waiting is either quiet concentration and visualisation, light banter for extraverts who find talking relaxing, or in extreme cases brisk physical movement like pacing up and down or stretching. People have even been known to run up and down staircases to work off excessive adrenalin, though this is not recommended in the minutes immediately before going into an audition.

Another crucial factor is the order of pieces, in cases where this is in the hands of the candidate. In musical auditions, as in performances, we have to assume that the first ten minutes will be higher in adrenalin, after which the system should relax somewhat. So where possible the first piece should be easy to play in the sense of being well prepared and predictably bullet proof, fairly loud to avoid shakiness, and fairly mechanical to get the system going. Pieces for the voice should be in an easy register and loud enough not to be shaky. It is better to take risks later and reserve the clever stuff for the last part of the audition. The primacy and recency effects in psychology mean that the first and last parts make most impact, so the start should be predictable and the end brilliant. Canny performers even prepare something technically ostentatious that is calculated to have a surprise effect on the panel – the equivalent of Bucks Fizz's winning gambit in the Eurovision Song Contest. This may be an unexpected turn of phrase, high note or pianissimo, for instance. Even cannier performers prepare a range of technical stunts of increasing difficulty so that in the moment of performance they can choose which level of difficulty they are confident enough to deliver without risk. Such a coolly calculated approach, with safe fallback options, is well worth developing and has worked well in practice, securing some important jobs for those that have used it. In the acting world, 'stunt' effects like Jane Seymour letting her long hair suddenly cascade down or Sylvia Kristel taking all her clothes off during the audition for *Emanuelle* have been equally effective.

Crucial to auditions and competitions is a sense of one's own importance. There are some ways of improving this which have been tried and found to be effective. The goal is to feel like a person of high stature, success and wealth. Travel by taxi; be driven rather than drive; book a comfortable hotel close to the place of audition. It helps psychologically to have a pocket full of money – say about £100 in cash. This is not far-fetched. It gives the feeling of being a person of worth, able to cope easily with anything that comes up, and has been successfully employed as part of the arsenal of self-confidence. The idea is partly based on an anecdote about guitarist Julian Bream, who reportedly likes to be paid in cash before gigs, to the point of having had so much paper money in his pockets on one occasion when he was paid in Italian lira that it was hard to hold his guitar properly on stage. Performers doing auditions are frequently hard up and in search of better career prospects. Nevertheless, auditions are a calculated risk and as such worth some degree of investment. Sometimes they are the only ways of getting to a desired goal.

Practical considerations

Practical advice for the day includes everything that makes you comfortable, relaxed, leisurely and powerful.

- Sleep well before the day.
- On the day make all travel extremely comfortable: taxis, trains, etc.
- If you drive, use a comfortable car, e.g. a large, whisper-quiet saloon with big, soft seats.
- Dress comfortably but with some degree of 'power dressing', e.g. some like the authority of wearing a hat.
- Plenty of time should be set aside for everything – nothing should be rushed.
- Focus on what you are doing at the audition – if music, then the composer and music; if text, then the text itself and its author. Centre in on the material before going into the audition room, so that you are already ready and only have to 'increase the volume' when you start.
- The audition panel is the least important factor – the most important is identifying completely with your own performance.

Enlist the help of your accompanists wherever possible. Make friends with them and use them as your emotional anchor during performance. Maintain good eye contact. Talk through the performance together and decide on aims and how to achieve them. You will then feel supported and not alone.

As the concert or audition approaches, visualise what the room will be like, who will be in it, what is likely to happen, and how to cope with any problems that may arise. It is often effective to visualise a 'worst case' scenario, both as a rehearsal of what to do should it actually occur, and more generally to remove the hidden 'catastrophe' at the back of the mind and turn it into a practical problem which can be dealt with.

Performance isn't just about what you 'look like', although many seem to think this is critical. Errors include:

- thinking if you 'look good' it helps make you sound good or perform well
- believing the performer must 'smile and look extravert' as a general policy, irrespective of the actual temperament of the performer (e.g. introvert, intense, rebellious, etc.).

What really makes the difference is:

- intense identification with what you are doing – whether music, dance or text
- large dynamic range
- control of timing – spontaneous slowing, speeding and creating space is extremely effective in causing suspense in those listening, who can 'perk up' their concentration dramatically. Listening to performances is often a mixture of interest and boredom, where the mind wanders quite considerably
- showing dominance over what you are doing, through timing, self-control and a heightened emotional range kept under control, i.e. 'power in reserve'.

Short film takes

The problems of preparing for an audition also apply to short film takes, such as those typically found in TV soap operas, in that you have to be ready to start at a moment's notice. The waiting and hanging around can raise the level of adrenalin, and since the takes are short there is nowhere for the adrenalin to go, leaving the actor hyped up. So the techniques used in pre-performance containment should be used. Stage actors can find these short takes very frustrating, since in the theatre a performance starts to come alive after the first ten minutes or so when the adrenalin has started to subside and the interaction with the rest of the cast is established. In the short takes required by most of the TV soaps this may never occur, leaving the actors 'all dressed up with nowhere to go'. There is the occasional long scene and even monologues in the soaps, and these, at least, give the actors a chance to stretch out and show some of their real dramatic abilities.

Public speaking, conferences, public appearances and the media

How is public speaking different from performing?

One essential difference in public speaking of all kinds is that the person appears as themselves. There is no intermediary 'shield' separating the person from the audience, such as 'the role' or 'the instrument' (the body or voice in acting). Actors – a number of whom are essentially shy people – can and do feel much more self-conscious when making speeches and other public appearances 'as themselves' than when appearing in role in their professional work. The 'self' is more exposed, and with it one's inner fears and perceived inadequacies.

However, it is not just shy or private people who fear presentations. Such fear can and does occur in extraverts, where it may be due to a lack of trust in others, a disproportionate fear of criticism by others, or a perfectionist feeling that 'nothing is good enough'.

Background factors that may pre-dispose to presentation anxiety

Possible factors behind discomfort with public presentations can include any of the following.

- Fighting with siblings – sometimes frequently or over many years – where the subject rarely or never won. This is a sort of conditioned helplessness pre-disposing to flight (fear) rather than fight (aggression). It may be worse if siblings shared a room, hence there was no way of escaping them and no 'place of one's own' in the house.
- A feeling of personal shame deriving from the belief that one's own family was not good enough. There may be a history of dislocated family life due to arguments, abuse, a large number of rowdy siblings, divorce, alcoholism, violence or the like. As a result, there may be an envy of other families, or even a wish to be part of another family. The feeling is that others are better, and so standing up in front of these other 'better people' exposes one to feelings of inadequacy. Since the idea of 'others' is uncomfortable, the presenter may feel more comfortable when the audience as a group of 'better people' is deconstructed down to individuals, each of which can be related to separately.
- A feeling of aloneness, of being suddenly emotionally deserted in front of others. This may be a panicky feeling as found in agoraphobia – the void is around one. It can also be linked to other phobias, e.g. driving on motorways. It can paradoxically be present in extraverts who seek others' affiliation but have to overcome personal discomfort or shyness to do so. Again, in this case deconstructing the audience down to individuals may help, because when individuals smile or

show acceptance there may be immediate feelings of relief, and a 'return to reality'.

- On the other hand, there may be a discomfort when people are physically close, just as when they try to become too psychologically close or familiar. The presenter longs for the comfort of being private, alone and away from the closeness of people.
- A feeling that one has to 'be very good' to avoid being made fun of, because of a history of being made fun of, usually by siblings, parents, teachers or schoolmates. The fear is of being thought silly, or a fraud. In actual fact a simple and usual definition of a 'presentation' is that the presenter knows more than the audience, otherwise why would it take place? Dealing with this requires strengthening the speaker's perception of his or her own competence.
- A history of having to be 'well presented' and 'behave correctly' in front of others, sometimes to exaggerated lengths. This emphasising of minute details of behaviour can repeat itself when standing in front of an audience – 'Do I look alright?', 'Did I do that right?', 'Is my voice right?', etc. The speaker's attention may concentrate on negative details, which is an unwelcome distraction and increases self-awareness. The solution is to focus elsewhere.
- History of being sexually shy from being 'looked at' or more by parents, siblings or others. There may be a need to consciously keep any sexual overtones away from the process of public speaking.
- A discomfort with groups, and a history of being something of a loner. There may even be a paradoxical inherent exhibitionism or rebellion from feeling excluded, and a desire to make one's mark. Communication starts to work when the audience is 'provoked' and a link made, such a positive audience response triggering a feeling of comfort. This is particularly true of 'forthright', emotionally direct people who hate two-facedness, and need a direct response to feel validated. It may work when the audience responds to an 'eccentric but honest' presentation of oneself.

Exercise:

1. *Make a list of six to ten people who you have heard speak in public. Write columns for their negative features and positive features. Consider each one in turn and write in the negative and positive features for each.*
2. *Make a list of the qualities you consider you personally have to offer an audience.*
3. *When you have done both these things, consider what sort of qualities you listed as positive and negative in other people, and then consider how these compare with your own aspirations.*

Analysis

The following is an example of an analysis.

- Positive features of 'good speakers': fun, wacky looking (dyed hair), natural warm personality.
- Own aspirations: I try to look correct. I try to make the content of the presentation as impressive as possible.

Analysis: 'I seem to have overlooked in myself the most effective quality I've admired in others – warmth, naturalness and personality. I've thought it 'incorrect' to amuse or entertain the audience and 'correct' to be as technically perfect as possible, to satisfy what I consider to be other people's expectations. Maybe what I've done is to project my own fears onto the audience. It isn't them who concentrate on revealing me as technically inadequate – it's me. I attribute my inner fears to them. If they respond to warmth and humour, why can't I allow those natural sides of myself to come out?

Strategies and helpful hints for presentations

- Deconstruct the 'audience' into individuals. A good way to do this is to speak to one person on the left and one on the right, alternating between them. This looks as if you are addressing the whole audience.
- Slowing speech. There is a common tendency to speed up in front of others 'to get it over with as fast as possible'. This is also partly because one feels one is not important enough to take up other people's time and attention.
- Learn to 'speak read', i.e. make reading sound natural and like speech.
- Write everything down if it helps, then look up as much as possible while reading. This also helps to naturally slow down.
- Make presentations short and to the point.
- Make a structure, and inform the audience of the structure, e.g. 'There are three main points to this. The first is...' This creates suspense – the audience is forced to focus to remember which point is being dealt with, so this helps avoid a lapse in attention.
- Use visual aids, which you can prepare well at your leisure.
- Try as much as possible to appear relaxed and smile – it relaxes the audience.
- Get involved with the material you are presenting and believe in it. Say it as if it's new and has just been discovered. It helps get the audience to believe it and pay attention.
- Control the audience like an actor. Use body language, pauses. Walk up to speak in an assured way. Giving the audience confidence keeps their attention and makes them respect you.
- Be the expert. You know more about your particular presentation than they do.

CHAPTER 5

Peak Performance and 'the Zone'

There has been much study in recent years into how to get special performances out of sportspeople, and this has led to the identification of a particular performing state referred to as 'the Zone'. This state is characterised by complete concentration on the task in hand, and a relaxed, easy feeling mentally and emotionally that gives an uncanny sensation of everything having a natural rightness and inevitability. It is as if you are not the 'instrument' that performs, but are passively present and some irresistible force is expressing itself through you. In the arts this is referred to as a Peak Performance experience, and the phenomenon has been observed probably since the ancient Greeks, or even further back. It is probably as old as performing itself. Anecdotally, performers seem to experience this extra effect maybe twice in a hundred performances. While previously it was regarded as a lucky accident, we now have a greater understanding of how to put ourselves in a relaxed state conducive to its occurring.

Self-management and awareness

There are two main philosophies, both with a long cultural history, that are important to the performer. One is based on control and management and is largely favoured in the West; the other is based on awareness and openness, and has been made popular by Eastern schools of thought. Both have strong benefits for particular aspects of the performing profession, and certain drawbacks for others.

The 'management' style gives us the self-management skills we need: assertiveness, negotiation, career planning, book-keeping, performing technique, and the ability to analyse and solve our problems objectively. The 'awareness' style is more holistic, and gives us the performance skills that depend on listening to and taking in the whole playing experience, not just our part in it. These are found in the 'Inner Game' technique (*see* page 88) and 'Zen' attitudes (*see* page 86 on).

The awareness model, from which Zen and the Inner Game are derived, is defined by many philosophies and methods that emphasise two main elements:

- a 'holistic' view of the world, stressing the interaction of all elements, and the 'flow' of such interactions and events over time

- the need for all individual elements in this holistic activity to understand and be 'aware' of the nature and consequences of their
actions.

Holistic activity is like an ant hill, where individual ants are aware of
their part in the complexity of their overall culture. It is also like the
'horizontal' or non-hierarchical example of a team game. This interde-
pendence is sometimes called a 'bootstrap' model – when we pull the
straps on a boot, one end tightens everything else up, and if we pull in
the middle it pulls the ends in. Any activity anywhere in the process
'acts on' and changes the rest of the process. No man is an island –
everything in the universe is connected to everything else. The rele-
vance of this to collective performing is obvious.

Further aspects of this holistic model can be found in all the Zen literature, and in the work of philosophers such as Hegel and Heraclitus
(*c.*500 BC), whose surviving fragments include sayings such as
'Everything flows and nothing stays' and 'You cannot step twice into
the same river' (i.e. the water in a river is constantly changing). Such a
model has found a lot of favour recently within the ecological and holistic movements.

This model is often contrasted with the cause-and-effect approach,
sometimes referred to as the 'Western' model. Because it forms the basis
of European science and thought, it is also called a Newtonian model
(after Isaac Newton) or a Cartesian model (after Descartes). It conforms
to the scientist's desire to control or manage events, and produce predictable and repeatable experimental results which are 'isolated' as
much as possible from external factors or 'variables'.

Such a 'cause-and-effect' model is easier to deal with than the holistic one as it tries to be as focused as possible, to eliminate 'everything
else'. The problem is that 'everything else' is still going on and may be
partly unaccounted for. This is like the performing situation where the
performer is aware of the cause and effect of his own role but less so of
everything else going on.

For those who like simple solutions and like to control events to get
predictable results, it is difficult to move from the cause-and-effect
approach to a more complex conceptual model. This is also a difficult
step for those in the 'pursuit of excellence' culture, which puts less
emphasis on 'equality and fraternity' and more on the 'freedom' of the
individual. Despite the rise of a substantial ecological movement, our
prevailing philosophy is still a vertical or hierarchical one, expressed as
'Anyone can be President of the United States', or 'There are winners
and losers in life'.

In terms of the performer, this management model contains some of
the following ideas.

- I act on things.
- The better I get at acting on things the more I influence things in my favour.
- As I become more successful than others at acting on things, I acquire more power and influence than they do.
- My superior power and influence give me control over my life, my goals and my environment.

This emphasis on the person controlling the environment is typical of psychologist J. Rotter's 'internal locus of control', whereby a person feels that life events are directed mainly by his choices, rather than by the environment or the 'external locus of control'. The importance of being a 'winner' is prevalent in the United States, and can also be found in other societies where individual wealth and success are valued. In a holistic model, however, there is a loser for every winner. One of the cornerstone philosophies of Western business practice is to make individual gains (or 'profit') at the expense of the total environment.

The awareness model contains some of the following ideas.

- Things act on me.
- The more aware I become of the infinite flow and wholeness of all parts of the experience called 'life', the more my awareness and understanding of it increases.
- Increased awareness and understanding makes me more 'in tune with' natural events.
- Being in tune with natural events makes my actions right for both my environment and myself.
- Harmony between all elements in the natural world increases the overall quality of life of these individual elements, and is more likely to satisfy their collective needs.

Such a model is passively aware rather than controlling, and proceeds via listening, noticing and understanding. It responds to events by creating new elements that fit into the whole, and emphasises self-knowledge, study and an 'ego-less' state of humility as the means of achieving mastery over one's environment. It emphasises the way things naturally happen, as in the Buddhist term 'karma'.

The awareness model, like the management one, has many additional philosophic, scientific, cultural and religious variations and flavours. Associated belief systems include the following.

- **Reincarnation** – all beings are connected to each other through the flow of time.
- **Astrology** – we are influenced by the position and movement of elements in the universe.

- **Paranormal or ESP (extrasensory perception) phenomena** – there are forms of communication that have been subjectively experienced which have no objective explanation.

These additional beliefs are a matter of personal taste, and can be accepted or rejected on a 'take it or leave it' basis. You can choose not to believe in a number of the spiritual expressions of this model while still adhering to its essential core: that life is a complex, inter-related activity, and that passive awareness of it produces understanding and harmony.

The awareness or Zen personality

The Zen personality is much the same as that suggested by W. Timothy Gallwey in his 'Inner Game' method. Significantly, it is also the most common 'artistic' personality found in the Myers–Briggs Type Indicator (*see* Chapter 1).

- Introvert – introspective, passive, understanding.
- Intuitive – complex, imaginative, holistic.
- Feeling – non-verbal, subjective, non-analytical.
- Perceiving – open, spontaneous, non-judgemental, non-planning.

The first two preferences are slightly paradoxical. Although the introverted personality is thought to be more conducive to creativity and more common in meditative pursuits, Zen would strictly speaking not consider that this duality existed: it would state that there is no internal or external, no inside or outside to the mind. It favours both inner meditative awareness and awareness of the whole outer world of the senses. In meditation, for example, the eyes are half-closed, focusing neither inward nor outward. The Inner Game tends to share this.

In the artistic personality the second preference is very strongly for intuition, which provides the creativity and imagination that underlies practically all art. The philosophic nature of Zen, and its sudden creative insights, is also nearer to the 'Intuitive' preference. Paradoxically, however, Zen appears to favour the senses, since our senses bring us the essential awareness of our environment. Since enlightenment may involve difficult conceptual leaps into the unknown, the journey towards it may actually be through the imagination and through meditative contemplation back into the real world of the senses.

Zen is certainly not about materialism in the sense of permanent objects with independent forms for which people feel greed. Its fundamental idea that all nature is a complex system or whole made of 'ten thousand' particles, all in a state of flow, is simple but at the same time more abstract than many would be able to grasp. So the world of sensation means 'every level of sensation, emotion, intuition and reason at one time' (*The Beginner's Guide to Zen* (BGZ)). Strictly speaking, Zen would again not admit there could be a dualism between the 'Sensing' and 'Intuitive' preferences. 'To see dualism in life is due to confusion of thought. The enlightened see into the reality of things unhampered by ideas' (Hui-neng in *BGZ*).

In Zen, intellectual analysis is one of the principal traps of the mind, and much effort is made to free one of it in favour of the actual living experience, so the preference here is for 'Feeling'. This is also true of the Inner Game, in which 'Thinking' is close to Self 1 (interference), while 'Feeling' is nearer to Self 2 (naturalness, trust). Since verbalising is a left brain activity and spatialisation a right brain one, Zen would also be a more right brain activity.

Zen clearly favours the spontaneous attitude, and the concept of the universe in a constant state of flow and change. It also teaches openness to this flow as the means of true understanding of and being at one with the universe. In terms of Inner Game theory, there is an equally strong bias towards the 'open and absorbing attitude'. 'Judging' is nearer to Self 1 (interference), while 'Perceiving' is close to Self 2 (awareness).

The managing personality
Typically esteemed in Western culture, the managing personality is most commonly found in high-school males in the United States and, not surprisingly, in managers. It is a typical 'managerial' or controlling personality, and the 'Thinking' part of it is typically masculine (as opposed to the 'Feeling' preference which is more common in American females). The managing personality, in terms of the Myers–Briggs Type Indicator, is the complete opposite of the artistic personality given above.

- **Extravert** – outer-directed.
- **Sensing** – realistic, objective, favouring tried-and-tested, step-by-step procedures.
- **Thinking** – analytical, favouring logic over feelings.
- **Judging** – making judgements and decisions to achieve goals.

Management skills have heavily permeated the culture of business and free enterprise, and show more signs of increasing than of decreasing in a world of technology and intensive trade. The success of the East in world trade, however, shows that Western cultures are far from achieving a monopoly of business supremacy, particularly in respect of the holistic working environments of the Japanese.

Zen and the Peak Performance experience
Zen is probably the best model yet for the performing 'peak experience'. The common features relate to a state where the flow experienced has a

magical rightness, the mind seems to have a heightened awareness, and nothing else seems to intrude on concentration. The following quotes are from *BGZ*.

The true Zen state has been described as: 'Always master of the situation, completely free to respond in any way, but at the same time totally involved in what is happening. In what is seen there must just be the seen; in what is heard there must just be the heard; in what is sensed there must just be the sensed; in what is thought there must just be the thought.'

Through this state one can reach the ultimate state of absorption: 'There are simply two degrees of absorption. Mindfulness is a state wherein one is totally aware in any situation and so always able to respond appropriately – yet one is aware of being aware'.

Mindlessness, on the other hand, or 'no-mindedness' as it has been called, is a condition of such complete absorption that there is no vestige of self-awareness. While the mind may start by focusing on certain elements, it passes to an holistic awareness: 'Try not to localise the mind anywhere, but let it fill up the whole body, let it flow throughout the totality of your being. When this happens you use the hands where they are needed, you use the legs or the eyes where they are needed, and no time or energy will go to waste'.

Zen emphasises the 'once-only' nature of experience. Every performance is a once-only event – if we experience it fully our actions are 100 per cent meaningful. It also emphasises the 'ego-less' quality of the perfect experience. The 'I' does not interfere in enlightenment, in which the death of those psychological patterns called the 'ego' is referred to as the 'great death'. Without the ego there is no division of experience into subject and object – 'because the mind has no definite form it can so freely act in every form'.

Awareness and the Inner Game

The *Inner Game* series of books has been a great help to sportspeople and performers. Designed for sportspeople, its theories were first applied by W. Timothy Gallwey to golf and tennis, and later to skiing. Consequently they were applied to musicians by the American classical double-bass player Barry Green in *The Inner Game of Music*.

Performers can find much that is useful in the Inner Game. Like many aspects of human knowledge, the Inner Game technique owes, in its turn, a debt of gratitude to its precursors, particularly to Zen and its centuries of tradition, and may be seen as a contemporary adaptation of its essential precepts.

The term 'awareness' is chosen in the Inner Game to describe the passively aware state similar to that achieved by Zen meditation and by performers who listen in an ego-less way. This global awareness is called Self 2, and the 'interference' mental activity is called Self 1. The preferred self, Self 2, is therefore open, non-judgemental and takes in the whole external experience, not just parts of it mixed in with one's internal brain activity. It responds to the flow of the performance and its overall shape, and so tends to be right brain spatial rather than left brain analytic. It also focuses on the moment, being in the 'now' rather than the 'what if'.

In sporting activities, such as golf and tennis, external awareness is simpler because all the external cues are visual. It is easy to 'watch the ball' and see the whole game revolve around it. The position and flight of the ball carry most of the cues needed to hit it accurately, and there is no need for internal dialogues and speculations in playing it. In the moment of hitting the ball, where it is going, what the opponent is doing or how the racket is being held are distractions to the 'flow' of the ball. The same is true of visual awareness in driving – watching the road ahead shows the flow of the traffic and how you need to react to it.

In driving, awareness of the flow of traffic also reduces the ego to a passive state. The focus is on others, not the self. The exercise of power and control by the egocentric driver is ultimately self-destructive because all the danger signals are in the external environment. The wise driver watches constantly, realising that he is vulnerable at all times. This vulnerability is one of our basic biological instincts: the animal in the jungle is constantly monitoring the sound of birds and other animals for the presence of the tiger; the animal drinking at a water hole is constantly looking around. The illusion that we are all-powerful leads to arrogance and disasters, and the whole of the martial arts emphasises exactly the same silencing of the ego and awareness of the action around us. The same is true of skiing.

External awareness and performance

How, then, does this external awareness relate to performing? Unlike driving or skiing, performing is not a dangerous activity, but it does require vigilance to external cues. The difference between performing and all of the above, however, is that it is not exclusively visual, but auditory as well. The visual cues are, nevertheless, complex – if you are reading a score in an orchestra, your eyes may be partly on the conductor, partly on the score, and your vision may be taking in the instrument or the audience. Then there is the added element of sound, on which a much larger percentage of concentration needs to be focused. So 'listen to the music' is for the musician what 'watch the ball' is for the tennis player. While 'listen to the music' works best for popular musicians, who do not have a score or a conductor to distract their visual focus, in classical musicians it needs to work together with ongoing sight-reading and attention to the conductor. In this case, the score is like a constant 'carrier frequency' around which the external music is 'modulated': the score carries the supply of information, and the player's performance is continually adjusted to the cues coming in from listening to the sounds around him. Soloists who play from memory can concentrate on the natural 'line' of the music, which can draw out a performance as if by a golden thread.

Where performances have the element of sound, and this applies to all voice-based performances like acting, what aspect of sound, then, should be listened to? Certainly not oneself to the exclusion of others (unless performing solo and unaccompanied). Many performers listen too much to themselves and too little to the overall collective performance. They even go into a performance with a 'blueprint' of what they intend to do, based on what they have been working on or want to try out, regardless of what their fellow performers want to do.

Such 'ego-trippers' destroy the flow of performance and conflict with other performers. Such a performer is effectively 'in a tunnel'. This tunnel-like perception not only cuts out essential cues in the performing environment, it also deprives the performer of the ability to react to the flow of the performance and respond with creative and unexpected solutions which fit into what others are doing. This is particularly true in jazz, as it is in all aspects of theatre acting where spontaneous interactions make a performance come alive.

Too much ego involvement destroys teamwork and diminishes the ability of others to be creative. Ego-tripping may result in flashy individual show or technical brilliance, but it disables the 'best' creative ideas of the whole performance. Audiences know this and respond best to the collective atmosphere of any performance where the interaction is obvious. Great listening can mean great performances, as testimony from all styles of performing overwhelmingly indicates. It also reduces vulnerability to stage fright and self-doubt, because shifting the focus from the internal to the external takes the weight off inner dialogues and anxieties.

Where to focus awareness in music

If 'listen to the music' is the first step in awareness, 'listen to what?' is the next. The easiest and probably best answer would be 'to everything'. Some things, however, have obvious importance in themselves. These include the following.

- The emotions in the music. The four main human emotions are happiness, sadness, anger and fear – most other emotions are variations on these. Some music has little obvious emotional state, the richness being in the musical 'argument'. Other music has obvious emotionality, directly expressed or evoked, and the musician needs to respond to that emotion – examples include the works of Mendelssohn (happiness), Rachmaninov (sadness), Stravinsky's *Rite of Spring* (anger), Sibelius (fear).
- The rhythm in the music. In popular and jazz music, flowing with the

rhythm is the difference between 'flying home' and 'trying to row the Queen Mary through an ocean of Mars Bars'. In classical music, where dance rhythms underlie many compositions, it is the difference between taut, natural rhythms with a spring to them – as Rubinstein plays Chopin – and shapeless, sentimental meanderings around a basic pulse. Expressiveness does not need to be outside rhythm – awareness of the rhythm can place phrases expressively within it, as Billie Holiday shows. Rhythm is not the same as tempo either – inside a fixed jazz tempo it is the individual components of the beat that matter – where the backbeat is and where the drummer is playing the hi-hat and ride cymbal. Within the same tempo, two musicians can be totally out of rhythm with each other, and the way to get the actual rhythm right is to listen. A Chicago shuffle is not the same as a New Orleans one; a Brazilian samba is not the same as a Los Angeles one. Certain beats need practice, like reggae and salsa, and practice starts with listening.

- The sound and dynamics of the music, and the balance between instruments.
- The meaning of the music. This may be expressed in words, with the meaning and emotions they contain; in the 'programme' content of the music, such as in Strauss's *Till Eulenspiegel*; or in the social and historical content of the music. Besides this, music itself has a natural structure with suspense and resolution, and a series of 'arguments' with phrases that question, elaborate, digress, modify or answer. This is just as true of a Beethoven sonata as it is of a 32-bar jazz tune or a 12-bar blues. This 'language' of music often brings us closest to what the music is saying. Sometimes the clearest place to concentrate is on the melody line itself, in the context of the harmony that supports it. For pianists a full-length Steinway stage grand piano gives the opportunity to constantly work with the sound, which can draw out the performance.

Besides the whole listening focus, global awareness also encompasses the body functions that produce a performance. These include posture, response to phrases, relaxed suppleness, breathing and physical movement. One of the essential ideas of the Inner Game is taking your focus away from what is inhibiting performance (Self 1), and transferring it onto what enhances performance. Any of the essential elements can be a worthwhile focus, and trial end error will show which is best in different situations.

A further finding of the Inner Game technique is that certain functions are better carried out semi-automatically – without constantly trying to monitor and control them. An example is drumming out a rhythm on a tabletop with your fingers while listening to music on the hi-fi or radio. If you try to control the precise activity of every finger, the process gets harder. If you let your awareness expand to 'feel' the overall rhythm within the global context of what else is going on, it gets simpler. It also seems to use less physical effort, as just the right amount of effort is automatically put into the movement.

Another interesting finding is that it can help to focus not on the global environment but on one single thing. While drumming with the fingers, for example, feeling elbow movement makes it easier. Like a mantra in meditation, this is useful in the first stage of diverting attention from unproductive interference. Once the mind is more relaxed – as in meditation – attention can become more global and take in the holistic experience. Try these things out and see the effects for yourself.

Trying and trust

The passive nature of awareness and its 'ego-less' quality may be a problem for some performers. Those who instinctively want to be 'in control' may feel that they are losing their power. They may prefer to think that the harder they try, the better the results. This may be one way of performing, but it has many things against it.

The act of 'trying' tenses the muscles and occupies the mind with distracting self-admonishments about doing better, not making mistakes, getting through this bit or doing that right. It takes up mental energy and space which is better used in listening and awareness. Those who 'psych themselves up' repeatedly during performances to the detriment of staying open to the wider environment may find they are on a downward continuum where the harder they try, the worse they perform. Trying may aid power sports, such as weightlifting, where the muscles have to tense up, but does little for delicate finger movements. In addition:

- Trying causes panic when it is the only method and fails.
- Trying causes 'blanking out' of the memory, as often happens when trying to remember names or when doing tests.
- Trying can have an obsessive quality to it which is attention-consuming.
- Trying is antagonistic to trusting your ability – if you can do it why do you need to try? Zen teaches that we have inside ourselves all the natural ability we need – we simply need to remove the obstacles to using it. Tao says the same, calling it 'doing without trying'.
- Trying makes us aware of the difference between succeeding through trying, and failing through not trying – as in the popular expression 'you're just not trying'. Success and failure divides art into a totally arbitrary set of opposing values which it does not contain in the first place. Failure, anyway, is something that should be positively explored as a dynamic situation with several means of escape, rather than as a static dead-end entity in itself. Permission to fail allows you to succeed.

- Trying is a form of desire, allied to envy, ambition and many other forms of self-fulfilment which are essentially selfish in nature. 'Can't you see how hard I'm trying?' is a defensive stance, not an open one.
- Trying is allied to 'force' and 'strain', and assumes difficulty. Like success and failure, this introduces the negative element of 'not trying hard enough', as in 'if at first you don't succeed, try, try and try again'. This in itself is dangerous, since over-strain ('no pain, no gain') can lead to injury. If at first you don't succeed, sit back and take a look at the problem, then wait for a different form of inspiration. As Fritz Perls, says, 'Trying fails, awareness cures'.

The Zen master Rinzai said, 'There is nothing extraordinary for you to perform – you just live as usual without even trying to do anything in particular.' The Inner Game theory equally points out such negative effects of 'trying', and suggests the term 'trust' as an alternative means of letting things happen naturally. Such trust is both mental and physical. Mental trust is the antithesis of the 'trying' inherent in perfectionism, and successful performers generally trust their ability and practise steadily and economically, rather than agonising over their talent and practising fitfully.

Physical trust is synonymous with economy of effort. Muscle power is not the basis of performance – it is the correct use of muscles that counts. Trusting your body without imposing the tension of 'trying' allows muscles to work within their optimum range. This is the range from total relaxation to somewhere below maximum tension. Within this range they are flexible and responsive, and raising the threshold of tension progressively cuts down flexibility and brings muscles closer to their non-functional limits.

The more relaxed you are to begin with, the more muscle range you have, and the more you are able to use the tiny forces necessary to make micro movements, such as small movements in close-up when acting, or playing music pianissimo – even pianissimo must be above the lowest threshold of muscle movement. Economy of movement also keeps muscle power in reserve, increasing stamina and long-term effectiveness. The correct amount of power is 'just enough to do the job', and leaves reserves for maximum effect where they are needed. Such muscle power is not a function of extra 'trying' in performance, but of regular practice to build up stamina. In performance, power can be achieved better by timing its release, as in karate. Again, 'effectiveness' is more important than 'trying'.

Such physical trust is the key to the violin playing method of Kato Havas, the Hungarian soloist and educator (Havas, 1986). The way of holding the violin and bow is loose, as gypsy violinists do. The more the player can trust that the violin and bow are safe and will not fall, the more the body can become relaxed, expressive and flexible. This flexibility spreads from the left thumb through the arm, shoulder, neck and torso to the right bow hold, arm, shoulder and body.

Trust is equally about letting the mind do what it does best with the minimum of interference. Like the body, the mind is a marvel of exquisitely fine capabilities. It contains instincts, memories, learned processes and a whole wealth of subconscious powers which, like the iceberg, are far greater than they appear on the surface.

Memory – one of the key elements in theatre and solo recitals – is a hugely underestimated power. Under hypnosis, memory is known to be capable of retrieving vast amounts of unrealised information. It works best when you are relaxed and can positively trust it. The term 'sleep on it' describes the problem-solving ability of the brain when asleep. Your memory not only stores information, it also indexes and cross-references it. The mind is constantly rearranging thoughts towards conscious goals, and improving memory by 'understanding' what needs to be memorised and storing it into more easily retrievable forms. Anyone who has crammed hours of notes into their heads the day before an exam and found that they are sorted into a recognisable form in the morning will have noticed this. So let self-doubt interfere as little as possible – trust your memory, and let it work for you.

Intuition is another mental power that works best when trusted. We do not need to analyse everything consciously to stay in control. Intuition contains its own 'analysis' of events, sounds and feelings, and is processed outside the rational brain. Again, our capacity for intuition hugely exceeds our estimations, and can supply a whole wealth of information that lies outside the processes of verbal logic. As Pascal puts it, '*Le coeur a ses raisons que la raison ne connait pas*' – our feelings reason in ways that lie outside the awareness of our logical brain.

The difficulty with trust is that it goes against so many of the ways in which we are educated to think. We believe we are functioning best when we are 'in control' through constant vigilance to our wishes and plans. We ignore that we may have more control through constant awareness of our surroundings and the flow of experiences of which we are a part. We force our brain to work hard. We ignore the ability of our brain to take care of itself. We try to manage ourselves without delegating our essential functions to the natural instincts of our minds and bodies. We become at times so over-managed that we are unaware not only of our surroundings and the messages they are constantly giving us, but also of our own inner space and how it naturally reacts to our environment.

A further difficulty with trust is with learned events. When once bitten, we are twice shy. If we are conditioned to believe we will throw up during performances we try to control it rather than trust that we will not. The same applies to musicians' fears that they will play out of tempo, forget the music, drop the bow, play wrong notes or lose their place in the music. We do not see trust as a way out of this dilemma because we do not 'trust' trust. We can say, paradoxically, 'I don't mind losing control as long as I don't actually lose control.' In other words, abandonment of control is not an option. And so we fill our minds with all sorts of controlling mechanisms which interfere with the whole process of awareness, and raise our ego to centre stage rather than letting it tick over in the background.

Such over-management becomes obsessional, and we occupy mental space with its checking procedures. Where this occurs, there may be a long way to climb down to a level of ego-less awareness. Any steps towards such trust are steps that will be rewarded with increased satisfaction in performance, even though the process may feel at first like 'the unbearable lightness of being'.

Will

Will is the least defined of the Inner Game terms because it is closer to the management concept. As such it has a lesser role in actual performance, and a greater role in all aspects of the profession that exist around performance – goal-setting, practice, career progress. It is fundamentally about 'shaping', a term used by psychologists to describe the act of modifying behaviour in a desired direction. At its simplest, it works in a trial-and-error form – the process of selecting the results that work, and correcting the errors that do not, so that we shape our progress in the desired direction and towards our main goals. Like the progress of a long-term career, it selects the useful and productive, and rejects the useless and unproductive. Will is therefore enhanced by:

- **goal clarity** – have a good idea of what you want to achieve – 'no aim, no game'
- **goal direction** – set goals, then modify them progressively
- **goal steps** – goals for today, this week, this year, the next five years...

Zen and creative thought

Inner Game theory is an excellent way of acquiring some of the basic ideas that would be present in a Zen approach to performing. It concerns itself not so much with the career management of the performer as with the actual performing experience. All those aspects of awareness, openness, intuition, trust and ego-less involvement are present in 'Self 2', the desired performance state. This relaxed concentration is called 'the master skill'. All that interferes is called 'Self 1'. The equation of the Inner Game states that total performance ability is the 'performance' minus the interference.

As in Zen, interference is characterised by 'thinking'. It is this exclusion of thinking that may not give a complete picture of performance, or indeed of creative activity in general. Many others have placed a high priority on brainwork, such as British poet and painter Dante Gabriel Rossetti: 'Conception, fundamental brainwork, is what makes the difference in all art.' The sort of 'brainwork' that interferes with performance in the Inner Game or enlightenment in Zen needs more careful definition if it is to be meaningful.

Zen is not entirely against thinking: 'Thoughts themselves are not a problem, it is possible to let the thoughts come and go without being distracted by them' (*BGZ*). It does, however, demote thinking to a background activity, and is against getting 'stuck' in thoughts. The interfering thoughts which intrude into Zen being are referred to as 'babble' or 'the mad monkey'. This is fairly close to the Inner Game description of 'traffic' – the running commentary which talks back and focuses on small parts rather than the whole.

It is easy to see that performance is diminished by mental digressions, anxieties that question confidence, and self-criticisms that impose 'shoulds' and 'should nots'. But what of the sort of brainwork that actually shapes the flow of our ideas and forms the foundation for our instincts and intuitions? What of the creative trial-and-error process which orders our art into logical structures rather than in random, goal-less directions? Without it we would perform without talent, and improvise nonsense. Our total artistic activity takes in both right brain spatial awareness and left brain analysis.

The thinking Self 1 may in reality be composed of two parts – interfering analysis and constructive analysis. Constructive analysis is something more than the passive awareness of Self 2, because while some of it is unconscious, other parts of it are conscious. It is true that this conscious analysis works best in a mental environment of trust and goal-direction, and relies on cues from awareness of the external flow of a performance. But the state of 'no-mindedness', as in meditation, has two drawbacks:

- it silences the creative-speculative thought processes which are constantly throwing up 'what if?' suggestions
- it roots experience in the here-and-now, while creativity is jumping constantly into the future.

The roots of the Inner Game in performance sports can prioritise the moment of play. But this is not the same as, for example, jazz improvisation, which is constantly speculative and idea-oriented. It may be that in the Inner Game's transition from sport to music the added 'compositional' element of jazz has been insufficiently allowed for, particularly given a natural bias towards the 'interpretive' aspects of classical music. Being in the moment may work better for interpretive music-making, but how does it allow for creativity?

Zen enlightenment has some elements of the creative process – it is a process of awareness which also contains germination, incubation and sudden insight. But again, the emphasis in Zen enlightenment is also on interpretation – understanding the universe and one's part in it. The truly creative mind is not just concerned with interpreting what exists. It is actively innovative. It does not passively wait for awareness – it constantly jostles with ideas, jumping from the first idea to a string of related ones. It does not think 'Apple, apple, apple, apple, appleness...'; it thinks 'Apple, William Tell, Switzerland, skiing, I need a holiday...'.

Creative speculation jumps ahead in a series of moves, just as in chess. The chess-player's mind is not in the 'now' at all – it is constantly several moves ahead, and being 'at one with the chess board and the playing environment' is not really of much help to the precise analysis of consequences, however much an instinctive global awareness of a situation may give strong hunches.

To be free to create, the mind needs to go where it wants to go – to access thoughts, feelings, analysis or the external environment. It needs to proceed via trial and error, integration, synthesis, symbol and metaphor. At times it gains insights from the 'now'; at other times it looks into the future and feeds back the results to the present.

So there is a place for rational problem-solving procedures within art, and in creative performance this need not be totally disabled. At the same time, listening skills in performance should always be present as a parallel awareness – mental 'management' alone is not sufficient to give the best performing experience. This is where performers with a planning preference may have most difficulty, and this includes ballet dancers and classical musicians. Demoting 'managing' mental activity during performance may need a 'quantum shift' from preferred Western cultural norms prioritising control, to a 'letting go', within which brainwork is a more free and relaxed activity. Performers with a naturally open attitude, such as most jazz musicians, may find this part easy. Ballet dancers and classical musicians who allow themselves to embrace this attitude may find, like Lord Yehudi Menuhin, that 'our control is best when we are least aware of it'.

CHAPTER 6

Managing Your Adrenalin

Most of us are familiar with the uncomfortable feeling of arousal and antic-ipation we get before speaking or performing in front of others. We also recognise the typical physical sensations that go with it – raised heartbeat, clammy hands, dry throat, fluttery fingers, 'butterflies in the stomach'.

Performers call it 'the pearlies', 'the shakes' or just 'stage fright'. Golfers call it 'the yips'. These days the term 'performance anxiety' is used to cover all the wider origins of such nerves. Athletes get it at the trackside, snooker players at the climax of tournaments, politicians before important speeches, businessmen and academics before giving presentations. Most of us will at one time have experienced it when giv-ing an after-dinner or wedding speech. 'Nerves' or the 'jitters' will be equally familiar to all those who have ever done examinations, driving tests, auditions and competitions.

Some of the most recognisable features of such anxiety are the thump-ing heart, swimming head and queasy feeling that affect us just before we are going to stand up in front of others. These are typically at their worst just before and in the first minutes of whatever we are doing. The cause of such bodily changes is adrenalin – a hormone that kicks in at such times.

Accompanying these 'bodily nerves' is the mental insecurity of being judged or intimidated by others, feeling inadequate, or feeling vulnera-ble to particular problems like memory lapses or the shakes. The many causes of mental anxiety can and often do precede the event itself – we may worry for days or even weeks in advance of an important presen-tation or show. This chapter and the next will deal with both aspects – first the adrenalin response that occurs in performance and then the longer standing issues and worries that underlie such anxieties.

The myths about performance anxiety

Let us start by looking at the common myths about such 'nerves'.

Myth: if your heart is beating fast and you have the shakes, you have stage fright

This may sound true on the face of it, but actually it is a myth. Rapid heartbeat, shakes and other symptoms are produced by adrenalin. But adrenalin produces exactly the same effects in other circumstances which are nothing to do with fear. For example:

- a person would get similar bodily symptoms when aggressively aroused, for instance before a boxing match or an important football game
- a person would get similar bodily symptoms when happily aroused, for instance during a sexual orgasm
- a person would get similar bodily symptoms when simply physically aroused and feeling no emotion at all, for instance when working out in the gym or running to catch a bus.

These three different sets of circumstances all show bodily arousal, but none are associated with the emotion of fear. The first two circumstances involve anger and happiness. The third tells us something even more important. We can feel physical effects like rapid heartbeat and fast breathing without any emotional reaction at all. It is crucial to break this automatic association between such physical effects and the emotion of fear. This point will be made several times during the course of this chapter.

Myth: there are 'good nerves' and 'bad nerves' – 'good nerves' can work in your favour

The English expression 'nerves' is very unhelpful. Why? Because the way we commonly use it, it has two meanings:

- nerves = adrenalin and the bodily effects of arousal. We say we are feeling 'nervy' when we are in this rather shaky state with our heart beating more rapidly
- nerves = the emotion of fear. We are 'nervous' when we have feelings of foreboding before an event or contemplate things going wrong.

As I have already stated, it is crucial to break this automatic association between such physical effects and the emotion of fear, yet the word 'nerves' can cement these two together. When people use the expression 'good nerves', or say of a successful competition winner that 'her nerves were working in her favour', it is usually an attempt to describe that state of arousal accompanied by a positive emotion of 'buzz' or 'challenge'. Because of the double meaning of the word 'nerves', one could get the impression that 'fear is good'. This is, of course, nonsense – as we shall come to see.

Myth: you need to feel nervous at the start of a presentation or performance otherwise it's no good

At first sight this seems perverse – why does one 'have' to feel nervous? But there is a lot of sense in this if we think of nerves as adrenalin rather than fear. Research has shown that most people have a rise in adrenalin before a performance. So if you feel physically over-aroused at the start of a presentation, this is actually to be expected. After ten minutes or so you will settle back into your optimum state of performance arousal and from there on things should go fine. On the other hand, if you are under-aroused even at the start, through tiredness or whatever, then you may settle back into a more apathetic state and not be alert enough to give your best.

Myth: you're only as good as your last performance

This is one of the most unhelpful expressions there is. It is usually used of performers but applies equally to the world of presentations and conferences. Most of us have spent years learning our knowledge and craft, and typically we can talk about this when we need to. This is the constant side of our ability. Subjectively, however, we can have wildly melodramatic ideas about how we imagine we have performed:

- we exaggerate isolated mistakes
- we look for the worst in audience reactions
- we overlook the many positive impressions we make
- we imagine that our colleagues or critics can 'destroy' us with their criticism, even though few ever can or do.

Such myths as the above have no place in a modern treatment of performance anxiety. They can be confidently replaced by much more helpful beliefs, as outlined in Chapter 7. The primary thing to bear in mind is that bodily arousal at the start of a presentation is normal. It should be simply accepted and tolerated as a discomfort, with its attendant rapid heartbeat, sweating and other drawbacks. By accepting it we can learn to manage it without panic.

In this way we can destroy the myth of 'nerves', and all the silliness of 'good nerves and bad nerves' and 'having to have nerves otherwise performances are no good'. The effects of adrenalin are not ideal. None of us would want to be in a state of rapid heartbeat, sweating, shakes and nausea out of choice, unless we were indulging in serious physical exercise. Some of the effects – such as the shakes – are visible to others, as when we loosely hold a piece of paper with notes on to speak from. But all these bodily symptoms of arousal are tolerable in terms of discomfort, and will predictably decrease during any presentation.

There remains only the many negative beliefs associated with performance anxiety. Such negative thoughts should be dealt with separately, and replaced with coping strategies and more positive attitudes, as Chapter 7 outlines.

Adrenalin and arousal

Adrenalin (also known as adrenaline or in the USA, epinephrine) is a hormone. Hormones are chemicals that travel into our body from the endocrine glands. Together with the nervous system, they help organise the body's behaviour and activity. Where the nervous system is very fast in response, hormones take longer to act and consequently longer to return to normal because they have to be carried to their targets in the bloodstream. The adrenal glands, part of the endocrine system, play an important part in our moods, our level of energy and arousal and our ability to cope with stress. In particular, adrenalin prepares us for what the body perceives as 'an emergency', facilitating changes in the body to cope with sudden action. It also sets up a kind of feedback system, or closed circuit, with our reticular system, which in turn stimulates more adrenalin to maintain the body in a state of emergency. This is one reason why it takes a little while for our aroused state to settle back to normal.

What is the adrenalin response, or the 'fight or flight' reaction

What does the body consider to be 'a state of emergency'? In our caveman days it was a state of confrontation, often with wild animals. These days we are left with the same bodily arousal mechanism. The trouble is that it goes off like a smoke alarm when the only thing seemingly threatening us is an audience sitting there peacefully waiting for us to perform or speak. Somehow we get it into our heads (and our bodies) that an audience means confrontation, and that's when the trouble starts. Adrenalin is produced on cue, and we are left to suffer its effects for several minutes whether we like it or not. Usually we don't like it, at least not for peaceful occupations like performing or speaking to people.

All those who 'perform' in any way in front of others seem to experience this adrenalin response to some degree in the moments when they start. Studies show this, and this tells us that we are all alike – adrenalin is normal and we all feel its effects. This dispels a further myth – the idea that some people feel the effects of adrenalin and others don't. We are all built the same way, so we may as well get used to adrenalin and learn to live with it.

Whereas the mental anxiety may be present well before the event, the physical adrenalin rise usually takes place about ten minutes before the start, and lasts about ten minutes into the event. After this it steadily drops as our focus shifts from anticipation of the event to the actual task in hand.

It is important to realise that:
a) the adrenalin reaction is *likely to occur at the start of any event*
b) it is a far better thing to *accept it and manage it rather than feel intimidated and start to panic.*

Figure 6.1   Changes in mental and bodily anxiety up to and into performance

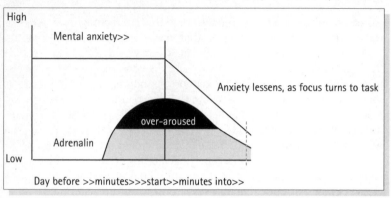

So, having accepted that adrenalin may accompany the start of a presentation or show, what is next? One thing that makes a lot of sense is – where there is a choice of how to structure any kind of presentation or performance – to start with ten or fifteen minutes of something that is bright, predictable and fairly easy to get through, even in an over-aroused state. This allows the hump in adrenalin to subside to a flatter level. Here we have one good reason why orchestral concerts should start with a bright overture – it gives the musicians a chance to have a good thrash around and get some of the adrenalin out of their system. This principle applies equally to all those who use their voice – vocalists, actors, presenters and public speakers. It can take the form of some personal greetings, a general introduction, a couple of anecdotes or jokes, a few thanks to people present, and so on.

Our typical reaction to an increase in arousal level is depicted by an inverted U. Performing ability steadily rises from nil arousal (e.g. sleep), through increasing stages of arousal (waking, coffee, shower, etc.), until it reaches the top 'plateau' of the inverted U. This represents the optimum zone for performing. When we are too aroused our performance ability starts to go down again until it reaches distress and panic. Ultimately we go into a state of shock, as in 'shell shock' or trauma, where we can hardly move at all.

Figures 6.1 and 6.2 show our optimum performing state in grey. The over-aroused state which occurs around the start of presentations, and which causes a drop in performing ability, is shown in black. As our focus shifts away from one's physical state and onto the task in hand – the content of the presentation itself – the adrenalin level drops, and the uncomfortable physical effects reduce to more normal levels. Performance level now reverts to the optimum zone shown in grey.

Even when moderately over-aroused we can still perform, because we are far from the state of shock. Despite the subjective feeling of being

Figure 6.2 The performance-arousal curve

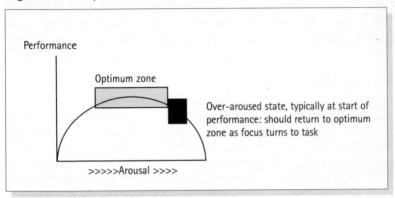

uncomfortable or even anxious, we can carry on with what we are doing. In fact, others may not realise quite how uncomfortable we feel – we seem to be speaking and acting normally, if rather stiffly.

It is possible for people to have differing performance 'styles'.

- Some like to be in the 'low risk' back area of the optimum performance 'zone'. This is more suitable for introverts who dislike too much stimulus.
- Some like to be at the very centre of their optimum zone.
- Some enjoy the 'high risk' front end, where the 'buzz' of performance nerves is part of the fun. This is the territory of extraverts and risk-takers.

Under-arousal: the effects of tiredness and stress

Tiredness and stress can have a negative effect on arousal and performance energy, and so cause anxiety. This occurs during the actual day of the event by:

- travelling long distances by bus/train/air before a show. Travelling can be quite energy draining, especially if it involves long mileages with many transport changes and shifts of luggage. A major tour can cover 20,000 miles
- jet lag
- having to drive to gigs and shows, typically for two hours or more
- over-exertion, such as carrying heavy instruments or gear
- too much activity, such as teaching and rehearsals
- low energy from hunger and irregular eating because of crowded schedules
- doing late gigs, such as in clubs open to 2 a.m. or later.

Stress and anxiety caused by the above can easily lead to insomnia or early waking, and therefore tiredness. Sleep problems tend to cause further stress, a vicious circle leading to consistently inadequate sleep – 4–6 hours instead of 7–9 hours. This is worse when touring, in all-night recording sessions or in late-finishing gigs where the body has to readjust from a nervous hyped-up state to normal sleep patterns. Touring performers often say that true tiredness only hits them at the end of the tour.

The after-effects of a performance can contribute a great deal to sleep disturbance – one is physically, mentally and emotionally aroused by performing and may need some time to calm down. The tired brain is likely to 'run over' events or mistakes repeatedly, or parts of the performance will not stop going round in the head. Over-concentration can cause irritability, and this contributes to insomnia. In addition, there is often pressure to party and socialise after the show, putting off sleep for many more hours, or even leaving sleep to a nap on the bus. A further problem is that the frustration of not performing to your best standards due to tiredness leads to further stress.

New research has shown that some people repeatedly stop breathing during sleep, then start again suddenly as if recovering from choking (sleep apnoea). Sleep is constantly disrupted, and the sufferer may feel very tired the next day without knowing why. This is made worse by age, which makes the palette less firm, by over-consumption of alcohol before sleep, and by obesity. The most at risk are overweight older performers who regularly 'drink to relax' before sleep and who in fact end up getting less sleep as a result. This problem is alleviated by reducing weight and alcohol consumption.

Tiredness can be cured by sleep, but anxiety or a poor physical state may inhibit sleep. There are a number of theories that say people can get by on fewer than eight hours of sleep, but in stressed people there is one other factor to consider: if your waking hours are stressful, every increase in sleeping hours decreases correspondingly the hours spent in waking states of stress. So in stressed subjects, sleep may be more important than for the general population.

A recent survey by British psychologist Dr Elizabeth Valentine showed that the best indicator of good performance is a subjective evaluation of ability immediately prior to performance – 'feeling in a good state to perform'. Somebody in a tired state is much more likely to have a pre-performance expectation of reduced ability. This may then act as a psychological programmer of a poor performance unless it is deliberately counteracted by positive 'psyching up'. We have seen that Geoff Wills (Wills and Cooper, 1988) found the greatest stressor of musicians was 'feeling that you must reach or maintain the standards of musicianship that you set for yourself', and tired and stressed musicians may be further depressed by the belief that they cannot reach the basic performing goals they set for themselves.

A successful performance clearly needs some degree of arousal and energy or it will be sluggish and inattentive, and tiredness progressively inhibits us from reaching this optimum level. On the other hand, the energy in a dynamic performance should not have a stress level which runs a serious risk of disorientation. The worst case is a positive feedback of tiredness and stress on each other: the performer does not have the real physical energy to cope, and the mind is constantly 'stressing up' the arousal level, leaving little concentration for the external needs of the performance. This is like the tired driver who tries to stay awake at the wheel, constantly psyching himself up to prevent losing his attention on the road.

Over-arousal: the 'fight or flight' response

The adrenalin reaction is also called the 'fight or flight response' or the 'alert response'. We have inherited this state of readiness and super-awareness from our biological ancestors the cavemen, and before that our distant ancestors the apes. In the wild our ancestors literally had to fight or flee when confronted with danger. A body in this state will do all the sensible things it needs to do to either fight or flee:

Physical change	Useful effects
Blood leaves the digestive system	More for major muscles
Blood leaves extremities	More for major muscles
Blood goes to major muscles	Helps fight or run
Sweating	Lose heat when running
Increased heartbeat	Raised action potential
Heightened breathing	Raised action potential
Decreased general focus	Raised primary focus

The general result was good for the survival of our cavemen ancestors, which is one reason why we are here at all. But however sensible for a caveman, tense muscles and sweaty hands do little good on stage. Anyone who has to address audiences will tell you that such changes to the body are often completely inappropriate:

Physical change	Undesired effects
Blood leaves the digestive system	Dry mouth, dizziness, nausea
Blood leaves extremities	Lose fine control, e.g. hands shake
Blood goes to major muscles	Body feels tense and stiff
Sweating	Uncomfortable, fingers slide on things
Increased heartbeat	Feel over-aroused and nervous
Heightened breathing	Can become light-headed
Decreased general focus	Lose track of one's surroundings
Increased primary focus	Obsessed with task one has to do

The effects of this discomfort vary – some dislike sweating because clothes become saturated and sweat patches can be visible. People who use their voice dislike the dry mouth, which is why water is routinely provided for speakers at presentations. They also dislike 'the shakes', because it causes tightness or wobble and results in problems for presenters with anything held loosely in the hands, such as pieces of paper with notes on. It is also the largest single cause of distress in violinists, since the bow bounces on the string. The term 'pearlies' for stage fright comes not from pearls of sweat but from the sound of the bow bouncing, which is just like the machine-gun rattle of a broken string of pearls bouncing onto the floor. People vary in how such bodily reactions affect them, from a lot to relatively little, and some may be more prone than others to particular effects like sweating, blushing and shaking.

The worst times for such nerves tends to be:

- at the start of the event
- if there is a sudden hush in the proceedings, so the performer feels 'exposed'
- if part of the performance is tricky, or the presentation involves technical aids like overheads, slides, etc.

Surveys of people who routinely face audiences show that experiences of stage fright are widespread. A study of actors by Fresnel in France found that 99 per cent confessed to stage fright at one time or another (Fresnel and Bourgault, 1996). Another study by Schultz of the Vienna Symphony Orchestra gives a good idea of how people are affected by the adrenalin response (Shultz, 1981). In the case of these musicians, some two thirds of players suffered mild to severe discomfort, around one quarter were not particularly affected, and the rest got a positive buzz out of nervous tension. A survey of orchestral members by British clinical pharmacologist Dr Ian James showed similar results: while nerves were seen as detrimental to performance by 60 per cent, 15 per cent thought nerves improved their performance and 9 per cent thought they made no difference.

This interesting statistic enables us to understand that the adrenalin response in people is not confined to the emotion of fear. The same performing state can be interpreted in three different ways:

- 'flight' – fright, as when rapid heartbeat makes us anxious
- no particular response
- 'Fight' – a positive buzz, or feelings of competitive aggression.

So the idea that some people 'get nerves' and others don't, or that there are 'good and bad nerves', is something of a myth. The truth is that all of us, when confronted with a performing situation in public, get some

degree of bodily nerves, or adrenalin, but not necessarily 'nerves' in the sense of nervousness and fear.

Now, if all of us seem to suffer the same raised heartbeat and associated symptoms, then the difference is in how this rapid heartbeat is **interpreted**, i.e. what **emotion** we feel and what we **believe** is happening to us.

- A panic reaction indicates an emotion of fear, and a belief that 'things will get out of control – I'll feel terrible and my performance will go to pieces'.
- A neutral emotional reaction indicates a belief that 'this is just a typical pre-performance sense of occasion, my heartbeat will go back to normal when I start to get into things'.
- A 'buzz' is caused by an emotion of elation and a belief that 'this is fun – I feel a real sense of occasion'.

Emotional labelling

In psychology, the James–Lange theory states that our emotions actually follow our bodily changes – 'we are afraid because we run away', for example, or 'we are angry because we strike'. In a similar way we could say that 'we are anxious because our heart is beating fast' or 'we feel fear because our bow arm shakes slightly'. While bodily states of arousal do not vary much from person to person, their actual emotional interpretation does vary considerably. The danger is thus of 'emotional labelling' – of attaching the emotion of fear to adrenalin.

There is a popular self-help book called *Feel the Fear and Do It Anyway*. Fear is not just a useful emotion in survival terms, it is an essential emotion. It protects us from life-threatening conditions in our environment. However, this is not the case with performances or presentations which are, with extremely rare exceptions (usually involving rock stars being mobbed by audiences), physically devoid of any particular threat. Fear is not appropriate on these occasions. So a better title would be *Accept the Bodily State of Arousal and Do It Without the Fear.* In addition, even using the word 'fear' can arouse anxiety. If you were to say, for instance, 'Don't think of pink elephants', then the phrase 'pink elephants' will already have been imprinted on your mind. You may not remember the negative, because the brain will tend to give more weight to the subject than to the context or grammar.

Emotions and beliefs

Our emotional reactions will then look for support from our thoughts and beliefs, so completing the feedback of body state > emotion > belief. So while one performer can feel elation and thoughts of positive challenge in response to a rapid heartbeat, another may feel fear and an expectation of failure. While one violinist may not be too put off by a slight shake, another may go into a state of panic and believe the whole performance is ruined.

The point of this is that anxiety in response to rapid heartbeat can be a 'learned' response. And if it is learned, then it can be unlearned. The negative response would probably be something like: 'Oh dear, my heart is beating fast – I feel nervous and I'm sure my playing will suffer.' The positive response, on the other hand, would be something like: 'Ah yes, I notice my heartbeat is a little more rapid, just as I would expect – I'm sure that as I get into the performance it will go back to normal fairly quickly.'

The crucial point is the *interpretation* – the actual physical symptoms are remarkably similar. The 'positive feedback' effect between physical cues, emotional responses and the beliefs and interpretations we give to what is going on is illustrated in Figure 6.3.

Figure 6.3 Positive feedback effect

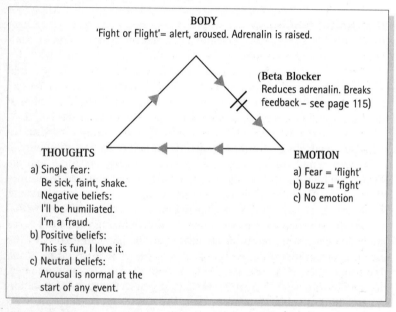

Breaking the feedback between arousal and fear

The crucial lesson to be learned from Figure 6.3 is to separate the states:

- body is body
- emotion is emotion
- thoughts are thoughts.

We need to break down this circle of reaction into its three parts, and then work on each. That way we can optimise our reactions for any event.

So when the body goes into a raised adrenalin state at the start of performance, the performer might like to take a step back mentally and visualise being like an airline pilot before take-off:

- check heartbeat – raised
- check sweating – slight sweat
- check digestion – slightly nauseous
- check muscle state – slightly shaky in the hands and fingers
- everything normal. Ready for take-off... whoosh... levelling off... welcome to the flight...'.

By the time we are about ten minutes into the show, the bodily arousal should sink back to a relative comfort level and the body as such cease to be so relevant, giving way to normal mental control. Again, a bit like flying.

To be sure we are dealing with stage fright and not other issues, it is useful to look briefly at states like phobias and panic attacks, as it helps to separate these issues and deal with them appropriately.

Stage fright as a phobia

In some performers stage fright takes on much of the character of a phobia, and in Fresnel's study of French actors, there was an additional phobia, such as fear of flying, claustrophobia or fear of mice, snakes or spiders, in 22 per cent of the subjects (Fresnel and Bourgault, 1996). There is a similarity between stage fright and claustrophobia in that once a performance starts it is delimited in both space and time – you cannot get off the stage and you cannot get out of the performance. It is like being on a train stuck in a tunnel, and likewise venues often have no windows with a view of the outside world. Some who experience stage fright as a phobia also suffer from claustrophobia, and particularly dislike stages without doors in the wings through which they could escape.

Overseas concert tours are even worse: you have to deal with the confines of aeroplanes and small hotel rooms; there is no escape route back to your family and the warmth of your own living room and bed; and you are surrounded by a wall of strangers speaking incomprehensible languages. In countries like Japan, facilities are also more cramped. Then, on top of this, you have to go on to a stage from which you cannot escape. Fear escalates as escape routes to familiarity and emotional safety appear progressively cut off.

Where phobias are present, it is helpful to deal with them separately, or at least acknowledge that the problem has a mixed origin.

Stage fright as a panic attack

Panic attacks are characterised by unexpected onset, and so are also different from the classic problems of performance arousal, where the onset is predictably at the start of a performance or passages of known difficulty. It is true that performances vary unpredictably in how well they go. Some experienced performers will say that playing to an audience of 2,000 people gives them a good feeling, whereas having to play their instrument in a television studio in front of two or three well-known musicians is emotional torture. Rock musicians who tour regularly will often say that stage fright, like good and bad gigs, occurs quite unpredictably: it may be on the third night of an otherwise good week, for no apparent reason. Even so it is usually related consciously or unconsciously to factors in the performing situation, whereas panic attacks may come from fears unconnected with performing itself.

In terms of physical triggers, the classic form of stage fright tends to be set off by a fairly predictable change in body state – the rise in adrenalin at the start of performing. This in turn triggers the emotion of fear, and familiar thoughts like 'I'll make mistakes'. Research shows that, like performance anxiety, panic attacks in general can also result from a sudden change in body state. But the difference with panic attacks is that there is no easily understood reason or explanation for the moment of onset. So it is important to ask oneself some basic questions. Are you, for instance:

- off colour, for one reason or another
- feeling the effects of a cold or flu coming on
- prone to other feelings of dizziness or strangeness which also happen when away from audiences, in which case it may be useful to see a doctor, since there can be organic causes such as thyroid problems.

Panic attacks can also be triggered by a sudden emotion of fear caused by some element in the environment. Sufferers feel suddenly hot and strangely 'spaced out', with a sense of foreboding, not unlike the reaction to phobias. In panic attacks where the source of the fear and the environmental trigger may be in the unconscious, it may take longer to bring the 'interpretation' to the surface.

In acting, there is another cause of panic – that of identifying so completely with a role that one suddenly has a sense of losing oneself, as happened to Charlton Heston when playing a courtroom scene in which his character, Queeg, was subjected to a gruelling cross-examination: 'When an actor puts himself in the character, or to express it in terms of possession allows the character to enter into himself, he feels the emotions of that character. It was not Captain Queeg that panicked under cross-examination in court, it was Charlton Heston. And for one surprising and disturbing moment Charlton Heston was suddenly and totally possessed by Commander Queeg.' (Wilson, 1991)

Liv Ullmann speaks of the same problem: 'There are two ways of crying: one is that you allow your character to cry, but the other is that you get so moved by yourself that you cry. And then you are in deep trouble because you are into self-involvement. The moment you feel too much private anger or private anguish you aren't in tune anymore.' Her vision of correct acting is of being an empty vessel through which emotions flow, but which is left still empty at the end of the performance – not possessed by the character (Wilson, 1991).

For all these panic reactions the end goal is the same – to rationalise the interpretation and so reduce irrational or exaggerated states of fear. Where possible residual fears should be dealt with separately, so they don't intrude on performances and presentations.

Hypervigilance to physical effects

It is well recognised that musicians tend to somatise more than any other group of the population (Miller and Kupersmuti, 1990). In an invasive state of anxiety our alertness to signs of distress can act like a 'hypervigilance'. The onset of even a tiny signal – sluggish digestion, slight shaking, changes in concentration – can be highly magnified by the emotions and interpreted as a 'worst' belief, which is then confirmed by further physical effects. Our attention becomes selectively filtered to let in those physical, emotional or mental distress cues which fit our current concerns, and tends to ignore cues outside this feedback circle. Ambiguous cues like raised heartbeat are thus interpreted as 'fear' rather than 'invigoration', because priority will be given – in a state of fear – to cues which fit a fearful interpretation. In depression the same thing happens – we give much more attention to sad thoughts and reminiscences because our physical inactivity and depressed mood filters our thought patterns. In both fear and depression our thought patterns become progressively more personalised and removed from the world outside our intimate circle of concern – reality recedes and everything seems to be focused on oneself, causing yet further distortions of what may really be happening.

The remedy for this is, again, to destroy the positive feedback effect of the circle by reversing one of the elements. We can reverse arousal by relaxation and breathing techniques, which in turn create a more tranquil mood. We can reverse emotional reactions to body changes by accepting them as natural. We can reverse negative beliefs by rationalising them. The brain then ignores the 'false' panic trigger, sees that there is no cause for alarm and passes the signal to relax on to the body. The body responds by relaxing and the rapid heartbeat and physical tremor declines.

Digestion and food before performances

Heartbeat and 'the shakes' are the most obviously exaggerated cues in performers, but some are hypervigilant to other physical effects of the adrenalin response, such as nausea. Digestive cues are largely ignored by the majority of us, but can act as a trigger in those particularly sensitive to their digestion – such as wind players or singers – causing them to feel sick or want to be sick. The same coping response should be made: 'Ah yes, I notice my digestion is queasy, just as I would expect – I'm sure that as I get into the performance it will go back to normal fairly quickly.'

The effect of nervousness on digestion raises the whole question of what to eat before performances and when. The worst foods are those, like sugar, chocolate or alcohol, which very quickly raise the blood sugar level, but then let it drop down below the original level, giving a perceived drop in energy. This leaves a choice between fibre-containing foods like bananas and oatmeal biscuits which are still easily digestible, and starchy foods such as pasta which stay longer in the stomach and release energy more gradually. The performer may want to experiment to see how much of which kind of food works best – high-energy diets for stamina, or reduced eating before performing to leave the stomach with less to digest. One favoured food seems to be fish, as it is high in energy and can also be digested easily.

Practical measures for managing your body state

Some of the keys to this are:

- breathing
- posture
- muscle relaxation
- chemical balance of the body (caffeine, alcohol, drugs, beta blockers, etc.)
- arousal state (amount of sleep, activity during the day, etc.).

One fundamental principle of anxiety reduction is that you cannot feel relaxed and tense at the same time – the one blocks out the other. Relaxation techniques of different kinds were found to be useful by 45 per cent in Fresnel's study of French actors (Fresnel and Bourgault, 1996).

Breathing

The simple rule for breathing is to count one for the intake of breath and two, three, four while breathing out. This ensures that hyperventilation – rapid intake of breath – does not take place, and that the emphasis is on the relaxing process of breathing out, where the shoulders are dropped and the body deflates. This is the first rule of combating acute anxiety and panic – deliberately drop the shoulders and then breathe out, as above. This should be done deeply, slowly and repeatedly until an improvement is noticed. Thereafter concentrate on regular outward breaths, keeping the shoulders dropped to reduce tension in the neck and arms.

Visualisation

As the body relaxes, you can then sit still, let your eyelids gradually close, and imagine a pleasant and happy scene. Often this will be a childhood memory, which is filled out in detail until it becomes a vivid source of tranquility. An example would be: 'I'm reclining in the back of a boat, gently rocking on the river on a sunny summer's day. The sky is blue and I can hear the water lapping at the sides of the boat as I quietly doze in the heat.'

Exercise

Another rapid relaxation technique is exercise. Some performers like to pace up and down before a performance to release tension. This is a logical response to the bodily changes involved in the 'fight or flight' mechanism, and tends to lessen some of the anxiety by using muscles that are charged for action. If you feel particularly 'charged up' with adrenalin it is not unreasonable to actually run up and down stairs or do some sort of physical workout for a few minutes. This should be timed to finish 10–20 minutes prior to going on stage, so that the body has time to regain its balance.

'Stopping' or shifting focus

If tension occurs suddenly in the middle of a performance, use either the technique of 'stopping' (or 'blocking'), which simply means putting the unpleasant thought deliberately out of your head, or the Inner Game technique of 'shifting' the external focus. Shift quickly from the 'stressor', such as fear of forgetting a passage or sight-reading a particular page, or the presence of the audience, to one particular non-stressful element. Immediate shifts of focus can be onto other people, the stage set, or some aspect of the piece itself. If there is a fear of right arm shake in a string player, shift onto the left hand. More generally useful focuses are the feelings of the author, lyricist or composer in writing the piece. Anxiety can close down your immediate field of perception, but when it lifts and you start to feel better, gradually enlarge your focus to the whole performance.

As well as the short-term methods above, there are other relaxation techniques which should take place at greater distance from the moment of going on stage. One widely favoured general trend is cutting down the amount of outside stimulation before important performances, known as pre-performance containment (*see* page 74). This reduces irrelevant distractions and focuses the mind on preparation. During the pre-performance period some kind of routine physical activity may also be helpful, such as putting on make-up, warming up or polishing your instrument. While some find chatting, television viewing and phone calls relaxing, others see them as annoying distractions and prefer to avoid them. Where there is a need for actual relaxation techniques, the following ones may be used.

Progressive relaxation techniques

There is a fairly standard relaxation method of tensing and releasing muscles one by one, from the feet up to the head, while breathing out deliberately and telling yourself to relax. To do this, sit in a comfortable chair, drop your shoulders and breathe regularly. Then start with the left calf muscle. Tense it as much as you can, breathing in. As you contract your muscles say to yourself, 'My muscles feel very tense.' Count to five and then let go quickly, breathing out at the same time. Count to five with your breath exhaled and tell yourself, 'I feel warm, soft and relaxed.' Then repeat the same thing with the right calf muscle. Go on to the thighs, stomach, chest, back, arms, shoulders and jaw. When you have finished, carry on sitting in the chair for a little while in a relaxed state and with a blank mind.

Biofeedback

Biofeedback techniques can be learned from an appropriate teacher, and include the following steps:

- rate the tension in your body on a scale of one to ten
- focus on the problem you want to deal with, such as a tense neck
- rate the problem in its present state between one and ten
- try to make the problem worse
- make a note of which muscles stiffen
- still focusing on the same muscles, try to decrease the tension
- make a note of anything or any movement that decreases the problem
- remember what you did and apply it again when the problem occurs.

Postural therapies

A number of posture methods promoting correct balance have been used for performers, chiefly Alexander Technique and Feldenkreis Technique. They tend to put the body into a more ergonomic and relaxed state for performing, which decreases some of the tension in the mind–body feedback loop that we have seen above. The message from the body to the brain is 'I feel relaxed', and the brain responds. Body language for performers can also help to 'ground' the mental fears by physically 'grounding' the body. In literal terms it can help to wear flat shoes and keep both feet on the floor when sitting, as well as balancing the body to offset playing any side-weighted instrument such as the violin.

Caffeine

Caffeine is contained in coffee, tea, cola and other 'high energy' drinks. If taken to excess it can cause tremor and anxiety, and these effects become more marked as one gets older. It should therefore be avoided at times of performance.

Beta blockers

Beta blockers are commonly used in cases of heart disease, and have found their way into the performing arts because of the effects they have on adrenalin. They 'block' the adrenalin response in the body and in doing so they reduce some of the unpleasant effects of panic, such as rapid heartbeat, shallow breathing and trembling. Consequently they tend to suppress emotional reactions like fear, and this in turn suppresses negative beliefs. Anxiety is decreased because the physical effects of anxiety are abolished and this is sensed by the brain.

They are commonly used by orchestral musicians (though those admitting to their use in surveys are around 5–10 per cent) and have also been tried out in sports like snooker, where a steady hand is vitally important (they are now banned in sport). The most important thing to know about beta blockers is that they should not be used under any circumstances without a medical consultation – they are dangerous for people suffering from asthma. Where they are prescribed, modern medical opinion is that their benefit is that of 'buying time', since they are particularly useful as a quick remedy for states of acute anxiety. In cases where performances have to be got through immediately and before any alternative psychological therapy can take effect, their use has been seen as one way of saving the performer from distress.

Those who take beta blockers are usually aware that their use is not the perfect solution, since all drugs have some degree of side effects (one stated side effect of beta blockers is nightmares). They keep them in the pocket in case they need a 'quick fix', typically waiting until about an hour and a half before the performance to see if they are needed. They thus take on the character of a 'rescue remedy'. In fact, 'Rescue Remedy' is the name of a Bach flower remedy which is claimed to have similar effects, and which some take as they would a beta blocker. If a sugar pill or placebo were substituted for either, there would be some emotional feeling of 'rescue' even if the drug itself did nothing, simply because the mental response changes to 'I'm going to be alright now' on taking a pill. Some musicians, in fact, take such small doses of beta blockers that the effect is almost notional. So the total effects of pill-taking are both physical (what it does) and mental (what you are expecting it to do).

One expert on beta blockers was Dr Ian James, himself an accomplished string player, and his description of their use contains the following (Winspur and Wynn-Parry 1998):

These drugs should only be taken for specific events and not on a daily basis. Usually they should be taken one and a half hours before performance. The only exception to this is nadalol, which should be taken 4 hours before. Most beta blockers last for 4 hours or so; nadalol lasts for 8–10 hours and has been called the 'Wagner beta blocker'. Atenolol has less effect on tremor than the others and is best avoided in string players. It has been claimed to have less effect on the bronchial tree than other beta blockers but still should never be used in asthmatics. Propranalol is destroyed at a variable rate by the liver, and certain factors such as whether one eats prior to a performance can make a great deal of difference to whether the drug works or not. Oxprenalol has a slight adrenalin-like effect of its own, as well as being able to block all the previously mentioned symptoms of fear. The excitement of performance is unimpaired by oxprenalol. Some performers have also reported that it enables them to think more quickly, thereby allowing them to execute those little feats of performance which have been carefully rehearsed but are all too frequently lost in the mêlée of the event itself. Beta blockers do not make one overvalue one's own performance. In this regard they differ from alcohol, where the reverse is true. If taken to excess beta blockers can slow finger movement. This effect becomes more noticeable at lower temperatures. Some beta blockers can cause a degree of insomnia. Frequently this is not recognised, as the performance itself may also inhibit sleep. It is important to realise that chronic stage fright often leads to depression. Beta blockers do not work under these circumstances. The reasons for this are obscure. The depression must be treated either with drugs or by psychotherapy and counselling.

The point about depression is underscored by Fresnel's study of actors in France, in which 12 per cent showed a depressive component in addition to stage fright (Fresnel and Bourgault, 1996).

Performers who do not want to become emotionally dependent on beta blockers or who want to find non-drug-induced solutions tend to come into therapy with the specific goal of stopping their regular use. They already have the knowledge, gained from using beta blockers, that they can perform without anxiety, and this in itself is useful. What they then want to do is find another way of predicting fairly confidently that they are not going to fall apart or experience acute distress. This can be done by psychological means which aim to replace controlling the problem with understanding it. As this takes effect the beta blockers are either phased out or confined to exceptional circumstances.

Summary of the 'fight or flight' reaction

- Adrenalin is a natural hormone that prepares us for 'fight or flight'.
- Our body produces it when it anticipates any state of confrontation or 'emergency'.
- The effects of adrenalin are uncomfortable but don't stop us doing what we need to.

- Adrenalin is much easier to control if we accept it and learn to manage it.
- Since it occurs most frequently at the start of any event, begin with something simple and predictable to break the ice.
- Our 'total system' consists of our body reaction, our emotion and our thoughts.
- Body arousal without the emotion of fear is no different from working out in the gym.
- Fear is just one emotion associated with adrenalin – buzz or no emotion is preferable.
- Our thoughts are much easier to analyse and get into proportion without fear.
- It is the combination of adrenalin + fear + bad thoughts that creates the classic form of stage fright.
- If we start by managing the adrenalin, we break the vicious circle.

It cannot be emphasised too strongly that one of the key strategies in overcoming fear of performing is to separate these three areas and treat them as distinct in their own right. This is the simplest and most effective way to break the habit of 'nerves'.

Having dealt with the physical symptoms of arousal in this chapter, we can now go on to look at the emotional and mental factors that can cause anxiety.

CHAPTER 7

Overcoming Performance Anxiety

In the last chapter we looked at how to manage the physical side of stage fright – the adrenalin response that takes place on occasions when we perform. We can see this in the diagram below, which we looked at in the previous chapter.

Figure 7.1 Changes in mental and bodily anxiety up to and into performance

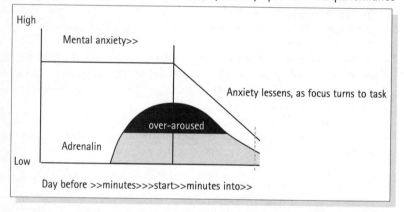

This diagram shows that while the physical symptoms of arousal typically occur just before and some time into the performance, the mental and emotional anxiety surrounding a performance can last for days or even weeks beforehand. Such pre-meditated worry also tends to recede during performance as the mind turns to the immediate task in hand, but because it is of a different nature to the actual arousal symptoms, it needs to be dealt with separately.

It is not surprising that there is some degree of pre-meditation before an important performance. Performing is a highly skilled business – it requires the equivalent technique of airline pilots or surgeons, who also have to concentrate for hours without being able to stop for a moment and walk away. No lives are at risk, but there is the added problem of having your work written up in the papers by critics for all to read. Some of the factors in stage fright can be generalised into a 'performing anxiety syndrome'. This may include:

- performing technically difficult material
- expecting to be criticised for not being note or word perfect

- coping with a number of unpredictable situational variables
- having to rely heavily on concentration and memory
- dealing with personality difficulties ('attitude problems') among fellow performers
- having to be constantly on top form despite rehearsals, travelling and transporting gear
- having to cope with exacting studio situations involving large sums of money
- having to deal with highly-skilled tasks in real time for three hours or more without stopping.

Some of the most common emotional responses associated with stage fright are the following.

Before the event
- Advance experience of anxiety preceding an event.
- Disturbed sleep, restlessness and stress before the event.
- A sense of catastrophe in which there is no proportion to the threat.
- An inability to think constructively and analyse problems objectively.

During performance
- Disorientation and inability to focus attention, e.g. on where one is in a presentation.
- A feeling of having forgotten one's craft, e.g. words, basic knowledge.
- Subjective feeling of loss of control – the brain 'goes blank' and the head is 'swimming'.
- Constant worry about the inability to perform successfully.
- A feeling of being alone or deserted.
- A sense of desperation at not having the power to deal with the event.
- A feeling of paralysis and inability to act, in which the body feels inert.
- A desire to escape or sabotage the event.
- A desperation to come to the end and get it all over with.
- An anticipation of failure and humiliation in front of others who expect success.

Maladaptive thoughts and behaviour

The presence of stage fright also can produce a range of behaviours which are maladaptive and make the problem worse. Examples include:

- vomiting before events, sometimes self-induced to avoid the idea of doing it in front of assembled people
- cancelling events for no reason other than the fear of not being able to cope

- turning up late or drunk in an effort to 'escape' the problem
- walking off during an event
- faking things or leaving bits out.

Maladaptive thoughts can be one recurrent over-riding fear. Sometimes such fears result in hypervigilance or exaggerated sensitivity to one particular feature of the adrenalin response, which is then blown up out of proportion, for example:

- being suddenly sick in front of or over the assembled people (feeling of nausea)
- suffering shake in one's voice or bow (tremor and the shakes)
- passing out (dizziness, tunnel-like perception).

Often such single fears derive from a previous 'freak' occurrence, which typically is unlikely to recur and which has not recurred since its first onset, for example:

- needing to suddenly go to the toilet and being unable to reach it
- dropping one's instrument or bow
- losing one's voice.

More general maladaptive thoughts and fears include:

- making mistakes which subjectively speaking 'ruin the performance'
- forgetting words or one's place in the piece
- fear of silences in the audience which draw attention and focus onto oneself
- being unable to do as well as expected, faking or feeling a fraud
- being stared at in an uncomfortable way, implying humiliating or sexual thoughts
- losing control of one's mental state, panicking or going mad.

Dealing with the different types of performance anxiety

For each performer, the particular combination of stressors may vary considerably: some are no problem, while others are. Dealing with the problem is a matter of identifying the particular elements that cause maximum discomfort, then finding the best ways of dealing with them.

The most commonly encountered forms of performance anxiety are the following (note that one or several can be present).

- Classic 'stage fright' – a learned anxiety response to previous bad experiences.

- Self-confidence issues, feeling a fraud or an outsider.
- Interpersonal anxiety – fear of disapproval or bullying by others.
- Burnout – anxiety over progressively diminishing interest and effectiveness.
- Physical injuries and problems that interfere with maximum efficiency.

The reason for being careful to separate the global term 'performance anxiety' into distinct areas is to optimise our treatment strategies. It is necessary to know what has happened to us in the past to give rise to such anxieties, and then deal effectively with such 'triggers' so they do not continue to disturb us in the future.

Self-confidence, interpersonal anxiety, burnout and injury are dealt with elsewhere in this book. The classic form of 'stage fright' is the main focus of this chapter.

Managing learned fear responses

The common type of performance anxiety usually referred to as 'stage fright' is often the result of a sequence of bad experiences. These are frequently 'first time' experiences, such as our first day in school, the first time we had to stand up and recite something to the class from memory, or our first time in a local youth orchestra. Such experiences can 'condition' our behaviour to associate fear and the prospect of failure with performing in public. This is known as a 'learned response'. As we have seen, conditioning can result in either a feeling of generalised anxiety, or can express itself as a repetition of particular facets of performance which have gone badly in the past, as seen in the maladaptive thoughts listed above.

Another cause of stage fright can be linked to childhood. An overprotective family member who constantly worries about the child, whatever he does, vividly imparts this fear to the child. This figure is usually a parent, and often the mother. The child then becomes afraid of the consequences of actions by empathising with the fear being expressed to him. Such fear can be of being away from home, mixing with strangers, eating certain types of food, going on aeroplanes or being in a big city. Since touring often involves all of these elements, it can be a debilitating experience if such imparted fears have not been extinguished.

Early this century, the Russian psychologist Ivan Pavlov did some pioneering experiments with conditioning and learned responses. Pavlov's experiments with dogs showed that a dog will salivate when expecting food. This he regarded as a normal response, so he called it an 'unconditioned' response. He then rang a bell each time the dog was presented with food. The dog 'learned' to associate the bell with food and started to salivate each time the bell was rung, whether there was food or not. It had 'learned' to salivate to the sound of a bell. Pavlov called this learned response a 'conditioned' response. The dog had been 'conditioned' to salivate to the sound of a bell.

Exactly the same happens with learned responses where we are the performer. The panic is not intrinsic in such things as talking or writing one's thoughts down on paper. With presentations, for example, we talk to groups of people without panic, and the large majority of us can manage to speak to a group of strangers competently when reading from notes. For feelings of panic to be present we must look for some association that overlays the activity, or some 'learned response'.

Onset of conditioning

The onset of conditioning can be very sudden, and two or three similar experiences – including non-performing disasters like being sick in the playground, or forgetting a recitation in front of the class – can cement the association. The obvious inner logic is the lurking threat that 'if it can happen once, it can happen again'.

Subject A

This clarinet player had bad food poisoning while playing in the school orchestra, and passed out during a rehearsal. When he came to he was on the floor, looking up at members of the orchestra standing over him and the conductor panicking and calling for the school nurse. He later developed a fear of passing out during a rehearsal, associated with the fear of dropping his clarinet and losing control.

Subject B

This girl had to run in a race at her school sports day. She arrived in a panic only seconds before the start of the race, after a large lunch and a bumpy car journey. After running a short distance she was violently sick, and fell on the side of the track, retching. Later that week she had to sing in front of the school, and again arrived late after a heavy lunch (mothers, please note...). She panicked, and ran off to the toilets where she was, again, very sick. As a result she developed a constant fear of being sick every time she had to stand up and sing in front of an audience.

The first thing that is apparent from these case histories is the real sense of drama we feel as we read them. It is not the performing that is dramatic, it is the 'catastrophic' fear of losing consciousness or being violently sick. They illustrate how such fears can be overlaid on performing. It is as if a bell goes off on stage and brings back an old historical panic that was the result of one freak experience. This old experience will not quite go away and haunts the unconscious as a reminder that things could get totally out of control.

Such panics are irrational. They are only rational in the sense that something like it actually happened once. But the chances of those exact circumstances being repeated are as unlikely as bells going off every time we eat a bowl of cereal. These initial responses were in the vast majority of cases conditioned by a particular set or cluster of stressful events.

Example of a cluster of stressors:
A violinist got up early on the day of a rehearsal, unable to sleep. He also noticed that he was coming down with a cold and felt slightly feverish. He spent the morning writing letters and on the telephone, and decided to have a short practice just before lunch, rather later than he had planned. Towards the end of the practice a string snapped, and he looked for a replacement. He was horrified to find he didn't have any, and quickly got ready to go out. His car was at the garage so he took the bus into town. Unfortunately the bus was late, so he got to his usual music shop half an hour before the rehearsal. To his horror they didn't have the string he wanted, so he ran out into the street towards the nearest music shop, which did have one. He couldn't find a cab for a while, and so ran several streets towards the rehearsal room before flagging one down. He sat down just as the conductor was coming on stage. After about three minutes he panicked completely.

Let us count the stressors in the above scenario:

1. Lack of sleep
2. Feeling feverish
3. Setting out later than expected
4. Equipment not working
5. Having to rush unexpectedly
6. Physical exertion and anxiety just before playing, increasing adrenalin
7. The humiliation of being late

How do I know it won't happen again?
The first thing to do in cases like the above is to make the sufferer from stage fright aware of the number of stressors in the original scenario. Having done so, you ask the question, 'Is it likely that this exact cluster of events will happen again?' The answer is almost inevitably no. The next question is 'So why do you think you will get the exact same panic response again, when circumstances will not be the same?' This is a difficult question to answer, and helps neutralise the pervasive idea that 'it will all happen again'.

Generally speaking, anyone who has fallen victim to such freak occurrences will say, 'How do I know it won't happen again?' We do not *know* that another world war will never happen again, but we do not plan our lives around it. If we did, everyone would have a bunker at the bottom of the garden with enough food to last a year or more. We carry on with our lives under the assumption that if freak events actually happen, we will deal with them as and when they occur. We do not allow them to stop us carrying on with the normal processes of living. Life itself is an unpredictable event, but it is generally safer than it is catastrophic. If the natural life expectancy is about seventy years, then this is what we base our assumptions on. Similarly, the natural expectancy of a performance is that trained professionals will do it competently, and this is what we should base our assumptions on.

Memory

Performing in public also requires control over your memory. If you have a memory lapse it disrupts the piece. Some performers are particularly fearful of memory lapses and believe, often wrongly, that they are prone to them. This can be worse as one grows older, since there can be a pervasive feeling of losing one's memory because of age itself. Not trusting your memory can further pre-dispose you to nervousness, which itself increases the likelihood of memory lapses – a vicious circle. Add to that the cumulative effect of a succession of memory lapses, even if these are no more frequent as the years go on.

There are some memory techniques that help, one being to learn a piece backwards so that in performance it becomes progressively more familiar. In the case of musical soloists it is not considered good etiquette to take the score onto the platform for recitals, but this is being challenged, not just in the case of difficult modern music but by world famous soloists like pianist Sviatoslav Richter, who would take the score onto the platform in his later years. Some soloists agonise over this choice. Others become conductors so that they always have the score in front of them – a little known reason why some well-known figures turn to conducting later in life.

Formalised ritual

It seems paradoxical that classical music itself is an expression of the most profound and unrestrained human emotions, but that in the classical concert hall this is carried out in an atmosphere more reminiscent of the reading of a will, with all the interested parties looking critically on and waiting for the essential details to be unfurled. The performer is expected to express all the raw emotion in the music in circumstances of great decorum. The popular club musician works in a much more relaxed environment. Since he can start again if he wishes, get up and walk out for a few minutes, eat a sandwich, have a glass of beer or talk to the audience a little, he generally suffers a lot less from stage fright.

In the world of classical music the audiences generally have money and social status, and behave in public with commensurate restraint. Occasions like the extremely informal and patriotic 'Last Night at The

Proms' in London show how pleasant music-making is when it takes place in an atmosphere of fun. Such evenings of entertainment were typical of concerts before the twentieth century, when programmes were longer, with more breaks, and included varied and popular items.

Today, classical musicians are bedevilled by stage fright during performance – this was claimed by 58 per cent in a survey by W. Schulz of members of the Vienna Symphony Orchestra, and is worst in Japanese orchestras, a country with very formal cultural aspects. It may be that the formality of modern classical concerts 'heightens the occasion', and that audiences enjoy this elevated mood, just as they enjoy dressing up and state pageantry; but moves back to more informal dress and behaviour have by common consent resulted in a more relaxed atmosphere which means less stage fright for the musicians.

Stage fright as a defensive tactic

There is a paradoxical way in which fear of one particular thing going wrong is used to eliminate fears of the whole performing situation. You would reasonably expect a top professional to be conscious of potential difficulties in any number of areas. In music, for instance, this would be fast tempos, long, slow tempos, pianissimo playing or modern scores. What one typically finds, however, is that one isolated area is used as a symbol or trigger for stage fright. In violinists it may be playing quietly at the tip or the heel, or playing in the middle of the bow; in wind players it may be playing quiet, exposed entries; in brass players it may be finding the perfect embouchure for certain passages, in dancers it might be a *grand jeté en tournant*.

Typically, such top professionals will say, 'If I don't get that particular thing in a piece I'm alright', like a driver might say, 'If I don't go over seventy miles an hour I feel there's no real risk', or a child might say, 'I'm not afraid of any animals as long as they are not snakes'. Since the risk is associated with just one thing, it is eliminated from everything else. In practice, this may result in the performer anticipating with dread 'the bottom of page 5' in the piece, but as soon as that is past, everything becomes alright again. Logic tells us that, when driving, there are risks other than speed, and that many animals besides snakes are dangerous. Focusing on one fear may be a lot easier than being engulfed by a whole number of potential threats.

This rather clever mechanism is like the Inner Game technique of focusing on one thing to take one's attention off other fears. The paradox here is why there is just one fear and not several, and why that particular fear can go on for years and years of a successful professional career where the sufferer in question says, 'I'm not really worried about the rest of my performing.' This paradox is not at all apparent, and is concealed by the fact that the 'particular stressor' is a real and genuine fear. If one *has* to worry as a matter of principle, surely it is better to choose just one thing rather than worrying about everything, particularly if that one thing occurs fairly infrequently.

Dealing with stage fright and the fear of things going wrong

We have seen many illustrations of how panic responses can be overlaid on performing situations. For those who suffer predominantly from feelings of fright, the following measures apply. The essential parts of unlearning these responses are:

1. Identify how the panic response became associated with performing in the first place. Take a detailed history, including other non-performing panic situations, if they are relevant.
2. Begin to dissociate the 'conditioned' panic from the essential process of performing. Monitor performances to identify and deal with any particular 'triggers' you may be sensitive to.
3. Acquire a conscious strategy of mental reactions to respond immediately to recurring triggers.
4. Acquire a sense of history and reality: the original 'catastrophe(s)' that caused the panic happened through a freak combination of factors that will not be exactly repeated in normal performing.
5. Acquire a sense of scale: nerves – however unpleasant – are not the same as utter panic. You can perform through them and survive.

Unlearning panic responses is not necessarily a case of extinguishing all fear in all circumstances, since this would be plainly unrealistic – performing is technically difficult and a large audience is a slightly awesome phenomenon. But a goal of reducing fear to manageable levels is attainable and can have a permanent effect. 'Being a bit nervous' is fine, and doesn't mean being out of control. Performers who take determined steps to conquer stage fright usually find they can make good progress. Working with a performer over time it is possible to accurately chart the worst situational variables affecting performance, and then factor them into performances, confront them, and reduce their power to surprise and upset.

During the process of replacing melodramatic fears with controllable nerves, there is usually a period of disbelief. During this initial period, feeling better alternates with feelings of increased nervousness – 'What if something goes wrong?' or 'How do I know this is really going to work?' Typically, recovery is achieved in a sort of saw-tooth progress, with better and worse days but a steady overall improvement.

With this improvement comes the last necessary step in the process, that of replacing one's negative self-image – 'I'm a person who suffers a lot from stage fright' – with a positive one – 'I get a few nerves like everyone else, but it rarely stops me doing my job, so I don't worry too much about it.'

Figure 7.2 Stage fright: classical conditioning (learned response)

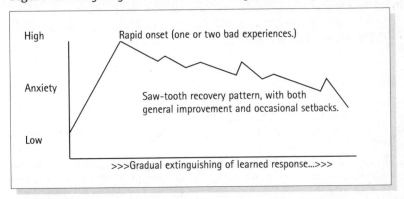

Cognitive techniques

Cognitive therapy consists, at its simplest, of identifying negative beliefs and thoughts, analysing them, and replacing inappropriate beliefs with positive ones that stand up to reality. The order of doing this is as follows:

- Identify the troublesome belief, e.g. 'If I make one mistake, the whole piece is ruined.'
- Analyse it and examine the evidence, e.g. 'What do I mean by 'ruined', and what do people really want in a performance?'
- Challenge the belief in the light of reality, e.g. 'Will people even notice it? Is perfection possible again and again in real life? Do people really put one slip before the total artistic effect of the whole performance?'
- Change the irrational belief to a better one, e.g. 'A few fluffs, though better avoided, are less important than the quality of the whole performance.'

This type of intervention is popular in counselling at present. Real gains can be achieved in relatively few sessions by concentrating on the problem itself, rather than the general background of the person.

Since performers can be emotional people who come to conclusions through gut reactions, a cognitive approach may at first seem foreign, since it means using our 'thinking' or analytical faculties. Even after a problem has been deconstructed, a new belief system will only really work after it has been internalised and translated into our own inner language. Because they use the analytic functions, cognitive techniques can supply the objective reality that a 'Feeling' world may need in order to see exactly what is going on. Proper analysis enables us to 'attribute' the problem to the right causes. So question whether the problem is:

- **Internal or external**
  Is what is going on: inside me – my reaction, my feeling, my fault?; or outside – someone in the cast, the band, external circumstances?
- **Permanent or temporary**
  Do I always need to have these feelings? Or am I really experiencing something temporary that may go away if I make it?
- **Global or specific**
  Does this feeling of unease affect everything – will I fall apart completely? Or does it affect just part of me – I will feel more nervous than usual but this will not stop the performance going successfully.

It can be seen from the above that narrowing down anxiety to specific things means far less likelihood of feeling 'engulfed'. An external explanation should be preferred to an internal one, a temporary occurrence preferred to a permanent one, and a specific reason preferred to a global one. The resulting effect might give the rationalisation: 'I'm feeling a bit stressed at the moment because I didn't get enough sleep, but I am confident that I can still perform up to a professional standard, and it is quite likely that things will improve as I get more into the performance.' On the other hand, concentrating on internal, permanent and global factors might give the feeling: 'I feel stress engulfing me for no reason – my whole performance is doomed from here on, and I don't know how I'll get to the end.'

To bring problems 'down to scale', you are particularly encouraged to avoid catastrophising. Learn to distinguish between anxiety and panic. One clever piece of self-persuasion is to divide stage fright into two distinct types:

- **anxiety**, which is uncomfortable but manageable and does not prevent performance
- **panic**, which is very debilitating and causes dizziness and disorientation.

You then persuade yourself that extreme 'panic', where carrying on is virtually impossible, is in fact most unlikely, and so all that remains is that sort of anxiety which is manageable. Consequently, when there is an increase in anxiety levels, the message to yourself is, 'This is controllable – I can deal with it'.

If you have lived through several performances in which you were uncomfortable but in which you got through the whole part and no real disaster or 'catastrophe' actually happened, you can make the surprising but true realisation that you may be more capable of surviving fear or terror than others. Far from being unable to cope – which is your subjective feeling – you are in fact able to perform through frequent episodes of anxiety. By reminding yourself that you can play through fear, you are telling yourself that you do not need to be afraid of it – you can cope.

Some other cognitive readjustments to typical belief systems are worth looking at and understanding. An example is adjusting your style of performance to suit your personality type.

- Extraverts – make good contact with the people in the audience, and allow yourself to feel good when they pay attention to you and show interest.
- Introverts – create a dialogue with the author or composer when you are on stage. Tell yourself that the audience is there to hear the work, not to look at you. You are 'not there', merely the vessel through which the spirit flows.
- Teachers (and those with didactic tendencies) – think of the audience as children. Show them what the piece is all about.

Social models for performing environments

The drama triangle

The Drama Triangle consists of three parts, as shown in Figure 7.3.

The 'drama' happens when the roles switch over, as when the 'persecutor' turns into a 'rescuer', or the 'victim' turns into the 'persecutor'.

The perception of the performer suffering from anxiety is that the performer is the 'victim' and the audience or one's fellow performers are the 'persecutor'. In this case there are useful switches that can immediately improve the situation. If the performer acts more like a teacher, trainer or all-round educator of the audience, then the performer can feel more like the 'rescuer'. If the performer is angry or irreverent – as in much stand-up comedy – the performer is acting the 'persecutor'. These two states can alternate, as seen in successful performers such as Dame Edna Everage, who shifts from rescuer to persecutor. The key is to avoid the victim role, and consequently its emotional quality of fear and vulnerability.

Figure 7.3 The drama triangle

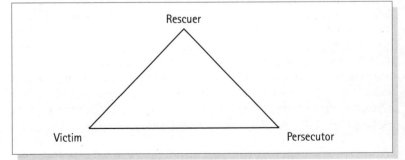

Figure 7.4 Transactional analysis in the performing situation

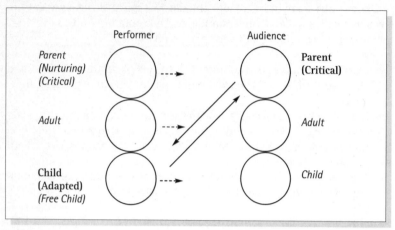

Transactional Analysis

In the TA model we refer to people as combinations of three 'ego states' (Parent, Adult, Child), and 'transactions' as being relationships between a particular ego state in the subject and another ego state in the object. In the performing situation, the performer typically feels as 'Adapted Child', while the audience or fellow performers are typically felt as 'Critical Parent' (James and Jongeward, 1978).

This case – where the performer feels the need to satisfy the demands of the audience – is shown by the bold text and solid arrows. A useful switch that can immediately improve the situation is for the performer to move out of the Child ego state into one of the other states, shown by italics and dotted arrows. The performer can switch into the Adult state, to get a more rational grip on the proceedings, or into the Parent state, either as Nurturing Parent (generously helping and informing the audience, who may then become more like the Child state themselves) or as the Critical Parent (as stand-up comics do when goading and making jokes about the audience).

Alternatively, the Child state may shift from the Adapted Child, which is reactive to a 'parent-like' audience or fellow performers and their perceived criticisms, to the Free or Natural Child, who simply performs happily in its own way, not caring about the audience, or plays with rather than against the audience – as seen in Woodstock and many other big rock concerts where the audience is encouraged to clap, dance and otherwise have fun as they would in their 'Child' states. The same is true of the 'Last Night of the Proms', when the audience dresses up and acts in a generally silly and fun way.

The Socio-Biology model

One Socio-Biology model (Dawkins, 1989) that is particularly useful is what is called 'The Prisoner's Dilemma'. In this model there are two participants. These participants have a series of transactions between them (like moves in chess) where each makes a move. The options are either 'Co-operate' or 'Non co-operate' and the scores are as follows:

Player 1	Score	Player 2	Score	Total score
Co-operate	3	Co-operate	3	6
Co-operate	1	Non co-operate	4	5
Non co-operate	2	Non co-operate	2	4

If we use this as a model for interaction between performer and audience or performer and colleagues, then the strategy of co-operate/co-operate clearly gives the biggest total gain for both parties. However, the situation is unstable in that if one party chooses not to co-operate while the other co-operates, the non co-operator instantly gains. The co-operator then becomes unwilling to lose out and switches to non co-operate. The overall strategy then lapses into non co-operation because although the total benefit to both parties is less, the chances of either party suffering a greater individual loss is avoided.

In the performing situation, the most effective strategy is obviously co-operate/co-operate. The total gain for performer and audience is greater, the atmosphere is good, and the event leads to satisfaction on both sides – like the rock concerts where the band gets the audience to clap and dance and the audience co-operates. The total result is reduced when the performer does not co-operate, i.e. makes no attempt to get the audience on his or her side or feels negative emotions for the audience. It is equally difficult for the performer when the audience is unresponsive, as comedians know to their peril. The worst situation is where performer and audience 'give up' on each other, resulting in boredom and bad feelings.

The strategy is therefore for the performer to 'co-operate' as much as possible, particularly in the initial stages, so as to bring an unresponsive audience round to co-operating. When this happens the eventual gains will outweigh the initial losses to the performer. Entertainers know this very well, and will 'work' an audience until it comes round, thaws out, and starts showing a positive response.

Becoming 'panic-free'

Stage fright has been described above as a whole variety of different and sometimes interlinked symptoms and beliefs. The more flexible the methods used to combat it, the greater the likelihood of success. Try out any or all of the methods described, choose those that work best for you and familiarise yourself with an anxiety-reducing routine that works predictably.

As your overall strategy for reducing stage fright starts to work, there is a typically enjoyable feeling that 'things are now better'. However, this is often followed not only by the worry that 'maybe it will all come back again' but the paradoxical idea that 'the longer I go without a disaster happening, the more likely it is that a disaster will ultimately happen'. This is no more true than the likelihood of a coin coming up tails after it has come up heads five times: the odds are still exactly the same. The odds of panic recurring are, in fact, infinitely less than flipping a coin because, in the overwhelming number of cases, the expectation of panic is built on isolated 'freak' occurrences which are extremely unlikely to happen again. Such paradoxical and habitual 'catastrophising' has been widely reported in studies of anxiety, and is part of the anxiety itself, not of reality. As the general anxiety lifts, the overall progress gets steadily better in a sort of 'saw-tooth' recovery pattern. There are still ups and downs corresponding to difficult performances and gigs, but these gradually flatten so that the worst cases are consistently less bad and the best cases are consistently better than before.

There is no such thing as a 'miracle cure' or 'getting better overnight just by doing this latest new technique'. Adjusting to reality means coping as well as possible with the constantly varying conditions of performing. The performer who becomes substantially more panic-free will, however, experience a new expectation. The old expectation that 'things will go wrong and I'll panic' becomes a new expectation that 'performing conditions may vary, but I sincerely believe and expect that I have what it takes to cope with that'.

What is needed to go with this new coping style is not just the new belief that 'I expect to be OK', but also a new self-image. When you become confident you may practise saying to yourself and to others, 'I don't panic unduly about stage fright.' Even better is to personalise this statement with a label – 'I'm a pretty panic-free sort of person.' Practising this label helps create the new self-image, just as saying, 'I'm a non-smoker' is more definite than saying, 'I don't smoke.' Both identify the new expectation, but personalising it really starts to make it sink in.

CHAPTER 8

Stress, Burnout and Unemployment

The stresses of the performing professions are well known in global terms, and recent surveys have also gone some way to itemise and assess the importance of a number of particular stressors. Added to the stresses peculiar to performing are the problems of burnout and depression, and the whole range of mental and emotional problems can be compounded by additional factors such as drinking and drug taking, alas all too common in the profession. It may be difficult to decide which problem is the priority and which to treat first – a burnt out performer may be stressed, depressed and frightened, drinking heavily and suffering a rapidly increasing incidence of stage fright. Alcohol and drugs are addictions with a different type of treatment plan, but fortunately the treatments for burnout, stress and depression have a lot in common and favour a healthy, active lifestyle with good sleep, holidays and an effective leisure programme.

The life of the actor, musician, singer or dancer is one of the most colourful of the self-employed careers. It is a fairly insecure and high-risk profession, offering both riches and poverty, but it also offers a steady amount of satisfying social and artistic feedback. Many are still working in the profession in their seventies and eighties, while those that give up full-time tend to retain an amateur or semi-professional interest. Despite the satisfactions of being in the business, there are a number of typical stressors which are acutely felt by some professionals.

Stressors

Stressors regularly faced by popular musicians have been well documented by Geoff Wills in his book *Pressure Sensitive* (Wills and Cooper, 1988). The following are his findings from a survey of musicians carried out through the Musicians Union in Britain, showing the stressors listed by one-fifth or more of those questioned. They have been divided for convenience into:

- career or professional factors
- situational factors in the actual working environment
- personal factors, showing subjective perception of anxiety or low effectiveness.

The actual percentage of musicians listing the stressor is given in brackets.

Career stressors
Worrying because of lack of gigs (38.6).
Difficulty in getting a good recording/management deal (32.1).
Having to sack a musician if you are a bandleader (30.5).
Conflict with record/management/agency executives who do not share your musical ideals (28.5).
Waiting for payment to come through from a gig/session (27.2).
Having to play music you don't like to earn a living (26.4).
Doing an audition (24.4).
Having to work when it is available, making it difficult to take holidays (22.7).
Worrying about the lack of pensions and benefits in the music profession (22.0).

Situational stressors
Instruments or equipment not working properly (44.8).
Having to read and play a difficult part at a recording session or gig (41.8).
Playing when there is inadequate rehearsal or preparation (38.2).
Effects of noise when the music is heavily amplified (37.4).
Endangering your life by having to drive a long distance after a gig when tired (33.3).
Having to play after travelling a long distance (30.1).
Doing sessions/rehearsals during the day then a gig at night (28.5).
Waiting around for long periods at the gig before it's time to play (27.6).
Getting musicians to deputise at short notice (27.2).
Playing a venue with bad conditions (23.5).
Doing a long tour (23.1).
Worrying about all the musicians getting to the gig on time (22.0).
Coping with an instrument that is physically difficult to play (21.5).

Personal stressors
Feeling you must reach or maintain the standards of musicianship that you set for yourself (51.3).
Stress put upon personal relationships, e.g. marriage (30.5).
Feeling that you need to become better known and/or better paid (28.9).
Feeling lonely or bored in strange towns or hotels when on tour (23.2).
Feeling tense or nervous during recording sessions as a session musician (22.8).
Feeling tense or nervous doing a live gig as a session musician (21.5).
Worrying that your ability to play will leave you (20.4).
Feeling that your musical ability is not appreciated by a musically ignorant public (20.3).

In the personal factors there is an obvious loading towards dissatisfaction with the quality of one's music-making, which is the highest overall stressor. This shows that musicians are particularly sensitive to how well they play and the overall quality of their gigs.

Performing as a Career

A number of different studies on musicians suggest that the vast majority (typically 85 per cent or more) are happy with what they do. Many other studies show a great number of detailed dissatisfactions with the 'profession' as opposed to music itself. This distinction between the 'artistic' and 'professional' sides of the business was well summarised by Berlioz as (roughly translated) 'Music – what a noble art, what a terrible profession.' The same is true of acting and to some extent dance, certainly in terms of the constant physical exertion. Concerns are:

* artistic satisfaction – the quality of work as perceived by yourself
* financial satisfaction – whether it offers the desired or needed standard of living
* social satisfaction – the whole image and status of musicians in society.

The last point is one with which performers have long been concerned. While many go into the profession because it can offer glamour and status, others feel society treats them as social lepers if they are not glitzy celebrities. To many it's still not a 'real job'. The 'worth' of a performer to society has always been an issue, because traditionally he or she is seen to do little 'labour' and produce no tangible 'product'. In many cases this is far from the truth, and one only has to look at the amount of money the arts and media bring into the UK as indirect earnings to see this. Nevertheless, friction between the 'average working person' and the artist includes:

* jealousy of musicians, actors, television personalities and artists in general because their talent enables them to act, sing, play or entertain people
* jealousy of and curiosity about the artist's lifestyle, fame and publicity
* resentment that the artist appears to get up late and spend a leisurely day doing what passes through his head
* misunderstanding or disdain for the impractical imagination of the artist in which, as the proponents of virtual reality say, 'Fantasy has replaced money as the unit of currency'
* total underestimation of the long and unsociable hours actors, dancers, musicians and singers habitually work.

There has always been a conflict of values between realistic, material people (*see* 'Sensing' on the MBTI in Chapter 1) whose lives are spent in administrative or physical work and artists who live in a world where fantasy is the key to sudden wealth that would take years to earn by repetitive labour. The gains, if they come, may be enormous: it has been said that ABBA made more profit in one year than the whole of the Swedish economy. But music, like gambling, is a high-risk occupation, representing high gains or high losses – it is possible for artists in the music profession to lose millions as well as gain them. Secure jobs are low-risk strategies – moderate gains but low losses.

Since realistic people represent at least two-thirds of the population, artists rightly feel they are treated as a minority. This does not mean that musicians are not 'normal' – everything that exists is actually normal. The so-called statistical 'normal curve' has a lot of middle values in the centre and a smaller number of extreme values at either end. Average-size people are normal, but so are short people and tall people – they all fit into the same 'normal curve'. Even if you took away the shortest and tallest and then redrew the normal curve, it would continue to have extremes at either end.

What is 'normal', however, is not what counts – it is the middle values of the majority that tend to become the norms of society. Artistic integrity does, however, have a value. While there is always a healthy middle-of-the-road market, there is also a definite value in uniqueness and the independent or 'indie' sector. Uniqueness is very collectable, as art or antiques show, and society pays enormous sums for it – this is simple supply and demand, since what is unique is in short supply, or is difficult to reproduce by anyone else. Unique is also new and unexpected, as in the previously unheard tracks and mixes sought by DJs. Such uniqueness may unfortunately only be valued when time has tamed it, which is small consolation to the likes of Bela Bartok or Charlie Parker and those who, while living, were at the extreme end of what was acceptable.

An artistic career is a constant choice of values. By and large, performers rate satisfaction higher than money, so their first aim is to get the art right. There are stressors involved both in over-achieving (fame) and under-achieving. Stress can also result from work overload or work underload. Overload can be travelling, rehearsing and doing two shows in one day, not to mention hanging about for sound-checks. Since overload can last for days at a time, performers may be chronically deprived of sleep and exist on a 'high' of excitement or stimulants, with a resulting 'come down' at the end of it. Underload can typically be long or regular periods of no work, where the artist begins to doubt his whole value and ability to perform.

The feelings of jealousy that 'others' are getting all the work because, for example, they are younger, more in vogue, more sycophantic and know the right people, do not help. One particular career stressor is 'not getting the rewards you think you deserve' – another way of saying that the standards you set for yourself are not being realised in your career, whether these be financial, social or personal.

Coping with attachment and family life

Actors and musicians have a particularly bad reputation for coping with commitments. Much of this criticism is unfair – like pilots and fire-fighters, many travel a lot, work unsociable hours and may be called out at the drop of a hat. This makes them 'environmentally' unstable, but not necessarily emotionally so. They are frequently caring, sensitive and fun to be with, and have a justified reputation for attracting people to them. They may be slightly easier to live with than racing drivers, but they still have a certain set of values based on individual worth and per-formance, and these need to be shared or taken into consideration.

Some of the typical performers' values tend to help them integrate with other people: they have high sensitivity and team spirit because they work in teams; they believe in feelings because their work is non-verbal, and they tend to find creative ways out of difficulties. Other aspects are non-integrative: they are competitive and tend to think they are right; they are used to alienation and can be defensive, non-con-formist and react angrily to criticism; they tend to prefer their own values, friends, lifestyle and even jokes. Such a generally defensive way of life sets a minimum value on commitment to social norms and a maximum value on individuality. Fitting this into the framework of commitment is not impossible, but may cause friction with partners and families who are left to take care of the day-to-day responsibilities of running a home. Possible consequences are that the performer will:

- change partners where conflict arises
- find a partner in the profession and share values. For married actors or musicians this can be one or more casual affairs with cast or tour members
- have a family 'outside' the profession and live another set of values when not performing. In many cases this represents a valuable financial and emotional refuge. Singers, in particular, seem to profit from supportive and preferably well-off partners for whom they are objects of endless fascination.

Many performers, such as orchestral players, as shown in a study of the Vienna Symphony Orchestra, seem largely content with family life. They nevertheless complain that work interferes with home and leisure life, and that holidays have to be rescheduled. The early careers of actors and musicians – in their twenties and thirties – is often a pressure point, where changes of direction or impulsive responses to events take place. They may become more stable as their careers progress, which may explain why later marriages can last longer than first ones. Later still, mid-life crises and anxiety over declining powers or looming retirement may cause a further stress point in relationships which partners have to negotiate. Dancers who have been through transition typically settle down in their thirties into stable family environments, after which they may remain contentedly in second careers.

Long or unsociable hours certainly put a strain on families. Many performers may not want to travel as much as their schedules demand, and when home may only really see the family at lunch or weekends. When also rehearsing and doing sessions or shows, they can wake to find nobody at home, go to work before anybody comes home and return when everyone is asleep. The effects on children and sex life are obvious. It helps when partner and children feel committed to the performer's success, not only financially but socially. Children hear their parents on recordings or the radio and see them on television, are admired by other kids, and benefit from the stimulating and lively social environment of show folk. Many do indeed make excellent parents, offering children a richness of fantasy that is particularly effective in early years. They may often be absent but they are rarely boring and may be much loved by their children. Other parents are so wrapped up in show business and themselves that the children feel ignored – particularly when both are in show business or one intimately supports the other as secretary, manager or PA. As is said in therapy, 'The children of lovers are orphans', and this is doubly true of 'showbiz' lovers.

Since arguments may often be about money, it helps when partners share a rather idealistic attitude to personal achievement at the expense of regular income. Poverty, however, is depressing, and those who make no attempt to meet financial obligations may be seen as selfish. Periodic adjustments of values or temporary jobs are one way of avoiding total family breakdown and a lot of regret later. Leaving the business becomes inevitable for some – particularly actors – when the last three years' annual incomes total less than an average wage for one year, and there are mouths to feed. Even so, the actor may be dragged away kicking and screaming, saying, 'I didn't give the profession up, the profession gave me up.'

Improving your life and career
There are a number of general remedies for stress.

- Encouraging yourself to take holidays. This can be difficult as it goes against the whole ethos of the freelancer as being always available for work. The fear is that others will get the work, fixers will promote others into his or her place on session and orchestral lists, and that work will dry up.

- Taking breaks with your partner. To keep relationships working, both partners may have to arrange to synchronise time off.
- Getting into a regular company, band or orchestra. This makes life more predictable and so less stressed, but may mean more touring and more tiredness. It also means auditions and trials, which are stressful in the short term and a reason why some freelancers do not apply for regular posts.
- Getting companies and orchestras to arrange more sensible rehearsal patterns, with better preparation for gigs. Britain is particularly bad in this area compared to the rest of Europe.
- Learning to negotiate better and acquire financial and business skills. This would remove some of the stressors around being manipulated by fixers, managers and recording executives, and being unable to handle late or non-payment, tax, pension plans and personal promotion and marketing.
- Taking more responsibility for your own health, sleep patterns and time-management, prevention being part of the cure.

Practical measures
Practical measures for making life easier include the following.

- Checking instruments and equipment regularly and carrying spares.
- Preparing better for gigs and shows and getting scripts and parts early.
- Turning down work that is clearly at the limit of or beyond your ability. Ask for details of gigs to assess the level of difficulty and stress.
- Intervening positively to get ridiculously loud music turned down to safe levels.
- Leaving early for gigs and shows.
- Talking more to fellow performers on a personal level to monitor their subjective states, and adjusting your attitudes and expectations accordingly.
- Getting help when you feel you need it. Do not wait for a problem to become a crisis.
- Structuring your life around work you enjoy as much as possible.
- Acquiring coping strategies for travel and touring situations.
- Increasing your overall confidence through self-help, and restructuring your belief patterns around your actual abilities.
- Eliminating through therapy the particular stressors that lead to stage fright and personal feelings of anxiety, frustration and inadequacy.
- Talking more to others about performance and techniques.
- Acquiring short-term coping strategies for dealing with actual stress in performance, so that you can quickly psych yourself out of feelings of distress.

- Learning predictable relaxation techniques that you can use when you need them.

Healthcare solutions to stress

Physical activity
Frequent moderate physical activity has been shown by a number of researchers to be an important factor in the treatment of stress and depression, even to the point of reducing anxiety levels as effectively as tranquillisers. Walking or moderate exercise of any kind is effective, and team sports such as tennis and golf add the element of company and competition. Outdoor activity is preferred, since the sunlight and the change in scenery are beneficial in themselves.

Routine busters
Stress, anxiety and depression close down the desire to experiment and take risks and tend to make the sufferer fall back on restricted routines, sometimes even of an obsessional character. For this reason, a degree of newness and challenge should be introduced – new places, new reading material, new activities. Since this may not be contemplated or may be resisted by the sufferer, such new lifestyle elements may need to be introduced sympathetically but firmly by concerned others.

Visualisation
Visualisation, as described in Chapter 3, is relaxing, particularly when combined with breathing exercises.

Diet
Stimulants like coffee and energy drinks can raise short-term energy, but when their effects wear off the drop in energy can be worse than a regime of cutting them out completely or using milder forms like tea. Herbal infusions are liked by some, and a milky drink helps sleep because of the calcium it contains. Protein and/or fatty acids in fish (preferably oily), eggs, beans, yogurt, soya, seeds and nuts help the diet and offset carbohydrates.

Humour and laughter
'Laughter is the best medicine' used to be the title of the anecdote page in the *Reader's Digest*, and modern research shows that it does in fact help restore and promote health. Some of it is purely escapist, our 'manic defence against reality', but laughing does have actual beneficial effects – it diffuses fear, it offers a sudden mental release from insoluble problems and ambiguities, it boosts the immune system and it brings back some of the happiness of childhood. Statistically, children laugh a lot more than adults, even though they don't get clever punch lines until they are older.

Meditation, yoga and silence

Noise is in itself a source of stress, so a quiet place accompanied by some sort of meditation or yoga is a very helpful refuge for the over-heated brain. Deep breathing exercises also help.

Massage

Stress can stiffen up the body and a good massage can be a welcome source of relief as well as a feel-good factor in itself.

Get a medical check-up

It is important to eliminate certain conditions like thyroid problems, anaemia and diabetes before looking at the psychological effects of stress.

Communicate

Stress, like depression, can lead to social and emotional isolation. A simple exercise to counteract this is to double the length of every daily verbal transaction, from buying a newspaper to talking to friends and family. The effects of this are quite striking – people around you feel more involved and respond willingly, opening up new areas of conversation and deepening existing emotional contact. As one cynic observed about life, 'So much to talk about, so little to say.'

Find appropriate ways of expressing anger

Stress may derive from people, events and situations that cause anger. Irritation, annoyance and displeasure are all expressions of the fundamental emotion of anger. It is not necessary to shout and become aggressive, but it may help a lot to admit the things that we are angry about. This can be the first step to fixing the situation.

Take action to fix long-term irritations

Unpaid bills, taxes, unfiled letters and documents, and general clutter act as long-term irritants, and taking action to fix them can give a substantial sense of achievement and mental relief.

Stress from interpersonal anxiety – attitudes of fellow professionals

One of the most stressful things that can happen to anybody – whether in the performing arts or in many other businesses – is to feel that others are out to undermine your career and frustrate you of your rightful opportunities. At its worst this can completely destroy people, who become paranoid, are unable to sleep and construct elaborate fantasies of doom, failure and isolation. Sometimes these centre on a single person, sometimes around a group of people or a whole organisation.

The effects of these paranoid feelings are out of all proportion to the threat, and to explain them it is necessary to invoke the idea that we are vulnerable to being 'cast outside the litter' in our primitive brains. Exclusion from a litter or a tribe in more primitive times would mean certain isolation and likely death from starvation or predators, and it may be some residue from this powerful instinct that still affects us when we feel the threat of exclusion or hostility from our immediate survival group. What is at risk is not our lives (though suicides are not unknown) but our careers, and by implication our professional lives and our future economic survival.

Anyone who has seen a number of severe cases of bullying, deliberate career destruction or bad-mouthing in the profession will be under no illusions as regards the severity of the possible effects on those unlucky enough to be singled out for such treatment. Bullying, destructive criticism, financial swindling and attempts to remove colleagues from work are, unfortunately, no strangers to the performing arts. Playwright John Osborne became so incensed by the destructive power of critics, he started a movement to fight back against them. It is not unknown for orchestral musicians to have nightmares about section companions or to walk off stage in disgust. Singers can take years to leave a teacher who threatens to bad-mouth them in the profession, or says that 'they'll never work again if they leave'.

Some colleagues just harbour bad feelings and resentment; others display criticism publicly. Some performers are always criticising others, some feel constantly criticised. Many do both – they feel critical about their own ability and then 'project' this on to others by criticising them instead. They then feel really bad when they suspect others criticise them. The criticism goes round and round – we dish it out, we take it in. One of the most stressful things a performer has to cope with is the 'attitude problems' of difficult fellow professionals. This happens in particular when touring and spending a lot of time with a regular company, band or classical orchestra. Typical of this is the tendency for critical or aggressive fellow performers to get 'under your skin' and cause feelings of anxious insecurity. Pit bands call this 'cabin fever'.

We know from the 16PF (*see* Chapter 1) that performers of all types have elevated critical tendencies and mild-to-pronounced suspicious feelings of others. We also know that criticism is internalised as self-criticism, directed onto others, and then projected back as a feeling that others are constantly critical of you. Popular musicians are also sensitive to 'attitude problems' because they already have a history of being manipulated, tricked and exploited. On top of this is professional envy, jealousy and the worry that others are after your work. At worst, performers can see colleagues as 'cynical', 'two-faced', 'greedy', 'ego-tripping' or simply 'always taking the piss'. Extraverts are wary of introverts; poor, idealistic performers are wary of rich, commercial ones; piss-takers of serious types; laid-back ones of those who are well organised. In addition, performers are collectively wary about bandleaders, management, agents, record and film companies, and so on – often for the good reason that their goal is to make money out of them. So the criticism and suspicion goes round and round – everyone complains and everyone suffers but little effort is made to actually reduce the general pool of criticism or make the musical world a less paranoid place to live in.

The fundamental attribution error

When it comes to anxiety over the attitudes of fellow professionals, one way of recognising and dealing with the problem is by seeing all these opinions, attitudes and suspicions as 'attributions'. An attribution describes any cause of apparent behaviour that you 'attribute' to somebody or something. Behaviour can be attributed to a set of circumstances – 'he's angry because his car was towed away this morning', or to a person's feelings and inner motives – 'he's angry because he thinks I can't play the music right'. The problem occurs where situational reasons are confused with people's motives. We all assume we have done something wrong at times. We interpret people's anger as displeasure with us, their tired looks as boredom with us, their failure to make contact as rejection of us. All too often these assumptions are wrong, as the following true story illustrates.

A New York actor was auditioning for a musical, and came on stage just before lunchtime on the last day of auditioning. As soon as he reached the front of the stage the producer (who he had auditioned for a short while previously) groaned and said, 'Oh, no, not again!' very audibly. The actor fled the stage on the spot, and remained angry and distressed until he happened to meet the producer a while later. 'How could you humiliate me like that in front of everybody,' he said angrily, recounting what he thought he had witnessed. The producer looked blank for a while, then his face suddenly lit up. 'Oh my God – I know what that was! We'd sent the messenger boy out for some takeaway lunch and told him on no account to bring back the tasteless junk food we'd had all week. I turned round as you came on and saw him coming towards us with yet another pile of junk-food takeaways. I must have said, 'Oh, no, not again!' pretty loudly – I guess you thought I meant you. Now you mention it, you auditioned very well a few months ago, and we had our eye on you for the part.'

Apart from being ridiculous when wrong, attribution errors cause us self-doubt we can well do without. The worst problem is the 'fundamental' attribution error – that of blaming ourselves for what we assume is our fault, rather than looking for causes outside ourselves. When the conductor is ratty, we assume we are playing badly; we do not realise his car was towed away that morning.

Other people's moods are referred to by a number of familiar terms such as 'vibes' or 'attitude problems'. We have an instinctive feeling that we do not want to deal with 'their stuff', but we may need to really train ourselves to disconnect our own feelings from the moods of others. As little children we will have blamed Mummy's bad moods on our 'naughty' behaviour, and we have a lot of unlearning to do to be free of this almost unconscious self-blaming tendency.

Dealing with attribution errors

- The first stage in retraining is simply to remind ourselves constantly that there are all sorts of possible reasons for the moods or actions of others. Had the New York actor done so he might have got the part. So do not start with the assumption that you are in the wrong.
- The second stage is to find out what other people's motivations actually are. Ask them, interpret their actions, look for reasons. Find alternative attributions for your feelings.
- The third stage is to create 'boundaries' between the moods of others and yourself. See fellow musicians as 'inside their skins'. Do this by visualising their emotions and personality 'contained' inside their skin, so they stop at the boundary of their skins. When you do this they will seem life-size, and will not 'spill over' or 'spread' towards you. Constantly remind yourself of this.

When other people seem angry, negative or critical, this may first and foremost be a function of their own situation and feelings, and possibly their own inability to cope with their problems. People in the grip of inner problems are naturally inflexible, unsociable, defensive or aggressive. By not responding to their bad moods you not only save yourself unnecessary grief, you are also more likely to bring them out of their negative emotions into the more positive emotion that you are projecting. All this helps cut out the negative feedback that can go round and round when the performing environment seems loaded with bad feelings.

Cultivating generosity

'Be kind to those you meet on the way up', the saying goes, 'because you'll meet them again on your way down.' Generosity is the complete antidote to criticism. By positively supporting others in the directions in which they want to go, much can be contributed to the collective happiness of performing. Duke Ellington demonstrated this to the world in his uniquely generous band arrangements, featuring the particular styles and aptitudes of soloists like bassist Jimmy Blanton and trumpeter Cootie Williams, for whom he wrote 'Concerto for Cootie'. Generosity is not just one of the fundamentals of ego-less performing and a non-judgemental attitude, it is the main secret of making others 'feel good'. And as American saxophonist Cannonball Adderley used to say, 'Fun is what happens when everything is mellow.' Feeling good is often the reason that lies behind hiring certain people time and time again. Performers who 'feel bad' are doing something to decrease everyone's ability to reach their best work, and 'if you are not part of the solution you are part of the problem'.

Putting others down can be deliberately avoided. This was demonstrated in a *Downbeat* magazine 'blindfold test' in which American saxophonist Sam Rivers awarded five stars to every piece of music 'because the musicians deserve that much for surviving in this business'. His interviewer was perplexed with his 'uncritical' response because it was unprecedented. There is a need for standards in music-making, if only to establish goals towards which to strive. Respecting such goals can, however, go together with supporting fellow professionals.

Close proximity

Life can be distressing when it involves spending a lot of time with someone you don't get on with at all. A performer may find him/herself touring with such a person, and having to put up with all sorts of annoying behaviour at rehearsals, shows and social situations, together with having to listen to criticism day in and day out. Performers have been known to walk off stage, argue out loud and even have recurring nightmares as a result of having to spend long hours right next to someone whose behaviour they find impossible. Particular string quartets are known to travel in different train compartments and even stay in different hotels.

Besides creating emotional boundaries, it may also be necessary to create working boundaries between what you will and will not stand for, so that the other person knows your limits, and between his time and yours, so he/she does not interfere with you off stage. It is difficult to say what is the most effective way of dealing with consistently annoying colleagues. One way is the 'short, sharp shock' of confronting the person face to face, alone or in front of others, saying exactly what is going on and what you are not prepared to tolerate. Another way is constant lack of response, or the 'silent treatment' used by the Inuit to discipline their children. To be effective, the latter has to be completely consistent and predictable, so that the lack of response extinguishes any point in the behaviour. Perhaps the best approach is a mixture of assertiveness and negotiating skills.

Depression

The periodic occurrence of depression is widespread in the general population, and as much as one-third of the population suffers from it at some point. The two serious forms – bipolar or manic depression and endogenous depression – usually require medical treatment, while the most common form, reactive depression, may be treated with either drugs or counselling or some combination of treatments. Depression is a problem in the performing arts, because artists are sensitive, imaginative and prone to emotional reactions, and because they take their careers very seriously and setbacks are taken as a personal assault on the core of their beings and the perception of their usefulness and success in the eyes of others. Reactive depression may result from general or relationship problems, but all too frequently it results from career difficulties, particularly opposition from colleagues or the threat of losing work and status.

Depression is best measured on a good depression scale, and the long-established Beck scale is as good as any. It is included in the book *Feeling Good* by David D. Burns (Burns, 1999), which also gives a range of cognitive treatments for depression. The Beck scale asks twenty-one questions about mood and lifestyle, covering characteristic areas such as the following.

- Feelings of sadness, tearfulness and disappointment.
- Apathy and loss of drive, both work related and sexual.
- Loss of appetite and weight.
- Feelings of failure, guilt, self-blame and punishment.
- Irritation and frustration.
- Loss of concentration and interest in things.
- Tiredness, sleeplessness and early waking.
- Worries about one's health and appearance.

Respondents rate their answers on a scale of one to four, one being no problem and four being a severe one. The answers are then totalled and scored on a scale ranging from no depression through borderline, moderate and severe to extreme depression. Severe depression should be a red alert for immediate intervention of some kind. Extreme depression should be dealt with immediately by a doctor.

Sufferers from depression may not realise the severity of their problem, since the onset can be gradual and since by its very nature it shuts down the emotional and mental alertness needed to react quickly and effectively to problems. There is consequently a tendency to drift progressively into anxiety and physical apathy, made worse by sleeplessness and a resulting general tiredness. In performers this alone is a serious problem. Because the sufferer tends to isolate himself or herself and resists physical activity, so worsening the problem, it is usually necessary for somebody to intervene from outside in a robust and prescriptive way, using any means possible to try to lift the depression until the sufferer has the mental alertness and ability to return to normal functioning. While the sufferer may earnestly want to feel better, the activity needed to do so may be stubbornly resisted, mostly because of the very apathy inherent in the problem, but the intervention must be persistent in order to succeed, to the point where it may feel as if the sufferer is being supported on a complex system of emotional scaffolding until there is enough progress for it to be removed.

A considerable problem with depression is the filter it puts on normal thinking. The main problem is 'globalisation' – the tendency to see particular issues as an overwhelming problem enveloping everything. 'I lost that part that I really wanted' becomes 'I'm a useless actor and I'll never work again, nobody wants me'. 'I'm having difficulties hitting high notes easily at the moment' becomes 'My whole range has gone to pieces – I'm finished as a serious professional performer'. It is as if the sufferer is wearing shaded black spectacles, seeing everything through a glass darkly and pulled out of shape as in a fairground distorting mirror. Not until normal alertness and vision is restored can the need for treatment be relaxed. Depression is a creeping and insidious state and should be dealt with immediately and as robustly as possible. Treating it takes precedence over most other activities, since while it lasts, the whole perception of reality is distorted and there may be associated risks like loss of work and even suicide attempts.

Dealing with depression

Dealing with depression is similar to dealing with stress and burnout – there should be an immediate increase in exercise, outdoor activity, socialisation with good supportive friends and relations, verbal communication, and the pleasures of life, such as hobbies and pastimes. A complete break may be needed, preferably a holiday. Holidays should be at least two or three weeks long so that the first week can be spent in winding down from the state of anxiety and the rest of the time in the enjoyment of simple pleasures. A beach holiday with sun and swimming is ideal, and decision-making should be kept to the level of 'Shall I have a swim or just lie in the sun; shall I have an ice cream or some fruit?' Hopefully such an undemanding state of relaxation combined with outdoor activity should induce some good sleep, which in turn should relax the system and promote recovery.

Cognitive therapy has been the treatment of choice for depression because it directly challenges the mental distortions and globalised thinking typical of the problem. A sheet is given to the sufferer to record the automatic thoughts that creep into the mind and to rate their emotional distress as a percentage. The sufferer is then encouraged to reconsider a thought such as 'I'll never work again', question its skewed logic and come up with a more appropriate statement such as 'I may be having a lean time, but there are a number of things I can do to get back on track, and in any case most careers hit the doldrums from time to time'. The emotional distress of this revised thought is then rated and is naturally a lower percentage than the previous one. In such a way the sufferer is forced into abandoning globalised thinking and into restructuring thoughts in a more realistic and optimistic way, so promoting a return to normalised thinking, which in turn restores general well-being, activity and alertness.

There is a serious risk of loss of earnings and position in an orchestra or company resulting from depression, just as there is in other high-stress professions like merchant banking where performance is carefully monitored by others and has to reach a continuously high professional standard. As with city corporations, the potential performance of the individual at his or her best is much valued, but a fall of ten to twenty per cent in efficiency cannot be tolerated for more than a short period. So again, there is reason for dealing with depression as fast and effectively as possible.

Employers are generally (but not always) understanding and tolerant enough to cope with a period of depression lasting a couple of months or so, and may encourage the sufferer to take a break and come back in restored health. They frequently want and need a progress report, and if possible some estimation of the outcome and possible date for a return to full function. Provided the employer is acting in the interests of the sufferer and there is support from the relevant union, and provided the sufferer agrees to it, the employer can be kept in the picture and all can work together towards a positive outcome. The employer may have to be told what to do in some respects, such as lifting any additional responsibilities, organising sick leave or dealing with colleagues who may have contributed to the problem with hostile or bullying attitudes.

Those involved should be careful, however, since there is always the possibility of dismissal and litigation, and each case should be carefully judged on its merits and implications. Unions may find it hard to intervene since both employer and employee may be members of the same union, and while they want to promote a successful resolution of the problem they may find it difficult to take sides. The Musicians Union, for one, is familiar with the problems caused by depression and has handled a number of cases with a generally sensitive and sympathetic hand, and the Equity Trust Fund has a range of helpful services, including that of a very good debt counsellor. All the unions in the profession are by now familiar with the medical and psychological problems of performers, and indeed actively fund a range of services.

Burnout

Burnout is a word coined in the mid-1970s, and its use as a description for 'physical, emotional, spiritual, intellectual and interpersonal exhaustion' became popular in the 1980s as a by-product of a lot of contemporary research into job stress. Though the focus of such research was the corporate world, clearly high job stress, personal frustration and inadequate coping skills are just as likely to affect performing artists, as has been shown in *Pressure Sensitive* (Wills and Cooper, 1988) which documented the stressors experienced by popular musicians, and was founded on a questionnaire circulated to Musicians Union members working as freelancers (see page 133).

Age at onset

The age typical of burnout is popularly assumed to be middle age, but it may occur at any of the following points.

- Late teens and twenties through an earlier start in the profession (child and early teenage actors, musicians and singers).
- 'Seven year itch': seven years after college, e.g. 28, when solo aspirations remain unfulfilled.
- Career plateau: 30–45, where early 'life change' factors apply.
- Late forties: mid-life crisis – Can I still manage? Will I have to make compromises? (Horns move from first (principle) down to third in the horn section, singers do less opera and more choral work.) For some this is the start of artistic decline.

Earlier onset may occur for a few reasons.

- Performing artists are starting earlier in TV programmes, popular music and dance and even classical music as the backbone of the media's 'youth culture'.
- The huge size and budgets of modern media companies and their worldwide coverage mean that 'stars' are hyped up very quickly to global celebrity status, and then required to meet the pressure.
- The importance of image and novelty rather than technical excellence and 'paying one's dues', and the substitution of studio-based bands for touring bands and studio sets for 'rep' means that newly created stars may simply not have the psychological readiness or strength of experience to cope.
- Our contemporary 'pressure to succeed' and 'pursuit of excellence' culture is forcing young people into pushing themselves harder in an increasingly competitive mental environment, where 'top ten'-type league tables and award ceremonies are everyday phenomena.

Stress types

Reasons for burnout can be:

- Under-work career stress
- Over-work career stress.

Under-work career stress is above all the realm of the actor, together with rock bands trying to make it in the business. The problem of chronic under-work stress is low self-worth and depression. With this is a subjective feeling of having no actual influence on anything – from agents to record companies – that will get work or a decent contract.

In successful popular and classical musicians it is often the opposite – over-work stress from schedules most people would consider ridiculous, e.g. up at 7.30, teaching in the morning, afternoon rehearsal, extra teaching in late afternoon then evening concert and not in bed before midnight. That may be a good day, out of town concerts or tours being worse.

Burnout as a loss of passion

Most – but by no means all – performers start their love affair with their art form, often at an early age, with somewhere near 100 per cent passion. The exceptions are those forced by parents or others into a routine of practising before any independent motivation or love of what they are doing has shown itself, and in these cases the roots of burnout may start at a very early age. But for those who start with a natural love of performing, burnout represents the gradual development from 0 per cent knowledge and disillusionment with the profession to the critical mass of 51 per cent disillusionment. After that the passion for performing goes into negative equity and progressive burnout ensues – practising, rehearsing and going on stage becomes more disagreeable than agreeable. This is 'spiritual and emotional burnout'.

Without knowing it, the performer has hit a career plateau where the typical work schedule is fairly similar day in, day out, and this applies equally to international artists as to rank and file performers. Energy of youth burns out revealing any number of underlying tensions, from performing nerves to worry about the future. Ambition

Figure 8.1 Burnout of primary motivation (passion) over time

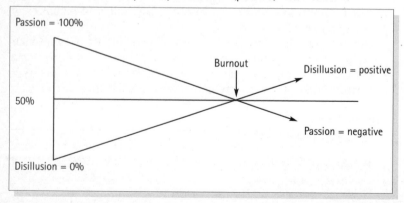

gives way to apathy and low performing buzz as careers become more predictable and less varied and challenging.

Burnout through prolonged performance anxiety

If there is constant and untreated performance anxiety for a long time, the subjective effect may be: 'I can't stand it any more – either I reduce the anxiety or I'm giving my career up just to keep me sane.' Loss of motivation may have caused a fall in professional standards which is bringing the performer close to the minimum acceptable level. Others may have noticed this for some time before it really hits home. To the performer it may be a sudden awareness that denial is no longer an adequate defence – technical elements are suddenly much harder than they seemed, and there is a realisation that one is only just coping. This sudden 'peak' in anxiety may be dramatically worse in performers who have become well known and have heavy schedules in the public eye, with advance bookings sometimes stretching ahead for months and years. Fear may become alarm and the performer fights against a desire to 'call for help', such as getting permission from a doctor or other specialist to have a short, long or complete break. The usual term used for the media is 'exhaustion' when a performer enters one of the celebrity clinics to recuperate.

Symptoms of burnout

- Don't practise or rehearse enough.
- Don't warm up before performances.
- Don't listen to other performers (orchestra or cast); just try to get own part right.
- Arrive minutes before performance.
- Tempted to or actually read papers/books in rehearsals.
- Have stopped doing solo performances, e.g. recitals, chamber work or one-person shows.
- May feel consuming guilt at falling technical standards which turns into stage fright.
- May turn up for work drunk or drugged as a way of dealing with nerves.
- May use alcohol, cannabis, cocaine or other drugs daily and lose track of pressing career needs or reality in general.

Is it depression?

Burnout may mirror apathy in other areas (marriage, sex, lapsed hobbies, lapsed sport due to being overweight). There may be several common depressive features, such as a sense of 'not looking back to birth but on to death' – fantasies one wanted to accomplish in one's lifetime may no longer be possible, particularly in career terms. Remember that the biggest stressor of popular musicians, which probably applies to all performers, is 'reaching and maintaining the standards you set for yourself'. In successful performers this is seen as a challenge, but when spirits are low and a career is perceived as hitting a trough, it can share depression's sense of anguish and 'futilitarianism'.

Recovering from burnout

Life on the 'mid-life plateau' can be successfully managed so as to give variety and enjoyment, but not in the same hectic, all-consuming way of the ambitious performer straight out of college, and not in the apathetic and jaded way where actual standards become progressively worse.

Increasing passion means reviving interest and commitment, while decreasing disillusionment means managing your life to prioritise pleasure, creativity and variety and decrease all sources of stress.

Dealing with burnout

Health priorities cover many of the stress reduction techniques and include:

- sleep
- pace work. Make periods of calm around important gigs
- say no. Eliminate the drudge of your bottom level of work. Alert the diary service to your particular needs
- get help with children where needed – in particular consider an au-pair, which can be very good value if you have the room. Your own freshness is imperative to your career. Positively recharge in time out – don't just vegetate or do boring household tasks
- take exercise. Be fit for tours which take you into overdrive. Work out or swim
- don't let teaching schedules overwhelm you. Organise teaching so it fits you, not the whims and exigencies of your pupils/parents – your own comfort is essential for good teaching. Have regular teaching deps or organise a co-op of available teachers to ensure deps
- get counselling if you suffer from stage fright.

'Feelgood factors' to schedule into your life

- Take regular holidays. Synchronise holidays with spouse where possible. Don't regard touring as satisfactory if spouse stays at home. On the other hand, if spouse is overworked also, don't overlook holidays alone.
- Communicate more, with other performers and your wider social circle. Keep in touch. Visit friends and vice-versa. Have dinner parties.

- Explore right brain activities, e.g. free improvisation or music therapy for musicians. Hardened professionals may become increasingly left brained. The right brain increases sensuality and so passion.
- Have at least one other passion – hobby, reading, sport, etc. The more interactive the better.

Career priorities

- After you finish the sharp ambitious rise in your career, expect a plateau. When you reach this, prioritise pleasure and important career moves and say no to work that interferes with this. Don't expect to continue rising (see Figure 8.2).

Figure 8.2 Long-term career management

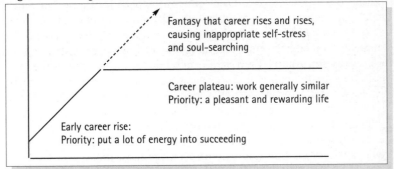

- Increase the variety of work, e.g. write plays, lyrics, sketches or articles, compose or arrange music, broadcast, produce or direct.
- Increase creativity – create your own work rather than relying on others. This ensures a personal contribution and a genuineness of personal cause and effect.
- Do regular solo gigs. Always be secure that you can do this and that you don't lose your nerve.
- Join with friends to play or try things out for the pleasure of doing it.
- Practise in a positive way – take out old pieces and try new ones as well as your regular exercises.
- If you have to deal with fame, keep control of interference from fans, the media, etc. Don't let others' expectations (teachers and parents who 'made you what you are', or managers who want to control you) overwhelm you or make you feel that you owe it all to them and not yourself.

Burnout may result in an avoidance of work in general, or self-imposed periods of not working. This breaks the 'golden thread' of passionate motivation that exists from the first love of our art which sets us on our path. Coming back to our art after a break may not feel at all the same.

That youthful energy may be replaced by a much more sober and adult type of motivation, with genuine worries as to whether the same high standards can be achieved again. This insecurity may cause self-doubt, and this may trigger performing anxiety.

Taking a break from the profession

Surveys in America and Australia suggest that 60 per cent of orchestral players reach a point somewhere in their careers where they are unable to play. Typical crisis points for performers include the following.

At college

The reality testing of competing with talented colleagues and seeing them get choice bits of work can make students realise abruptly that it is harder than anticipated to keep up with the best. In the case of musicians, changes in technique suggested or demanded by new teachers can be quite disturbing when they destroy a 'natural' or self-acquired technique, like an embouchure, a familiar way of holding an instrument or a fingering technique. Even when such changes work well in the long run, they are difficult at first. At worst they may cause an acute 'crisis' where anything and everything is tried out as a desperate way of getting back to a method of playing that works. This may cause such a drop in self-confidence that giving up for a time is less stressful than continuing.

General small-talk in music colleges and stage schools is often about who can do what, how many hours people practise their parts, and who is doing what audition. Students are prone to checking up on each other by listening outside practice rooms and going to shows and recitals, increasing the pressure that already comes from teachers and parental expectations. Pleasure from performing may be lost in the stress of keeping up with the expectations of everyone involved, particularly if parents are paying large sums of money for the course.

Another reason for dropping out at this stage is being pushed too hard, or forced to do activities or studies that seem boring or unproductive. It may be necessary simply to stop, for the sake of preserving your identity. There may then follow a period of reflection where a decision is made to perform at an amateur level, to give up completely and do something else, or to take up a different role in the profession where there is less pressure. If there is a whole family history of performing, then a break may be a symbolic gesture that things have to change. This break is best made naturally, but can be made at the cost of a temporary emotional breakdown or a physical 'problem' that gives a reason for stopping that others can accept.

In your thirties

The reasons for burnout at this stage may be similar to those at college in terms of ambiguous motivation. Pressures may, however, have built up gradually over a long period rather than coming to a head. Other reasons for problems at this stage are simply getting bored with performing, a dislike of constant touring, feeling you have reached your maximum potential and that it is time to pack it in, or finding that work is tailing off and other professions offer better career conditions. There may always have been a second potential career in the background, and this may eventually become that much more appealing. Artists of all kinds like variety and challenge, and may benefit from change, even when it means harbouring regrets about what they are losing.

Another reason for giving up in your thirties is loss of peak bodily function. This is typically the age when ballet dancers give up, and to a lesser degree it applies to singers or people who have a fairly strenuous stage act. Things start to work a little less well than before, then conspicuously less well. It becomes noticeable that you are no longer being hired for the same work, and then work may start to dry up completely. The answer to this may be – like boxers – to quit while you are on top. Physical factors may be felt by the artist in terms of loss of function, but they may also be perceived by the public in terms of getting older and losing the golden image of youth. You may suddenly start to realise – despite attempts to conceal or deny it – that the public has turned to younger artists. Time to become a chat-show host, journalist or record producer! A further reason is starting a family, particularly for women. The break may be temporary or fairly permanent, since many agents are unwilling to proceed with the careers of women who pass the age of about thirty-five.

In mid-life
By mid-life and beyond, almost all the above reasons may have been relevant. It is said that after the age of forty one stops looking backwards to birth and starts looking forwards towards the end of life. This reassessment may be quite profound, prioritising the quality of your life and what you want to get done inside your lifetime. There may be some things that need to be done: writing books, travelling, moving house, visiting family. If there are adequate means available, performers may retire early so that other goals can be ensured. Some never retire as such, but pass the time agreeably, playing golf and socialising, and do occasional guest roles and chat-show appearances.

Psychosomatic Reasons
There are a number of psychosomatic reasons for a breakdown in performing ability. The symptoms in these cases include physical ones, but there is a feeling among a number of health practitioners that psychological factors play some role. It may be a bodily problem or 'a body in rebellion'. Often doctors cannot actually find anything wrong. The message inside the system may be 'this is too stressful – you must stop', and

the indication to stop may come from the body if it does not come from the brain first. External symptoms may reflect a larger unhappiness, like a marital problem, a sexual or financial frustration, a bereavement or something that destroys confidence or causes depression. There are, however, some particular conditions that lead to loss of physical function and mental anxiety, and this is a particular problem in dancers who have to perform a whole range of demanding movements, as indeed do musicians.

Loss of function in musicians

The importance of physical function, in particular the hand and arm, in music-making is so absolute that any technical or physical malfunction hits at the heart of the musician's self-confidence, and is easily exaggerated and dramatised into a more global 'problem' which may occupy the forefront of the musician's worries until both physical and psychological dramas are normalised. Frequently encountered problems of instrumentalists include the following, which are quoted from *The Musician's Hand – a Clinical Guide* (Evans, A. in Winspur, I. and Wynn Parry, K. 1998).

(a) String players

The violin is a masterpiece of bad engineering. Not only is it difficult to hold under the chin, but the right hand bowing action is a perfect example of awful human ergonomics. Given the starting premise that performers are prone to hand shake due to the effects of adrenalin induced by confronting a large audience, and a further ordeal by fire of their peers, section leaders and conductors, the very last thing they want to hold in a shaking hand is a metre long wooden object which will go through a motion of several centimetres at the opposite end of a minute hand movement of a few millimetres. It is hardly surprising that string players refer to stage fright as 'the shakes'. In consequence, the performance psychologist makes friends with large quantities of our national violin sections. The same is true of violists to a lesser extent, and so on down the scale to cellists and bassists, who suffer considerably less as the bow gets shorter, heavier and lower in grip, and so present in increasingly infrequent numbers. Less often, violinists present with left hand problems involving vibrato. If wrongly applied this can lead to overuse-misuse syndrome, which is dealt with on page 159.

(b) Wind and brass

Wind players are more rarely seen for hand shake – there is no bow and the hand is conveniently on the keys. Even the embouchure is less shake prone, particularly in the case of the clarinet. But brass players are beset with embouchure problems – particularly the horns, but also the trombones and trumpets – and dystonia (*see* page 158) can be an insoluble problem leading to premature loss of career.

(c) Keyboards

The primary problem of concert pianists is the fear of memory lapses. Having said that, performance nerves do affect hand technique through shaking and sweating, and if this is the case a general reduction in anxiety should be undertaken by the psychologist. Where the problem is overuse-misuse syndrome, this is dealt with on page 159.

(d) Plucked instruments

Both guitarists and banjo players are liable to dystonia and overuse-misuse syndrome.

(e) Percussion

Percussionists may suffer overuse-misuse syndrome as their fellow musicians do, and have added technical worries like over-hand/under-hand choices of grip and the whole question of how and where to practise, and how to avoid boredom when using practice pads rather than the real kit for reasons of noise.

Problems of psychological loss of function

The early literature of Freud contains some classic accounts of 'hysterical conversions', notably that of Anna O, where there was a somatisation including some loss of hand function following the traumatic death of her father. Freud's conclusion that where there is inadequate emotional reaction and working through of a trauma such as death, the outlet for expression might be through the body, is equally true to this day.

An example was the case of a guitarist who, following the death of his father, which had not been worked through, had a sudden loss of right hand dexterity on stage in the presence of a 'father figure' who he looked up to musically. This loss of dexterity was not present in practice, but continued to occur on stage, and through working through the events of the time he was able to fully recover his hand function.

Cases less 'classic' than the above can also be usefully treated by the same methods, though in some more paradoxical cases of arm and hand problems the origin remains stubbornly rooted in the unconscious. The patient may not see the utility of pursuing a longer process of sleuthing round the unconscious where the apparent problem is physical, and a frequently heard plea is 'can't you send me to a hypnotist who will root it out and cure me in a few sessions'. The image is closer to the vaudeville stage hypnotist than the clinical hypnotherapist, whose attempts to teach self-hypnosis and professionally examine the root causes appear to be a severe letdown of expectations.

Provided that a good working relationship is established to achieve some psychological benefits, progress does take place and after a while patients may recover. This, unfortunately, is not the case with dystonia, and every effort should be made to obtain a correct diagnosis of a specific problem.

In the case of psychosomatic pain, one alternative for the brave psychologist is simply to bluff it out and refuse to collude with the problem. Provided the psychologist acts with extreme authority and directiveness this may work, as it did when Freud treated the conductor Bruno Walter for a difficulty in conducting with the baton. He carefully directed Walter to take a holiday in Sicily for a definite period of time, stating with absolute certainty that the problem would disappear on his return, which it did. While few mere mortals would be so authoritative, the lesson in not colluding with the problem is the foundation of modern pain management and is well learned.

Physical losses of function

(a) Dystonia

Dystonia is a neurological movement disorder characterised by involuntary muscle contractions and postures, which can affect any part of the body including arms, legs, trunk, neck, eyelids, face or vocal cords. It can be misdiagnosed – e.g. as vocal abuse, carpal tunnel, or a psychogenic problem – and its importance underestimated, since there is no pain and it does not present a catastrophic loss of function like overuse-misuse syndrome. Dystonias are actually more serious and harder to cure completely, and are caused by new and unwanted neural pathways interfering with habitual movements - finger or larynx for instance. Two antagonistic functions, like extending and contracting, then contradict each other causing 'disobedient' movements.

Musicians are typically affected by focal dystonias affecting one part of the body, most often hand or embouchure (usually in the jaw and corners of the mouth), which are task-specific and related to certain instruments. Early symptoms can appear as momentary lapses, technical problems or insufficient practice, and in brass players can appear in one part of the register. Over weeks and months performance problems become worse, and neither practice nor rest helps. Pianists typically are affected in the right hand, and spasms cause the fingers to contract and curl under when playing. String players are more affected in the left hand, guitarists, wind and percussionists in either.

Since this is a neurological problem, the psychologist needs to give support and in many cases careers advice, and deal with anger and feelings of loss, but should not be optimistic about tackling the problem itself. There are now effective sufferers' support groups giving information and help, and complex rehabilitation schemes which offer partial success, but the gains have been more with hand function in pianists and guitarists. Progress with embouchure problems, which have ended the careers of some notable brass players (trumpet, horn and trombone), is still problematic, though botox (botulinum toxin) can be used. It can be heartbreaking for a doctor to tell a performer that his or her career is ended, and nobody should underestimate this unfortunate condition at the present stage of medical knowledge. Hopefully advances will improve the situation. Those seeking help on this difficult subject should look up the websites on page 245.

(b) Overuse-misuse syndrome (RSI – Repetitive Strain Injury)

What is often referred to as 'RSI' seems on the face of it to fit the cases of professions such as keyboard operators, and has thus been seen by the various unions protecting the working conditions of journalists and other frequent keyboard operators as being simply 'overuse'. This interpretation was originally used for pianists, violinists and guitarists in which it is most often seen. Performing arts specialists dispute this and claim it is better interpreted as not only 'overuse' but also 'misuse' of the body – particularly resulting from practising for long periods in a psychological and physical state of stress and inappropriate posture, for instance before important exams, auditions and competitions. The difference in emphasis is important not only for diagnosis but for prevention and treatment. The treatment for 'overuse' is considered to be complete rest, while that for 'misuse' is much more complex, including psychological help with stress reduction, practice attitudes and posture correction.

Treating overuse-misuse syndrome

The first difficulty both the client and the therapist have to grapple with is 'how much of the pain is physical and how much psychological in origin'. Typically the medical specialist will find some initial problem, e.g. inflammation, and there will be an accompanying diagnosis from a physical practitioner of 'misalignment', 'bad posture', etc. No indication is usually given of what percentage of the problem is manufactured in the mind, and indeed such a calculation would be very difficult to achieve. Typically the inflammation improves to the point where nothing shows up on scans, and the postural issues have been dealt with in a number of sessions, with advice on how to use the body better in future. At this point the pain should go away, but in a significant number of cases it doesn't.

The psychologist may not know how much of the pain perceived by the sufferer is physical in origin and how much is due to hypersensitivity, or exaggerated by the mind, and usually there is a combination of both. Gains can be made by trying to help in desensitising the mind to pain. One enlightened GP described the main function of the brain as 'ignoring things'. This useful advice – that the brain would cease to function if it were not able to prioritise what needed to be attended to – goes a long way towards describing the necessity of persuading the brain to ignore pain rather than 'noticing it' constantly. Even where organic function is restored, the image of pain can linger, because it obeys the laws of classical conditioning laid down by Pavlov – rapid onset, followed by slow desensitisation. Pain is no longer actual but a dramatically over-sensitised perception, which the brain is unable to let go of. The psychologist's role here is in facilitating this process of desensitisation.

Other parts of the treatment may deal with:

- loss of function, and the emotional stages of loss
- careers advice if and where the medical advice is complete rest
- tendency to hypochondria, which musicians are particularly prone to because of their heightened imagination, sense of drama, self-involvement and non-verbal focus
- dealing with sabotage. Performers 'pushed' into a career on stage, e.g. by parents, may physically break down as a defensible way of opting out and preserving their identities and alternative career goals
- dealing with perfectionism. This is a personality type that seems prone to physical breakdown. Since high stress is invested in being perfect, there may be a tendency to over-practise or practise obsessively and unproductively.

Dealing with loss of function and psychosomatic problems

Dystonias and RSI, while physical problems in their own right, have psychological components and consequences that lead to sufferers often seeing a number of practitioners.

Sufferers from these and other more psychosomatic problems are known to doctors as 'fat file patients' because of the number of consultations they have with various practitioners in search of a possible cure. The initial treatment plan usually requires a prompt intervention by a medical specialist, in conjunction with a physical/postural specialist (usually a physiotherapist), which should serve to diagnose the nature and extent of the problem and the overall nature of the treatment plan, which may go on to involve the psychologist and possibly other practitioners as appropriate.

Where there are a number of people being consulted, a coherent treatment plan is essential not only for the correct treatment of the problem, but crucially to gain the patient's confidence in the recovery plan that is to be put in place. Without one centralised team approach, the patient will show every desire to browse around all sorts of plausible practitioners, and go 'grazing' up and down Harley Street in search of top specialists, all of whom point out both the perceived focus of the problem and a helpful intervention. If no attempt is made to co-ordinate the treatments offered, the patient will rapidly end up substantially out of pocket, totally confused and mistrustful of everyone involved in the alleged solution of the problem.

Since the psychologist will rarely be the first practitioner involved in a case of physical pain, it is crucial that those involved in the initial assessment present a realistic picture of what the psychologist can and can't do, so that the patient comes to therapy sessions with the right attitude. An example of the 'wrong' attitude is a referral to a psychologist which goes along the lines of 'I'll send you to Mr X, who is very good with performers and will surely help sort out the problem'. The patient is quite likely to infer that Mr X is, like the medical model just experienced, a person who will give a clear and helpful diagnosis followed by an equally clear recovery plan.

The reality of the psychologist's work is that even assessment is complex – the mind is by far our most complex organ and is not easily examined. Time is required to assemble the jumble of psychological factors potentially involved, and even more time is required to see those factors that stand out as priorities. Yet more time is required for the patient to comprehend and accept his own problem – for the blindingly obvious reason that any material in the 'unconscious' is by definition not yet in the 'conscious' mind. More time again is required for the patient to accept and accommodate changes in perception, attitude and actual behaviour that might eventually help solve a problem or avoid its recurrence.

A cherished medical colleague of mine once wryly observed that 'the difference between doctors and psychologists is that with psychologists nobody dies and nobody gets better'. Humour aside, this could well be borne in mind as an initial approach to the 'softly, softly, catchy monkey' nature of the psychologist's approach. Sufferers hang on to the idea that pain is felt in the body so the problem should be in the body, therefore physical practitioners should offer more of a cure. They may feel that talking about pain is fruitless. Given the high levels of desperation and frustration performers feel when contemplating the loss of their life's work and ambitions, this is not surprising, but nor is it helpful.

What is helpful is the attitude that mind and body are closely related in a constant feedback loop, and that a positive change anywhere in that loop may have knock-on gains on the total performance system. Such an holistic attitude may be anathema for the impatient sufferer seeking a clear solution, but it is particularly appropriate in these cases. On the other hand, the psychologist should be realistic in assessing where no good is being done and the client is wasting time and money, and refer back to other specialists for second opinions.

(c) Personal injury (PI)

Personal injury is something that affects performers, and litigation can be the result. Where this happens it is important to separate the roles of the forensic psychologist, whose job it is to fight the corner of the injured party in court as an expert witness, and that of the confidential counsellor, who must on no account get involved in the legal proceedings. The victim leads a double life while waiting for the court case, sometimes a delay of several years, on the one hand maintaining the state of injury which is deserving of compensation, and at the same time attempting to recover enough function to carry on with one's career.

This unenviable double life takes an enormous toll on the inner mental state of someone who is grappling with all sorts of stages of loss, with their attendant angers, depressions and utter frustrations. Employing the services of the best possible forensic psychologist – preferably one who does PI cases day in and day out and knows all the legal angles and the most effective lawyers to use – frees the personal counsellor to be client-centred and explore the real personal issues. The client may try hard to get everyone he or she sees to write a favourable report which can be added to the lawyer's case. The temptation to get politically involved in the court case itself, which might involve disclosure, taking sides or questioning the veracity of the client, should be resisted by the personal counsellor.

Losses and gains

One positive result of time out, besides recuperation and recovering emotional strength, is the chance to do something else for a period of time. If this is done well, confidence may be gained which carries back over to performing. Such confidence may be a welcome indicator that one has other potential talents besides performing, and this then acts as a firmer basis to the 'performing self'.

Those who have had problems that have led to a period out of performing may experience a mixture of losses and gains. Losses can often be the breaking of the 'golden' thread of magic that stretches right back to childhood. This thread is a source of great energy and sometimes has a sort of sacred quality to it – that of an unbroken commitment. Those who give up and return speak of a strong feeling that 'things will never feel the same', and report a wiser and sometimes more distant attitude to the profession. There are a number of distinct stages of loss. Typically these are as follows.

- Denial – 'I can't believe it's happening.'
- Bargaining – 'If only I had...'; 'If only it had...'; 'Why did it have to...?'
- Anger – 'It shouldn't have happened'; 'I'm angry with it/everybody/the world/God...'
- Depression – 'I feel down, lonely, sad, regretful...'
- Acceptance – 'It's happened, I'm still here, I have friends and other things to do...'

These stages do not necessarily happen in this order, and some reactions are stronger than others or may last longer. All the stages are normal, and experiencing them has a positive long-term effect of 'getting through' the loss. Understanding these stages can be helpful for dancers or musicians who have to give up playing for a period of time for reasons such as injury or RSI. If any of the stages seem to be lasting too long, the help of a counsellor may make the process easier to get through.

Gains can be the result of substantial increases in self-confidence or objectivity. If one has become good at doing something else, that inner security can be transferred sideways into professional confidence. And being able to stand outside the profession may give all manner of useful insights that can be acted profitably upon. Big problems become small; solutions become that much more obvious. Like riding a bicycle, performing ability and talent do not really go away. It is possible to pick up a career again – not at the same point by any means, but with the same capacity to perform, once limbs and joints have regained their flexibility.

Long-term strategies for overcoming and learning from failure

Hope may be one of the virtues, but its other pole is disappointment. One danger is to build expectations on an exaggerated degree of hope, because for most people bad things can happen, have happened and will happen. If life is built on hope rather than a healthy sense of reality, disappointment can catapult a person into depression, despair or even 'heartbreak'.

Relying on a continual cycle of hope and disappointment is a naïve strategy for success. Better is to adopt a long-term strategy which allows for failure at any or every stage, but does not exclude later success. Steady progress towards excellence is achieved through a positive attitude – setbacks become learning events, as crucial to doing well as success itself. The goal is a steady increase in potential, not a roller coaster ride of hope and despair. Important factors are attitude, bravery, belief in the power of hard work, positive response to threat, achievable goal-setting, flexibility and constant reassessment of the situation. As they say in the world of music hall, 'It's not over until the fat lady sings.'

A career setback like a bad appearance, show or film, or a book project being turned down, is not a catastrophe – it is a setback. It helps to focus carefully on the incident in question ('Thursday was a bad night') rather than 'globalising' setbacks ('I'll never, ever be able to walk onto a stage anywhere again'). And when setbacks do happen, it is important to learn to recover quickly, otherwise chronic stress can turn into depression.

Studies with nurses in Accident and Emergency units show that recovery rates from traumatic experiences vary greatly between individuals. Those who suffer most long-term stress are those who take weeks or more to recover from bad experiences, which linger in the mind and disturb sleep. Those who suffer the least stress are those who can mentally and emotionally deal with problems within a few days, after which recovery is quite rapid. When thrown by a horse, as the saying goes, get straight back on it again.

Unemployment

Unemployment is an unavoidable part of the performing arts: because talent and opportunity favour the few, many are left without work. Unemployment has obvious effects on the emotional well-being of artists, and a further question is whether some are more prone to unemployment than others. Some idea of how to answer these questions can be found by looking at a sample of unemployed people in the performing arts.

We have some interesting personality profiles on long-term unemployed performers in the Arts Psychology Consultants databank. These come from a number of six-week courses devised and run at the Hammersmith and West London College by Arts Psychology Consultants, between September 1989 and June 1990, under the Employment Training Scheme. The courses were conceived for any unemployed people working in the arts, and favoured musicians, visual artists and actors in that order – there were three writers, a handful of film and television people, and only one dancer. All were long-term unemployed, and the age range was late teens to late fifties, with a mean of somewhere in the thirties. About two in three were selected from the pool of unemployed applicants, and a large number of these were intelligent and talented, some having excellent previous work records.

On the Myers-Briggs Type Indicator they scored unusually high on 'Perceiving' (P), and this is one crucial feature that stands out in the whole profile. This is unusual even for the general population of performers, and suggests a marked lack of planning and organisation as

Figure 8.3 MBTI preferences for unemployed performers

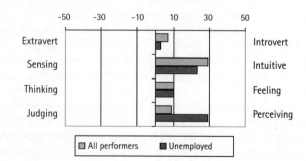

being a large contributing factor to unemployment. This P preference favours creativity and is found in the highest creatives (judged by peers), but the lack of organisation, procrastination, and inability to decide what to do may mean that there is a tendency to end up doing nothing. The 'Feeling' focus – marked with musicians but less with actors and film people – adds emotionality at the expense of rational decision-making and does not help work prospects.

Figure 8.4 16PF Factors for unemployed performers

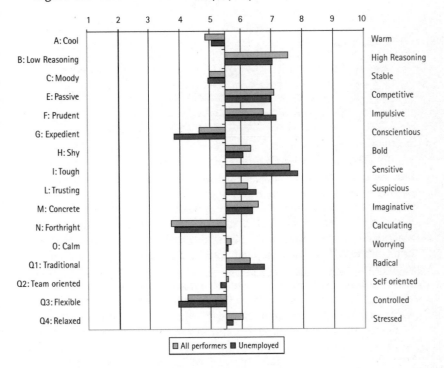

The Cattell 16PF shows high intelligence (B+) around the 115 IQ mark. A number of researchers including Crockenburg in 1972 have proposed a threshold model for creativity, above which it is independent of intelligence and more dependent on personality factors, and the IQ for the threshold has been put at around 120. Intelligence in this group clearly did not guarantee work, and personality factors appear more important. The group was imaginative (M+) – musicians 6, actors 7 – and creativity was very high, just as high as working professionals, in fact.

The group scored around average for warmth (A+) and emotional stability (C+). Interestingly, their score on neuroticism was only average, while anxiety was more elevated, suggesting a more reactive or environ-

Figure 8.5 16PF Second Order Factors for unemployed performers

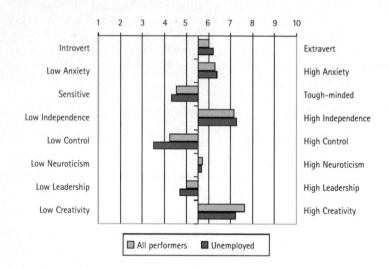

mental cause for anxiety than a temperamental one. One contributory factor was suspiciousness (L+) – musicians 7, actors 6 – though the composite anxiety score was higher for actors than musicians.

Extraversion was above average, contrasting with the slightly introverted preference on the MBTI. This was due to higher scores on social boldness – competitiveness (E+) was high and so was impulsivity (F+) and boldness (H+). The group did not lack ambition or social presence, though they might be easily put off by adversity since sensitivity (I+) was unusually high. Tough-mindedness was interesting – women score higher at 5.9, while men score very low at 3.7. In addition, the group was much more forthright and naïve (N-) than shrewd and calculating.

Independence was high at 7.3 and so was rebelliousness, both free-thinking (G-) and radicalism (Q1+) being elevated. The sociopathy score for our group is elevated at 7.28. All this underlines the dislike of structure and rules.

Self-sufficiency (Q2+) was average, but self discipline (Q3+) was low, with actors the most undisciplined. Low scorers tend to be untidy and leave things to chance, as seen on the MBTI (P) scores. Scores for superego control are notably low, between 3.1 for actors and 3.8 for musicians, with male and female both at 3.5.

In terms of Belbin's team roles, unemployed performers are very similar to the whole group. They are less perfectionist and less able to take orders, and higher on the more argumentative Shaper.

Vocational scales are given in Figure 8.7, and scores show the number of times the particular skill was rated in the top three.

Figure 8.6 Belbin Team Roles for unemployed performers

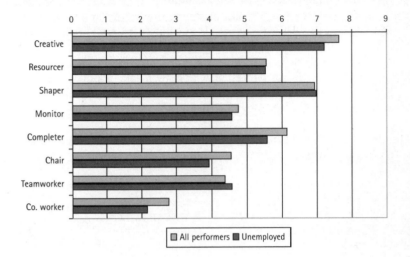

Figure 8.7 Occupational Interest scores for unemployed performers

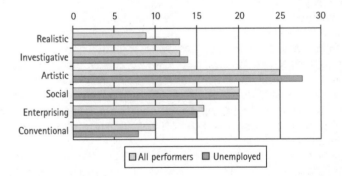

When subjects identified their top three interests, far and away the main preferences were for artistic and social skills. In fact they scored noticeably higher on artistic interests, stubbornly clinging on to their art despite lack of work. Enterprising skills accounted for 15 per cent – lower than the average for performers, which may explain their unemployed situation. This group rated 'Persuading people' low on job values. The way the questionnaires were filled in shows that subjects liked the idea of interesting and varied projects and being able to manage people and be important. They did not seem to like the actual jobs by which one got power and influence, and disliked having responsibility for people and even competition. Investigative and realistic skills were similar, but conventional administrative skills were almost non-existent at 2 per cent, again showing a positive dislike of structuring things in a businesslike way. This also gives the lie to the old idea that actresses should become temps – nothing could be more boring in their eyes. Since on Holland's job scales the overwhelming number of arts careers are listed as combinations of ASE, this correlates well with known data. It also confirms the prevalent MBTI types, INFP and ENFP, which are typically related to the arts, counselling, psychology and caring.

Job values of unemployed performers – number of mentions as highest/lowest

Most preferred job value		Least preferred job value	
Creativity	38	A predictable routine	55
Artistic work	29	A well-known organisation	22
Communication	21	Competition	20
Variety	17	Persuading people	18
Friendship at work	15	Physical challenge	16
Learning new things	14	Fast pace	13
Money	13	Working alone	13
Recognition	10	Pressure	12
Challenge	9	Peace	10
Excitement	9	Responsibility	10

The most preferred job values were Creativity, Artistic work, Communication and Variety. Next came a cluster including Money, Learning new things and Friendship in the workplace. These values correlate closely with the high 16PF scores for creativity and independence, while friendship, communication and contact with people reflect feeling values. Money is only seventh, showing some truth in the idea of art for art's sake.

The least liked values were overwhelmingly the 'organisational' ones: A predictable routine and A well-known organisation. Next came some of the enterprising ones: Physical challenge, Competition, Persuading people, Fast pace and Working alone or under Pressure. Also disliked was having to take responsibility for people. Since some of these values would occur for a successful and busy self-employed artist, this asks the question as to whether these unemployed subjects simply could not muster the self-confidence to survive under pressure. Interestingly, Challenge and Excitement were high values, but were pursued within the art form rather than in real life.

Conclusions from this interesting data are that unemployed performers are intelligent, highly independent and creative, characteristically intuitive, imaginative and oriented to the future and new possibilities rather than present realities. On the face of it they seem as gifted as working professionals and in some cases more so.

So where is the problem? This group is low on superego strength, organisation and willpower. They are radical and rebellious and dislike external aspects of organisation such as a predictable routine, admin. work, and working for a well-known organisation. What is much worse is that they have great difficulty in internalising enough self control and organisation to structure their own work, and are poor at valuing and selling themselves. Instead they tend to avoid decisions, procrastinate and work in binges. In sum they appear rebellious but not yet self-actualised; reacting against external authority concepts but unable to interiorise their own authority over themselves. They appear to be naïve at heart but outwardly suspicious of others. It is as if there is an inner venturing childlike quality which, as a result of anxieties, frustrations and disapproval by others, not to say being ripped off financially, has become mistrusting, aloof and critical. All were unusually sensitive and prone to worry and stress, though they do not appear to be fundamentally neurotic.

The six weeks of course work included a lot of focus groups, some individual work including the personality profiling, some projects which they devised and carried out themselves – each group made a film using the media studies equipment at Hammersmith College – and some radical new ideas like music therapy groups for performers, which worked so well under the inspired leadership of Pixie Holland that they continued for years after the demise of the course itself. The artists on the course grouped together and called themselves 'The Isolationists', exhibiting in the *Economist* building and elsewhere, and the musicians became much more positive about their work.

The course was scrapped after one year because it did not fit the Government's targets of getting people back to work. Obviously, unemployed artists considered themselves to be self-employed freelancers and had no wish to change that status. In fact the figures for sending people back to work were the worst in the whole scheme, at one single person in total! This is a reflection of the whole government attitude to both self-employment and the arts. The members of the course found it very helpful and positive feedback from participants was extremely high.

General factors in unemployment

All performers experience some fear of being unemployed. This can turn into fantasy and superstition. The telephone, for example, can take on 'magical' qualities for the freelancer; as one actor said: 'It controls my emotions – it can lift me from depression to elation in three minutes.' Many feel a permanent fear of being unavailable or out when important calls come through, sometimes putting off holidays, even going out of the house. With an answering machine there is still the fear that the caller might be in a hurry and book someone else. These days performers routinely use pagers, mobile phones and diary services to stay available.

External factors for unemployment include economic recessions, cuts in grants, closure of clubs and theatres. Periods of lack of work can also happen when writing a book, composing, putting together a band or rehearsing. But above all, unemployment is the scourge of the acting profession. Where business-people suffer from over-work stress, actors suffer from under-work stress. The figures on unemployment from Equity do not make happy reading. At any one point about one in five actors is working. The tale of haves and have-nots continues with the figures for earnings in the profession – again, about one fifth of actors earn the lion's share of the income, and if the income is averaged out such is the effect of the low earnings of the unemployed that the average income for a male actor is below the national average wage.

Women in the profession have a worse time. Their average income is even less, and in addition they have the whole problem of when and if to have children. Actresses who fall pregnant early on may go through traumas deciding between a baby and a career, and may be quite unjustly faced with the prospect of an abortion which they may feel secretly about for years after. And since the large part of a woman's career may be as a twenty- or early thirty-year-old this can push back children into the late thirties where all may not go so well. There has been a growing trend in the profession for actresses past forty to adopt children, which may be a reflection of this problem. Certainly the age of thirty-five can be traumatic – agents start clearing their books of the actresses who haven't made the transition into mainstream roles or 'character roles'. If children don't take you off the stage, the agent might do the job.

This scourge of unemployment and its associated problems is the main factor that gives the profession its reputation for insecurity, and it is justly deserved. The jobbing musician, by comparison, is usually doing a gig or a function during any particular week, doesn't need an agent and doesn't have to be too ingenious to get musical work of one kind or another. Ballet dancers are protected by the companies they work in, and so are many classical singers once they are established. There are a number of companies in the acting profession that do give such security to the lucky (the actor's catchphrase in TV interviews is always 'Well, I've been very lucky...'), but the main protection of the actor may be a TV soap or a West End run. This brings another set of problems again.

The lowest job value for performers is 'A predictable routine', and with a long run that is exactly what happens. At a conference about the profession an eminent academic presented the results of a large survey on unemployment in non-arts professions which had highlighted job continuity as the principle goal, and made the mistake of concluding that what was true for the rest of the population was equally true for actors, musicians and dancers.

When I pointed out that 'A predictable routine' was in fact the lowest job value in the arts, and by some way, he was nonplussed. The actor David Suchet, who had just opened in the West End, sprang to my defence and pointed out that actors began to yearn for change and variety after even a week of a production, but a predictable routine was in the very nature of a long run, and of course good business for all concerned. A number of other actors added their voices to this, concluding that there was a 'homo sapiens' of whom most statistics were valid, and a 'homo performans' who was quite a different life form.

Transition and resettlement in dancers

Many performers give up working through burnout, injury, unemployment or other reasons. Dancers are a little different in that they know in advance that they will give up, and even approximately when. Technically speaking, all dancers become unemployed at some point, usually in their early thirties. Since this is part of being a dancer, it is well provided for in the case of the major dance companies, and is referred to as 'transition'. The shift into another career is known as 'resettlement'.

Dancers in Britain, as in Canada and Holland but more so than in many other countries, have a very effective support mechanism to deal with transition and resettlement, and it is this programme that provides us with much useful data on their personalities and values, which come from the Arts Psychology Consultants databank on dancers referred for career profiling. Career profiling is typically done around the transition point, though dancers are increasingly requesting such a profile some years before the actual moment of transition.

Dancers recognise that they must finish their main career in their early thirties – character roles sometimes take them on for some years – and increasingly want to plan for the change by starting various courses well in advance (such as getting a pilot's license), both to acquire skills and to get a taste of certain occupations to see if they like them. This was somewhat frowned on by some in the dance company management as counterproductive to motivation while dancing, though the modern attitude is that it settles the insecurity of the dancer in the face of change. The Dancers Career Development Trust also likes to hand out a one-off sum of money to cover a major career move, which typically includes a college course and some money for hardware needs such as computers.

There is no reason why such a personality profile should not be valuable to dancers at any point in their dancing career, and might even help with understanding personal and artistic qualities such as extraversion, leadership, creativity and anxiety. It may also be asked whether the 'self-doubt' of the dancer – given the single-minded training and frequent lack of wider study areas – is partly self-ignorance. The statistics for the 56 dancers seen at the time of calculation were as follows.

Figure 8.8 MBTI preferences for dancers in transition

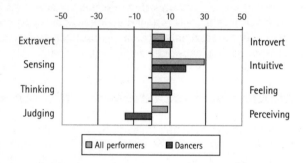

This shows that in this particular sample, dancers are more introverted. Two-thirds are imaginative ('Intuitive'), the other third practical and realistic ('Sensing'). Three fifths are 'Feeling', the other two fifths are 'Thinking'. Two-thirds are structured and planning ('Judging'), while one-third are flexible and open ('Perceiving'). They are thus the only group of performers to score positively for Judging, all the rest being Perceiving. No doubt this is connected with the constant structure and ritual of their practice routines.

The first thing that is noticeable about the 16PF profile is that scores are fairly central, rather than extreme, and this 'balance' does seem a factor not only in the physical poise of dancers but also in their mental equilibrium. Another indicator for this 'balance' is the anxiety and neu-roticism index, which is not only appreciably below other artists such as painters and musicians, but even in the case of neuroticism, slightly below average. This may surprise dancers, who may internally feel inse-curity and low self-esteem, and externally believe some of the mythology that they are poor communicators and unqualified for any-thing but dance. But other data in other countries such as Canada confirms this very closely. Dancers themselves are not neurotic. They do a difficult job with passion and commitment, and maintain profession-al standards arguably higher than in any other art form. At transition, confusion may arise between the inherent stability of the dancer and the enormous instability of the life transition, with its attendant confu-sions, depressions and anger, that they are required to experience. In this respect it is the process that creates anxiety, not the dancer.

Figure 8.9 16PF factors for dancers in transition

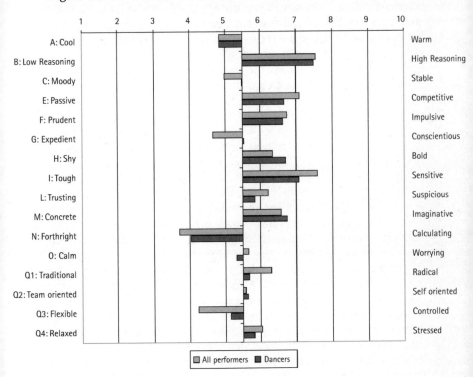

Figure 8.10 16PF Second Order Factors for dancers in transition

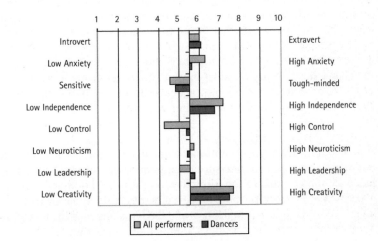

The intelligence curve of this sample of dancers shows a peak at a point equivalent to the top 15 per cent of the population. This sample of dancers is clearly intelligent, and of well above average personal potential. Why should this be a surprise to some dancers who still dwell in low self-esteem? It seems that something in the feedback between dancers, their peers, their teachers and the general public is creating a mythology which simply does not stand up to analysis. We have, on the contrary, to explain our findings of high potential by the fact that this sample is already highly selected – it contains those dancers who 'made it' into the profession. However, it is these dancers that make up our major dance companies, so these are effectively 'our dancers'. Within the sample were also a number of independents, and the independents were no less intelligent, though they had made it in a different part of the dance world.

The creativity profile of dancers is particularly interesting. Unlike the smooth 'normal' curve for the general population and the raised curve for general arts subjects, it has two clear tendencies. There is a lower creativity score representing about one-third of the sample and a higher creativity score representing the other two-thirds. This suggestion that there are two groups of dancers – practical ones and imaginative ones – is exactly mirrored in the Myers–Briggs profile, which shows that one-third are realistic and practical and two-thirds imaginative. It may be hypothesised that these are the dancers who identify with the physicality of dance and who, like sportspeople, live in the moment and get a certain intensity out of the heightened experiences of real life – challenge, movement, fun, material rewards. This realism is a very positive indicator of success after transition, particularly if self-employed.

It is, however, fairly untypical of the arts as a whole, which is a much more abstract dimension in which 'virtual reality', fantasy and the world of 'what could be' rather than 'what is' holds more allure. This abstract world contains more metaphor, more symbolism, more duality, irony and ambiguity. Whether or not the dancer is called on to portray such symbolic duality and conflict (which is much loved in the Russian culture), it is an inherent dimension of choreography and frequently of the classical repertoire of ballet music. The trade-off for such abstraction can, however, be a lack of practical realism which may have to be taken into account in planning second careers.

Motivation in transition

Practical dancers at transition may want to continue with something physical e.g. in sport and leisure or physiotherapy, or material e.g. in business and administration. Creatives, on the other hand, will want to express their creativity in choreography, directing their own dance groups, or outside dance in the arts and media, or in creative tasks within other disciplines, for example, running one's own company.

Belbin's team roles shows the following tendencies:

Figure 8.11 Belbin's Team Roles for dancers in transition

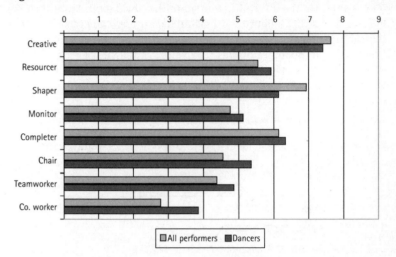

The average creativity score is predictably high, and the Researcher and Shaper are good. So is the Completer, a somewhat perfectionist role showing dancers' pride in getting everything meticulously right. Organisational roles like Chair and Team Worker are good, and the Company Worker – dependable and obedient – is higher than other more rebellious performers like popular musicians. Added to this is the data on job values, shown below.

Job values of dancers – number of ratings in top 3

Most preferred job value		Least preferred job value	
Creativity	19	A predictable routine	25
Communication	15	Community work	19
Artistic work	13	A well-known organisation	15
Money	13	Working alone	15
Challenge	12	Persuading people	13
Variety	10	Taking risks	12
Friendship at work	9	Physical challenge	11
Learning new things	8	Competition	10
Contact with others	7	Precision work	8
Recognition	7	Pressure	8

These values are largely in accordance with other arts subjects (see page 20). Ironically 'A predictable routine' and 'Working for a well-known organisation' are both typical of a dancer's working life, so there may be a distinct atmosphere of 'grin and bear it' in the major companies about some aspects of the work. These values are absolutely typical of artists, with 'A predictable routine' being anathema to most.

At the end of the decision-making process, the dancer should be fairly clear and happy about choices, and also understand clearly all the steps in the process and exactly how such choices have been arrived at. The predicted outcomes of this sample of 35 tally quite well with the actual outcomes of the overall number of dancers dealt with by the Dancers Career Development Trust.

Occupational preferences (Holland Self-Directed Search):

Figure 8.12 Occupational Preference scores for dancers in transition

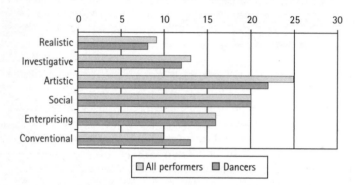

The trends among dancers to different types of career in recent years are interesting. Many more are going into computing and technology and into business, some in a self-employed status. More are going into helping professions like counselling. There has been a large shift away from the arts – numbers interested in a further arts career have halved in four years – with dancers increasingly finding the courage to make a clean break. Lower level admin and secretarial work has all but disappeared, which is quite correct for a group of people of high intelligence and achievement, but a departure from the low expectations dancers previously had of their work prospects.

Dancers are still pessimistic about how they will get through interviews with their relative lack of education, and it is often helpful for the psychologist doing the careers profiling to write a letter to the university or organisation in question affirming the positive qualities of the dancer, and the success of dancers in general after transition. Such a reference will aim to dispel any mythology concerning dancers and underscore their considerable positive personal qualities:

- high intelligence
- dedication and capacity for hard work

- self-discipline
- punctuality and conscientiousness
- performing ability to large audiences at an early age
- ability to earn and manage an income of £20,000 or more while others are still at college
- communication ability, including verbal *and* visual/physical.

All this amounts to a potential to do very well. Studies of the academic progress of dancers have revealed several to be high achievers in the top flight of their courses, and a number of later careers reveal similar determination and personal effectiveness. Where the psychological problems of transition have been sympathetically and positively dealt with, including support, warmth and encouragement from friends, partners and those assisting transition, the considerable talents of the dancer may be liberated to work. They may then go on to work with a new set of goals and hopefully a new and different passion which may result in rewards other than the ecstasy of the dance, the feeling one is special and the constant feedback of applause.

Summing up the data on dancers in transition shows them to be:

- fundamentally similar to all other artists, but with a more 'balanced' profile
- highly intelligent, typically within the top 15 per cent of the population
- not inherently more anxious than average, despite the anxieties of transition itself
- divided into a practical one-third and an abstract two-thirds
- likely to favour second careers in Arts, Social, Business or Science and Technology fields
- Likely to do well academically and use their personal skills to their benefit.

Getting older in the profession

Getting older can introduce a number of potential stresses.

- Becoming out of fashion or dated.
- Becoming bored, and 'coasting' rather than improving.
- Becoming disillusioned or 'bitter and twisted'.
- Having to defend your professional abilities against a hungry new generation.
- Having to deal with natural physical decline, including loss of high-frequency hearing, weight gain, decline in absolute intelligence and responsiveness to new problems, plus a number of aches and pains.

- Having to deal with particular physical effects, such as contact dermatitis (common in cellists); varicose veins (common in bassists); shoulder, neck or back pain (common in drummers); and a variety of possible injuries in dancers.
- The risk of your livelihood being stopped short through certain serious medical problems like arthritis, rheumatism, broken limbs, multiple sclerosis, Parkinson's disease or dystonia.
- Getting tinnitus (buzzing in the ears) from continual exposure to high sound levels. The particular danger of high sound levels is that the full effects may only be experienced years later, so – as with smoking and drinking – there is no instant way of detecting damage. Not only that, but levels above the permitted maximum (100 dbA for 2 hours or higher than 105 dbA for half that time) are regularly produced by both PA systems and some instruments themselves (drum kit, amplified guitars, large brass section playing fortissimo). A drum kit, for instance, can reach 112 dbA, which in theory should only be experienced for about thirty minutes at a time. High sound levels have been linked not only to hearing damage but also to narrowing of the arteries, raised blood pressure and even some alteration of the chemical balance of the brain with possible personality effects.

Managing one's career is a difficult enough thing to do even without the added stresses of the profession, and some practical help is given in the following chapter.

CHAPTER 9

Career Management

Celebrity, fame and the entertainment industry

Celebrity and fame are somewhat interchangeable terms these days, though in theory fame denotes a higher level of achievement and a wider renown. The nature of fame has changed substantially since the advent of the mass media, and where it was for centuries the realm of heroes and cultural greats, it is now heavily biased towards contemporary figures that appear on our TVs, cinema screens and CDs. Polls show that Britney Spears is considered more influential than Jesus Christ, and the statistics for obituaries in British newspapers show that media figures make up about two-thirds of those considered important enough to remember. Musicians make up 10 per cent to 15 per cent of the total, and actors, film people, TV presenters and other media personalities about 50 per cent. Sportspeople make up 10 per cent and politicians about the same.

Since 'fame' is in simple terms the fact of being known to large numbers of people, and the media is the obvious way of disseminating information and entertainment, it is hardly surprising that the faces most often seen in the media, and the stars hyped up by the opulent advertising budgets of the fame industry multinationals, are the people that are most widely recognised around the globe. Since performers and media personalities make up well over half of the fame industry, there has been an increasing emphasis on becoming famous within the performing arts in recent years. The media has given itself heart and soul to the creation of new celebrities, with talent shows and programmes to pick new singers, actors and entertainers showing astonishing success with the public, who flock in droves to buy CDs of their newly created stars. And with the advent of sophisticated statistics to show viewer and consumer ratings for everything put before the public, sheer popularity is paramount and critical acclaim is secondary. There has always been a debate as to whether stars are phenomena of production or consumption, and certainly phone-ins and viewers polls are tending to shift the nature of the star to the viewer's choice.

How much the dumbing down is a circular phenomenon which feeds on itself through appeal to the lowest common denominator is debatable, but the whole process seriously affects the high end of culture, with classical and jazz record sales barely reaching 5 per cent in many countries, arts budgets slashed, and whole orchestras disappearing or doing commercial work to survive.

This shift in the performing arts towards celebrity and entertainment has a number of implications for performers.

- The range of skills in demand has altered – pop singers are routinely expected to be thin, fit and able to dance well rather than play instruments. Consequently, training routines are more centered on the gym than the music academy.
- The large quantity of media appearances necessary for a successful performer – many in close-up – has resulted in a huge increase in cosmetic surgery of all kinds and an emphasis on looks as the foundation of charisma.
- The requirement of speaking effectively to the public and handling one's image has spawned a whole PR and media skills training industry – a spin-off from the political spin-doctor industry.
- Ageism is becoming a substantial (though largely unaddressed) problem in the industry, as performers become increasingly teen-oriented because of looks and youth appeal.
- The word 'wannabe' has entered our vocabulary to describe largely talentless youngsters with 'premature celebrity syndrome' – the desire to be the centre of attention on the basis of ambition alone rather than solid skills and 'paying one's dues' in the trade. This may be a cynical observation, since the queue of young hopefuls at Hollywood's door in the Golden Age of film certainly pre-dates the modern wannabe, and the stage mother phenomenon probably dates back to Salome.
- Youngsters are assaulted by elaborate publicity campaigns to glamorise and sell the major stars on whom the multinationals depend, and by comparison the money spent on publicising the higher arts is derisory and makes little or no impact on sales. Consequently, taste changes over generations.
- The popularity of computer games and adrenalin sports have fed back into the film industry, spawning an endless succession of outdoor action movies saturated with elaborate stunts, chases and shoot-'em-ups. Such formula movies have in turn created an expectation of constant action and stimulus – something due in part to the remote control unit with which viewers can flip channels at the slightest sign of boredom. The demise of the narrative movie has created new types of movie actors – men and women with strong physiques and good muscle bulk and tone, who look good in close-up and need less rhetorical skills than the theatre requires. Unsurprisingly this has helped the crossover of a number of famous sportspeople into the movies.
- Computer technology has created a new type of star – the computer-generated graphic. On the heels of computer-simulated

environments, like those in *Titanic*, come whole films based on computer-generated characters, and with photo-realism becoming increasingly lifelike we are soon likely to see synthetic stars replacing real ones – a situation not lost on Hollywood's agents who are feverishly manoeuvering to secure rights for the stars that provide the voices and movements for these new creations.

The above points describe the phenomenon of popular entertainment, but there is one key element which counterbalances all of the above and encourages independent low budget productions and the freedom of the individual to innovate and find new markets. That is the Internet. Cheap technology has transformed the experimental side of the industry – huge hit records can be made in a musician's front room, artistic output can be displayed and distributed via a website, camcorders can make all manner of public access material from the serious to the completely self-indulgent, and artists can in certain parts of the industry promote themselves effectively without the need for agents.

Performers are thus caught in a pincer movement between large-scale formulaic entertainment – the fiefdom of the multinationals like Warner and Sony – and the anarchy of the Net. This makes the politics of an industry in the throes of such upheaval quite difficult to determine. Should the young performer sing, dance and work out in the hope of getting into the mainstream entertainment side of the industry, or acquire computer skills, Midi equipment and camcorders and try to sell the results through the Internet? This polarisation has tended to categorise a whole new generation within the performing arts – there are the performers and there are the techies (referred to as 'geeks') and creatives (see *This Virtual Life*, Andrew Evans, 2001). Gone are the days when you simply bought a guitar, wrote some songs and looked for a venue for your new band – life is more complicated and it takes other skills to get to the top. It may even be more profitable to 'play' a DJ's turntable than an instrument.

Coping with celebrity

For those performers in the mainstream entertainment industry, celebrity brings not only obvious rewards but also its own set of unique problems. Overnight fame, in particular, can bring a raft of life changes, as singer Rosemary Clooney remembers: 'There's a euphoria that comes with it, where you're not prepared for that kind of lifestyle, the unending escalation of earnings, people that you meet that you had no idea in the world you would ever associate with at all. And you're really not prepared for all of it happening so quickly. It's hard, very hard.' (Boller and Davis, 1987)

The emotional dislocation of sudden change has been studied by Holmes and Rahe (1967) and expressed as a table of life change factors with scores for the severity of their effect on people. Overnight fame can include quite a number of factors, as shown below.

Marital separation	65
Business readjustment	39
Change in financial state	38
Change to different line of work	36
Change in responsibilities at work	29
Outstanding personal achievement	28
Change in living conditions	25
Revision of personal habits	24
Change in residence	20
Change in social activities	18
	Total = 322

In the original study, life changes were related to physical illness – scores of 200 to 300 over one year brought health problems to over half the subjects during the following year. For a figure over 300, the number rose to three-quarters. So the physical effects of stress are serious enough to advise those whose careers hit sudden take-off to carefully stagger their life changes over time. Whatever the temptation to embrace the rewards of money and fame as fast as possible, it may be advisable to keep family and friends in close contact, possibly put off moving for a year or two and, where relevant, put off changing the line-up of bands unless necessary. A salutary account of how too much too fast can affect the overnight sensation is given by Olivia Hussey (*The Telegraph*, 4 March 2002): 'I grew up with the whole world watching. One moment I was just a girl acting in a movie, and then I was internationally famous, touring the world and getting mobbed, giving endless interviews. I was exhausted. I couldn't wait to get out of the spotlight. So I went home and hibernated for more than a year. I was a recluse. I didn't go anywhere. I didn't do much of anything but sit at home.'

Personalities and fame

Fame and life in the limelight is easier on extraverts, who have a much higher capacity for constant stimulus (they are referred to as 'stimulus hungry') and who naturally talk more and are more at ease with strangers. As we have seen from personality statistics, however, there are a good number of introverts in the business, and this includes the acting profession. Introverted actors have a harder time than most because the public wrongly assumes that if they can be commanding and charismatic 'in role', they can reproduce this at any time as themselves in real life. Not so. Some famous names are too shy to comfortably make a speech at a wedding, and go home quietly every night where they phone a friend and listen to Mozart, or maybe a bit of Brahms and

Liszt. Wild horses wouldn't drag some famous names out to party through the night. Neither hell nor high water would persuade other rabble rousers into a peaceful eighteen holes of golf with a close friend.

Introverts therefore need to be strict about privacy to avoid overload and burnout. Garbo used to return to Europe between films, preferring nature to civilisation. Others hide behind 'no comment' and simply smile. All are prone to over-work stress, but the constant unending amount of stimulation, people, noise and activity can put celebrities in clinics at various times in their lives. Often this is through a combination of stress, drink and drugs, but sometimes it is simply exhaustion. It is an overlooked fact, but 'going off sick' may be the only way of getting a desperately needed month's holiday when the diary is full for the next three years. Agents overlook the need for time out when dollar signs are flashed in front of them, but at the risk of health breakdowns. Fame favours the fit. Stars of today work out to add muscle bulk and tone for action roles, but fitness is crucial to pop musicians on tour – Sting takes his personal trainer with him and is mentally, emotionally and physically fitter than performers half his age. Prevention is hugely preferable to intervention in the crucial question of health.

Fame also favours the analytic personality rather than the emotional one (MBTI 'Thinking' rather than 'Feeling' – *see* Chapter 1) for a few reasons. Analytic thinkers are better at structuring their thoughts and arguments, can make tougher decisions and tend to be more logical in their choices. Emotional stars like Marilyn Monroe were much more vulnerable in comparison. Perhaps most important of all, analytic types are sensitive to injustice where emotional types are sensitive to praise. Since love and praise are particularly fickle qualities in the fame industry, the ups and downs of popular and critical acclaim can be hard on the warm-hearted celebrity who relies on being considered lovable.

The advice to all performers needing to deal with large numbers of people is to create and develop a harder business side – even if this directly conflicts with the sensitivity and emotion needed for professional work itself. This tougher self can be turned on and off as necessary, and is essential for dealing with agents, managers, production and the media. It protects against financial and business vulnerability, and also the many personal demands made on the celebrity.

'Altitude sickness'

Yul Brynner observed that 'They like you until you're standing on a pedestal and they hand you an Oscar. Then they say, "How did he get up there – let's knock him down."' There is a particular feeding frenzy that can attack stars who fall out of grace and lose the respect of the general public, particularly after media scandals of one kind or another. But all are prone to falling out of the public eye. As people say in the profession, 'Be nice to the people you meet on the way up – you'll meet them again on the way down.' There is a finite amount of glitter within the glitterati, and it migrates from old to young, from the established to the new sensation.

The fear of falling from grace is probably one of the reasons behind the prima-donna attitude of stars. While it is important to send out constant status signals to the media and management in terms of the paraphernalia of staff and hotel rooms appropriate to a star of such magnitude, it may be more important for the stars to persuade themselves of their continuing importance. As we have seen in Chapter 3, we all have three ego states – the superior, the actual and the inferior. But while most of us dream of stardom, stars actually live it, so it becomes the level of actual achievement rather than a fantasy. The only available fantasy is thus the inferior one – feelings of being a fraud and being found out one day. This fantasy undoubtedly gnaws at the minds of many in the public eye, and is behind the actor's perennial superstition and his chat show catchphrase 'I've been very lucky'. The antidote to such gnawings is self-affirmations of the constancy of one's talent, as found in Chapter 3. Prima-donna behaviour may be effective in short, sharp bursts, but multinationals are not unable to tear up million dollar contracts, as some recent well-publicised cases have shown.

Fame as an identity crisis

One of the hazards of becoming famous may be a slide towards self-absorption, as Dr Glenn D. Wilson writes in *Fame, the Psychology of Stardom* (Evans A. and Wilson G, 1998).

Anecdotes of the narcissism and grandiosity of the stars are abundant. Reviewing the autobiography of Kenneth Williams (*Just Williams*, 1985) in the *Sunday Times*, George Melly noted that although 'living through almost 60 years of turbulent history and profound social change, he (Williams) recorded no thoughts on anything unrelated to himself'. In his *Diaries* (1993), the world's worst plane crash, in which 574 people were burnt to death in Tenerife a few minutes after he landed there, is mentioned only as the reason his bags were delayed, causing him to be furious about having to go to bed without washing or changing properly. John Kennedy was reportedly so fond of his own image that he had the White House filled with mirrors so that he could admire himself frequently. Marilyn Monroe regarded herself as so indispensable that she would almost invariably arrive late on a film set, or not at all, if she felt disinclined. According to Norman Mailer, during the filming of *Some Like It Hot*, 'on a good day she was two hours late, on a bad day, six'. Val Kilmer is said to have had film crews and extras at Pinewood Studios instructed not to make eye contact with him. This may have been one of the traits prompting Marlon Brando to remark that

Kilmer was 'confusing the size of his talent with the size of his pay cheque' (*Sunday Times*, 25/8/96). Elton John tells the story himself that once when he was staying at the Inn on the Park in London it was very windy outside, so he phoned down to the desk and asked them to stop the wind (*Observer*, 5/3/95). In all these cases, the observation that these celebrities 'have become too big for their boots' needs to be tempered by recognition of their underlying vulnerability.

Dealing with fame

To avoid fame 'going to your head', make changes gradually where you can, and keep seeing familiar faces who act as a reference – most often close friends and family. This helps you to digest mentally what is happening. Identify where it is important to say to yourself 'success won't change me'. And stay healthy – eat a balanced diet, take regular exercise, and build in periods of relaxation to your lifestyle.

While it is necessary to play out the status game for the media, it is also important to stay humble. The expression most commonly heard on chat-shows when well-known actors are interviewed about their lives and work (apart from 'I'm currently appearing in...') is 'I've been very lucky'. Why is this distrust of the 'fickle finger of fame' the byline of the acting profession? Simply because it is quite possible to be here today and gone tomorrow, particularly when youth starts to fade. You are indeed 'lucky' while you are in the public eye. Fame is an 'optional extra' in your career – the 'tinsel' that falls on you and then falls away again. This is true for all but the legends. Humility and realism in this way preserve a sense of scale and avoid the pride that goes before a fall. If you feel fame exceeds your expectations you will not be mortified to find that in the end it leaves you back where you expected. It will at least have given you a lot of experiences and useful contacts while it lasted.

Another thing about fame is that it signals reaching the top level of the profession. And from the top the journey may be down – either slowly or, in some cases, quite suddenly. This may be difficult to cope with unless there is a 'plan B' for dealing with life after fame. Good examples are buying property, investing wisely, opening an interesting company, going into production, writing a book, starting a family or becoming a chat-show host. The most fulfilled of the ex-stars are those with new careers or families to occupy them.

On a purely financial level, keep mortgages and borrowing at realistic levels. A commitment for five, ten or twenty-five years can be a nightmare when money suddenly dries up, unless you have the equity to survive it and sell up for a profit when the going gets rougher. Houses are a medium risk, instruments a good one (especially old stringed instruments like violins or even classic guitars), studio electronics an extremely bad one, unless you are hiring equipment out for a profit, because it all goes out of date in months or years. 'Lifestyle' spending is the worst of all – running up debts to finance holidays, parties and shopping sprees with members of the 'jet set', whose money comes from much more predictable sources like business or family fortunes, and who may desert you as soon as your glitter or cash fades away.

Keeping a clear boundary between fantasy and reality is vitally important in handling your own self-image and your image in the eyes of fans. You may go 'into role' for a stage act, adopting particular clothes, a particular image, even another name. Off stage you can be confronted by fans or simply ordinary people who still see you in your 'role' rather than as yourself. At worst, you become the focal object of fans who can have identity crises to rival that of any star, as Glenn Wilson describes (Evans A. and Wilson G., 1998):

> The word fan comes from the Latin *fanaticus*, meaning someone inspired to frenzy by devotion to a deity. There is indeed a certain religious fervour in the behaviour of many fans. Just as football fans worship their heroes on the pitch and perpetrate violence out of 'loyalty' to their club, so the fans of Hollywood stars and pop singers create for themselves a sense of identity out of following the movements of their idol. They attend performances, collect records, photographs and other memorabilia, create and visit websites on the Internet, and meet up and talk with like-minded others. They may try to infiltrate the life of the star as much as possible, sending them gifts, attempting to engage them in correspondence or conversation, and imagining that the object of their devotion reciprocates awareness and interest. Or they may live vicariously through the star to whom they have attached themselves, fantasising at some level that they are that person, enjoying all the pleasures and privileges of their life style. One obvious way of identifying with the idol is to try to look like them. This may be achieved by imitating their clothing, hairstyle, make-up, accent and general mode of behaviour. If the latter is somewhat anti-social (e.g. drug-taking or destruction of property) this can get the fan into considerable trouble. Some fans even go as far as having plastic surgery to look more like their idol (Herman, 1982). Look-alikes may make a career themselves out of imitating a famous person (e.g. appearing in advertisements and opening fetes), but there is a danger of over-identification, such that the imitator loses sight of who they really are. At least one 'reincarnation' of Marilyn Monroe has committed suicide, apparently in order to complete the identification with their idol. Sometimes even the stars model themselves on an idol. When Debbie Harry claimed she was a reincarnation of Marilyn Monroe, it was unclear whether she was living in fantasy or delusion.

To some fans you can be yourself, to others you will never be anything other than a public image. I remember sitting at a table with Chet Baker a few months before his death, just after he had played the first set at a jazz club. A journalist came over and asked for an interview, and Chet Baker asked him what he wanted to know. 'Oh, the usual things, why you sound like Miles Davis, why you have a reputation for drugs and hard living...' As he got up with a somewhat weary look to sit with the journalist at a quieter table, I said, 'It's a shame they never ask you anything personal like "what's your favourite colour".' 'Yeah,' he said laconically. After the interview he went onto the bandstand and played the whole of the second set. A full hour-and-a-half later he came back to the table, sat down, turned to me and said, simply, 'Violet.'

Children and fame

Identity crises later in life can be worst for children suddenly propelled into fame through starring in popular films. Not only did they have to suffer the ambitions of stage mothers who used them for their own ends to get into the industry and mingle with celebrities, they also had to suffer the role reversal of paying for their parents' lifestyles and, to crown it all, having nothing of their own childhood, identity or even money, left at the end of the day, as is recounted in Evans and Wilson ('Fame, the Psychology of stardom', 1998):

> Child actors frequently ended up effectively penniless at the end of a profitable career. Edith Fellows on her twenty first birthday 'returned to Hollywood to collect her childhood earnings, held in trust by a California bank under the terms of the Coogan Act (named after Jackie Coogan, this required parents to invest at least half of the child's income) and received a cheque for exactly $900.60 – the amount she had earned every week at Columbia. Tragic though it was, Edith's story had a familiar ring that made it almost commonplace.' (Cary, 1978) Nor have things improved significantly. Heather Ripley, who was only seven when she played Jemima in *Chitty Chitty Bang Bang* (1968) said, 'I wish I could sue for compensation. It was child exploitation. I can't listen to that awful accent they made me use without squirming, and they paid me peanuts. Most people assume I get money every time it's shown and must be rich. In fact I only got six or seven thousand after it had been invested for ten years'.

Prevented from acquiring an adult sense of money, child actors were required in a general sense to keep their childhood going for years after they had physically outgrown it – claiming, paradoxically, that they had never had a childhood at all. Many felt pushed into a movie career they had never wanted – 'there's a difference between walking on stage and being pushed from behind', as one star put it. They developed stage fright as a result of being dropped into situations they could barely manage, despite the commonly held assumption that children never suffer stage fright. Worse still, they experienced several problems through confusing their movie personality with their real identity, to the point where they ended up literally hating their movie persona: 'I felt as though a long delayed time bomb had finally detonated and what self-esteem I possessed was disintegrating all around me. I loathed everyone and everything that was even associated with Hollywood. My wrath turned inward, beaming its murderous rage toward someone I had come to hate more than anyone else in the world – Baby Peggy. She was the one who had done it all to me. She was the one who kept me captive, without any self of my own. She was the one I would have to destroy if I was to survive.' (Cary, 1978)

Those that enjoyed childhood fame were vulnerable to problems like suicide, under-age sex and addiction to drugs and alcohol. Given such a strange role reversal with their parents, whereby they 'parented' their own parents, both financially and emotionally, it is hardly surprising that the lives of child actors are a unique psychological case study in themselves. Many sought whatever therapeutic help was close at hand in order to resolve their identity crises, or later joined organisations with good emotional support systems. This could range from three years of counselling from Dr Arnold Hutschnecker (author of *The Will to Live*) in the case of Jackie Cooper, to analysis in the case of Dickie Moore. Heather Ripley – as nice a person as you could meet – is active in New Age movements under the name 'Banner Heather'. Christian Science was a refuge for Marcia Mae Jones and the Catholic Church for Baby Peggy, who stated that, 'Although no longer living under my parents roof I found I still could not free myself from the lifelong pattern of wanting to make them happy by giving them money. Perhaps I still needed to feel essential to their happiness in order to feel loved.' (Cary, 1978)

Many have found it difficult to form emotional attachments later on in life. Diana Serra Cary's first husband had 'married Baby Peggy', not herself. 'I for one had no idea of who I was or where I was going. All I knew was who I had once been and that was a tough act to follow.' (Cary, 1978) Other child actors married several times – seven in the case of Mickey Rooney; eight in the case of Liz Taylor, who was not the only one who 'sought movie-like solutions to problems. If a story did not end happily, Elizabeth would interrupt and say "Oh, don't end it this way, I want it to end happily".' (Cary, 1978) Some were only able to find happiness well away from their pasts. Deanna Durbin settled in France with her third husband, and Heather Ripley fled to Ireland and hid away for years to avoid attention after *Chitty Chitty Bang Bang*.

Later child stars may have been spared some of the hothouse atmosphere and excesses of that period and escaped more lightly, but much of what they recount covers the same ground. Here is a similar quote from child actor Michael F. Blake:

> Speaking as a former child actor I can confirm that we don't retire. We are forced out of a job by growing up. We are then put into the unenviable position of having to choose a new direction for our life and career. We got very little career advice – some child actors might have gotten advice from older actors or directors on a personal level, but none ever got any advice on a general level from the unions (SAG or AFTRA) in Los Angeles. The industry should do more for child performers, but sadly they never will. Some go on to use drugs, rob dry cleaners, appear on TV chat shows and generally say to the world 'feel sorry for me, I'm no longer important'. Then there are those who either move into fields behind the cameras (I became a make-up artist) or just simply move on to other fields, raise a family and live a pretty 'normal' life. Make no mistake about it, being a child actor can be tough. Your career is pretty limited time-wise. And it can play on your psyche when you are no longer needed by the film and TV industry. Happily, there are more former child actors out there living a normal life than the ones who make the cover of the National Enquirer. (Michael F. Blake, 1999)

Heather Ripley – who left the movie business completely after appearing in *Chitty Chitty Bang Bang* – is not so optimistic:

> The stress of the whole ordeal traumatised me so much that I have Attention Deficit Disorder, which I didn't have before the film. I can't hold down a job or keep relationships together, I have very poor organisational skills, I suffer from mood swings, anxiety, paranoia, stress, depression and alcoholism and have been through a couple of periods of drug addiction. My parent's divorce was doubly difficult for me as it was partly caused by them being separated for 14 months during the filming, which I internalised a lot of blame for, and subsequently I was effectively alienated from my entire family with the exception of my father and grandmother. I have only recently got to grips with most of my problems after six years counselling at the Findhorn Foundation, and have re-established a good relationship with my mother, who did not speak to me for 10 years. Kids should absolutely not be encouraged by their parents to seek fame at an early age. Fame, in itself, has little benefit and many disadvantages. I think that if I had continued as an actress – though I am a damn good actress – I would be dead or insane.

This is a particularly poignant illustration of the dangers of experiencing too much fame too fast, where a child from a small village community whose parents have no knowledge of the film business is catapulted into a major role. This demonstrates the need to stagger significant life changes and learn the ins and outs of the business first, as described on page 182. It also shows yet again the effects on the larger family unit when the mother bonds closely with the daughter due to the filming, and how an emotionally immature child's mind can internalise blame when things go wrong.

Success in the business

When asked what he would do again, the R&B legend Chuck Berry memorably remarked, 'I'd go to business school first, then become a musician.' Success in any aspect of the performing business, except possibly the regular dance companies, requires some degree of business skill. Typically you need to communicate often and effectively, by telephone or through recordings or publicity material. You also have to manage yourself like a one-person business, and this is helped by having some sort of career or business plan. Given the typically 'Feeling' and spontaneous nature of many performers, it is not surprising that management skills are foreign at first sight, but fears about not being able to cope are largely unfounded – performers are adaptable, intelligent and resourceful. They are well able to learn computer skills or simple book-keeping, and may even design artwork or promotional material. And while many may dislike the ethics of marketing, they can be surprisingly good at it if they try. The alternative to effective self-management is a 'can't cope' attitude, opting out of many essential aspects of the profession that could enhance your career. Being organised is a confidence booster, and proves to yourself you are on top of life, not that life is on top of you.

Making a business plan

To be fully effective, a career plan should be as detailed as a business plan – after all, as a self-employed person the musician is effectively a 'sole trader' in business terms. Having a clear and achievable career plan is a motivation in itself – 'no aim, no gain'. This should be done as soon as possible, and preferably formulated at college rather than in a sudden urgency upon leaving. Questions to be addressed include the following.

- What is the main area of choice: performing, directing, writing or composing, teaching, other? What secondary choices are involved?
- What are the styles envisaged: classical or contemporary work, electronic, jazz, popular, West End, TV, session or studio work? What mix is contemplated? Will lucrative styles subsidise chosen artistic ones?
- What is the level of income aimed at? What is the lowest acceptable, and how is it achievable with the type of work envisaged? What level

of income represents adequate motivation to stay in the profession or support a family?

- How will work be obtained? Joining a band or company, diary service, fixer, agent, personal contacts, hanging out with influential people, advertising and marketing oneself, international competitions, responding to ads and auditions? All of these and more?
- What is the most artistically fulfilling choice? What is acceptable, and what is unacceptable?
- What is the expected scenario in 1, 2, 5, 10, 20 years and at retirement? Will there be a switch of career (e.g. 10 years as a performer before going into teaching or administration)?

Answering these questions first gives you a chance of putting together an effective career. Ignoring them makes the business a game of chance where you are at the mercy of anyone and any offer you get.

Self-promotion

Selling yourself requires a whole repertoire of promotional activity.

Publicity material – photographs
Photographs should be:

- recent
- of good detail and contrast, but with a variety of grey scales so that they will reproduce effectively on formats such as photocopiers
- probably black-and-white, though colour has more impact and is getting cheaper with the introduction of affordable colour printers
- varied in their poses and attire, from the formal to the informal, and with or without props or instruments
- natural – particularly avoiding the terribly overworked cliché of 'expressive hands' framing the face – or if arty, then original and with genuine impact
- life size – the face and features must be right in the foreground unless an effective middle-distance shot is available
- done to a professional standard, whether by professional, enthusiast or yourself
- made over to you – you need to have copyright to reproduce publicity material at your convenience, not that of the photographer. This entails getting a letter of release and either the negatives or large prints that can be reduced/copied and reprinted. If the photographer wants to keep the negatives, get a signed agreement for terms and fees of reproduction
- ready to mail out, i.e. kept in sufficient numbers.

Artwork

A graphic artist can put a total publicity package together, and the benefit of this is that any logos or visual effects will be used throughout. The following are usually included:

- CV
- business cards
- letterheads
- compliment slips
- publicity brochure with photo(s)
- A4-size posters
- larger posters (A3 plus) if required
- artwork for cassettes, CDs, videos, etc.
- folders for packaging all the above.

As with photographs, the same recommendation exists about getting a letter of release to give you the copyright, especially in the case of distinctive logos you will use as your trademark. The fee for the copyright should be agreed and paid at the same time as the first batch of printed material. If you keep the artwork yourself, this leaves you free to use different or cheaper printers. If the graphic artist keeps them and prints economically it can be more convenient. Be prepared to negotiate over artwork. Look for someone who does a lot of it and can show you a portfolio you like the look of and which includes the sort of material you want.

Beware of artists who have not done much of this type of work before, including friends of friends. They may have no idea of what to charge, what to do or who keeps copyright, and you may end up not speaking to each other or even suing. If you want to use them for their artistic merits or because they will 'do you a favour', then go ahead, but make certain all arrangements are precise and mutually agreed from the start. Do not put up with any evasiveness, however good-natured in tone – no purchaser of a service should accept a vague 'we'll see how it turns out' or 'we'll cross that bridge when we come to it'. These are usually a sign of unprofessional conduct and can just as easily act against you as in your favour. This is a clear case for assertiveness and negotiating skills.

Curriculum vitae (CV)

The CV of a performer is somewhat different from the usual one outlining education, work experience and hobbies. While it should be equally adult in tone (delete all minor teenage activities like 'president of the school stamp-collecting society'), it should give only the major qualifications and grades and leave more space for actual professional experience. Where colleges are mentioned, give names of teachers, particularly if they are well known, and all recitals and prizes. With repertoire, start with a full list of all repertoire you have and where you have performed, and from it make a working list which shows you in the best light. Include any commissions, own compositions, large venues and well-known fellow performers. All material should be honest rather than exaggerated, but should also be assertive and complete. Understatement is of no use in a CV.

General rules for CV-type material is that it should be:

- on good grade paper, including glossy, textured or coloured paper where appropriate
- A4-size, which is cheapest and easiest to print. Be a little wary of graphic artists who suggest impractical solutions because they want striking images for their own portfolios
- printed in a pleasant typeface. 'Typewriter' style fonts like Courier are not effective. Serif fonts (with curls and squiggles) or sans-serif fonts (plain ones) give either a traditional or a modern image
- pleasantly set out on the page, using space as well as print for effect. Lists like dates and venues should be neatly arranged in regular columns down the page
- accompanied by photographic material. For a more professional look, incorporate pictures within the CV by scanning photos into a suitable computer and printing them inset in the CV. This is not at all difficult, and print outlets can do it quite cheaply. A scanner is now fairly cheap, so you could do it yourself
- chronological, either moving forwards in time – which shows a clearer artistic development – or backwards, starting with the most recent engagements. The latter is easier to read in a hurry and so has become accepted in the job market sector, but it may be more confusing in terms of a performing career
- relevant to the use to which it will be put. If work as a singer is required, play down other work as pianist (list 'best results' only). You may want to make up a few different CVs if you are multitalented. In most cases list creative work, particularly if recorded or performed in public. This shows a valuable added dimension to a personality
- above all designed with the reader in mind. Put yourself in the position of someone opening your publicity package. Go through the actual motions of opening it and reading it, and note your objective reactions. Try this out with friends. Think of the typical working day of the person opening the package – how many such packages does that person get in a day, what do they look like, what is likely to get noticed, what is likely to get thrown straight into the bin, what is the current state-of-the-art technology (colour photos, CDs, DVDs?), what is outdated, what is strikingly new? If you are quoting prices,

what is the market like – are you expensive but good, over-priced, average or attractively cheap?

- designed to take account of any change in status like address or telephone number. Get adequate copies printed at a time, with easy arrangements for change, rather than an 'economy package' of 2,500, of which 2,000 get thrown away when you move. You can 'design in' changes, by using small sticky address labels or putting addresses on the contents of folders rather than on the folder itself.

Particular items for inclusion are the following:

- personal information – date of birth, nationality, driver's licence, brief family details plus any famous family members you want to include
- education – schools and colleges, plus private teachers and summer schools/special courses
- exam and competition results – list all good results, or placings in important competitions. Restrict non-performing exams to the essentials
- hobbies and interests – should be deliberately more 'human' and informal and designed to show that you are an interesting and well-rounded person. Active hobbies (oil painting, playing tennis) are more effective than passive ones (going to the cinema, reading), and interesting pastimes of an informal nature are fine ('presently renovating an old fisherman's house')
- professional experience – should easily fill half of the CV. If this is limited, cut down the rest and include every single engagement plus details of repertoire to pad it out. Repertoire should be performable at time of writing, since it may be asked for in response to your mail-out. Those with longer careers have more choice – include the most prestigious venues, programmes and fellow performers in detail, and the rest in summary form ('also toured Japan and Spain'; 'recent work includes...'). Future bookings should be included as far ahead as known
- critics' quotes – select quotes from major publications (newspapers, performance industry magazines) rather than minor ones (parish newsletters) unless you are at the start of your career and that is all you have. Make friends with the press and inform them of all career moves, major recitals or recordings so you are likely to get maximum coverage
- agency – if you have one, use this as your business address. If not, write 'Agency – self', and include either your home address or a post-office box number. List a professional telephone number, which can be ex-directory to protect your home address. A professional number should be different from your usual home number so you can put it

on an answering machine with a proper, businesslike message (not 'This is the number for Ali, Marti and Snooky. Marti is on holiday until the 13th')

- fees – if you quote them, update them regularly and make it clear whether they include or exclude accompanist, travel or hotel. If you are VAT-registered, note this.

Publicity and marketing aids

Agents

Agents are essential for actors, comedians and musicians who want to get booked regularly. There is no real substitute, though actors' collectives are better than nothing, and run by each member of the collective putting in a day a week. Internet agencies are in their infancy, and have yet to yield results.

PR

PR agencies are useful as a short, sharp shock when you have a very public event. They get concentrated media coverage by knowing people on first name terms and persuading them to use you in editorials, on covers, or to fill empty space just before print deadlines. They are not cheap, but pay off if used wisely and sparingly, as in creating enough media exposure to get you a deal or good agent.

Press cuttings

If you attach a lot of importance to press coverage, join a press cuttings agency, which will collect all reviews and inform you of all occasions when you appear in print.

Diary services and mobile phones

A diary service is useful when you are away from the telephone for long periods, since it accepts work on your behalf. This often makes the difference between work going to you or going to someone else. If you have conditions for the work you accept, make this clear to the diary service – they usually accept anything within your usual professional field. Mobile phones are another way of staying in control, and are now commonplace in the industry.

Computers and the Internet

Being equipped with your own computer is a cheap and effective way of cutting down on publicity costs. It also means that you have a word processor to write with and can do your tax effectively on a spreadsheet like Windows Excel. Peripherals include a good colour inkjet printer, a scanner to incorporate photos and a fax modem. Decide whether to buy a desktop or portable system and where you are most likely to use it.

Portables are more expensive and have inferior monitors and keyboards, but are extremely practical. Musicians who already use a computer for music-making can use these for all of the above, as long as there is no conflict of space or time between one use and the other.

The Internet is becoming essential in all kinds of businesses. You need your web page, preferably with a permanent address ending in .com or .co.uk, and also an e-mail at that address, so you are free to change service providers. Your web pages can then contain photos, CV, recordings and any other publicity material. This is good for actors who can enclose a whole range of photographic material and even video clips, and for musicians who can sell their recordings over the Internet or in downloadable form. Some rock bands are doing brisk trade over the Internet – it can be a very powerful tool.

Books
The performer's bookshelf should include some basics such as *The White Book*, *The British Performing Arts Yearbook*, *Spotlight*, *The Music Week Directory* and the *Musicians' Union Directory*. These are an invaluable source of data on the profession, venues, agents, clubs, record companies, management, competitions, bursaries, festivals, publishers, journals and other societies and services.

Magazines and Internet sites
Subscribe to whichever publications will keep you up to date with news, competitions, auditions, vacancies and equipment for sale. Examples at the time of writing are *The Stage*, *Music Week*, *Classical Music*, *The Strad* and *Studio Sound*. Internet sites are now as effective as magazines, and can be located through the many search engines available.

Filing system
It helps to keep details on record of fellow performers and contacts in the profession with a brief note of who they are and in what context they were met. This can be kept in a personal organiser, a computer database, filing cards in a box, or any other convenient means. Computer records are probably best, since they can then be printed out in a variety of formats or transferred into personal organisers and back. A small filing cabinet is invaluable for storing correspondence, scripts or sheet music, accounts and all the things that usually clutter up bookcases, cardboard boxes and plastic bags.

Union membership
In Britain, it is not expensive to join Equity or the Musicians Union (MU) at its basic level, and it serves two important purposes. First, it ensures that the union exists, and has the clout to defend the performer's livelihood in all respects – from negotiating rates to supporting medical

services. Second, it offers you a large number of effective services – the *Members' Directory*, regular information on lost instruments or gear, reports of unreliable fixers, cheap instrument insurance and support for hardship or legal action. Given that we have particularly good unions in Britain, membership is strongly recommended, if not essential. It can do a lot more for you than you may realise.

Other societies

This is less important than membership of Equity or the MU, but for certain key issues many societies do invaluable work and offer worthwhile benefits to members. Prominent and important societies include the Royal Society of Musicians and the Incorporated Society of Musicians, both of which are well worth joining and giving support to. Details of these are found at the back of the book.

Making demos

These days recorded material means both audio and audio-visual. Both include a bewildering array of formats, which tend to expand much quicker than they settle down into accepted standards. We are in a particularly volatile period of 'format wars', caused as much by cynical marketing and bloody-mindedness between the major manufacturers as by genuine technological progress or benefits to the consumer. First decide which of the formats to use. Then the following steps are recommended.

- Make sure you package the demo in an attractive way, preferably in a total package with your other promotional material. Put a clear label with your name, address and phone number on the tape or CD itself, not just the box – tapes get thrown around and mixed up. Address all material directly to the person you are targeting, not vaguely to the company. Ring up in advance to get the name, correct spelling and title of the person concerned, and ring back to make sure he or she has received it.
- Make sure any audio or videotapes are set to start in the right place and do not need to be spooled or turned over. This does not apply to discs.
- For an audio demo include two to four songs, with the best first. The first seconds and minutes must be effective because the demo will be ejected the moment boredom sets in, particularly if the person playing it is going through a very large pile. The songs included should vary in tempo, mood and key (often overlooked). Lyrics and details should be supplied in a printed format, not handwritten. For a videocassette, one song is acceptable, though more are better. A video of a live event is permissible if the sound and camera work are good.
- Make sure your video/audio recording is of professional quality. If it

is not – and this applies to anything unprofessional – leave it out. Acceptable quality means clear and detailed pictures in good lighting, and hi-fi sound with a full frequency range and a dynamic noise-free response. Copies of analogue copies are not acceptable: make a good master, e.g. on DAT or VHS hi-fi stereo, and then make all cassettes off that master. If SCMS (Serial Copy Management Systems) copy-inhibit circuits are present (e.g. on DAT machines), then buy a special box to disable them, available from studio-equipment suppliers. You have copyright of your own material, so you are not infringing copyright by making demo copies.

- If you are doing your own promotion, get a press officer, 'plugger' or popular club DJ to push the demo consistently for a short period in the hope of a quick kill, such as a first contract with a small independent label. When signing contracts, get them checked extremely carefully and sign only for as long as you want or need to, reserving the right to make future changes without financial obligation once the period of the contract has expired.

Employing business professionals

It is the job of managers, agents, accountants and lawyers to be good at business skills. Since you pay them, you employ them, so in theory they should do what you tell them to. In practice, their management and negotiating skills can be quite intimidating, and you need to make sure they are directed at others who can further your career and not yourself. So any written agreements should be analysed in detail before commitment, preferably with advice from your union or another reliable independent source. Once you have protected yourself, a good team of professionals backing you up can do wonders in launching and managing your career.

Assertiveness

Positive behaviour designed to get the results you want or need is not a passive process, and requires a more practical, cynical and hard-headed approach than would normally be employed with friends and acquaintances. This may be a learned process which goes against the grain, but it usefully protects against being exploited by those in the profession who have such skills in abundance.

The major problem for many performers is their 'nice' bits – their generous, sincere and feeling nature, and their tendency to be naïve and see the best in people and situations. When it comes to negotiating, this is the absolute opposite of what is required, and all these 'nice' bits must be resolutely put aside. The performer does, however, have some potentially useful personality traits: above-average intelligence, creativity, spontaneous reactions, listening and learning skills. To these needs to be added a completely objective approach to what is being negotiated, without a trace of sentimentality or generosity. Artists of all kinds are critical and can analyse situations, so with practice this can be done. In time, they may learn to take pleasure in negotiating for the variety and creativity it can involve, and for the protection it gives against being taken advantage of by others.

Exercise: How assertive are you?

In a situation with someone close to you where you are simply not getting what you want, is your voice typically:
1. Raised or shouting?
2. Calm and controlled?
3. Pleading or whining?

You find yourself complaining about being unjustly treated. The person you are confronting seems uninvolved, and a little abrupt. Do you find yourself:
1. Looking at the person aggressively to make him look away?
2. Maintaining normal eye contact?
3. Looking down a little as you speak?

You are in a situation with some other people where you feel they are wasting time and you want to get on and do something. Do you express your impatience by saying:
1. 'Come on, let's stop wasting time and do something'?
2. 'What do you think about moving on to something else'?
3. 'Would any of you mind very much if we sort of...'?

Someone close to you enters the room muttering in an obvious state of anger. There is no obvious cause for it. Do you react by saying:
1. 'Now look here; don't take that tone with me'?
2. 'You look angry. Why?'?
3. Nothing, or moving to another room?

A fellow musician plays badly on a job you are doing, leaving you frustrated by the performance. Afterwards do you:
1. Start criticising?
2. Ask what went wrong?
3. Feel embarrassed, pack up and leave?

Feedback
Work out if you answered mostly 1, 2 or 3 to the above questions, then consult the feedback below. However your answers came out, do not

expect to be 'perfect' at once or even at all. As with all cases of modifying behaviour, small gains can be reinforced with practice.

Mostly 1s
Your typical behaviour may be seen by others as a little forward or aggressive at times. You will find that the assertive alternative may be equally effective and may leave other people without any defensive or bad feelings.

Mostly 2s
You seem to have made a good start towards positive, assertive behaviour.

Mostly 3s
The person absorbing the bad feelings may be you. You may feel that with a little practice, and starting with small but positive gains, you can use words instead of silence and come away from situations with positive thoughts rather than a feeling of 'I wish I'd...'

What is assertiveness?

Assertiveness is not passive behaviour, such as when you want to say something but do not. This is the notorious: 'Waiter, there's a fly in the soup' situation – you pull it out by the wings and somehow convince yourself that flies are clean, sweet-tasting little things, then drink up the soup because you do not like to make a fuss. But neither is it aggressive behaviour, demonstrated in confrontational statements such as: 'Now just you look here, I've got shares in this company.' Aggressive behaviour tends to get negative results because people do not like it. Assertive behaviour gets positive results because it is constructive and can be done pleasantly.

Assertiveness is not exactly manipulative behaviour. This may produce short-term results, but it loses friends in the long term and is usually characterised by indifference and insensitivity to other people's feelings and wants. Assertive behaviour recognises these, and so can get results without losing friends. In particular, assertiveness is not arrogant or 'superior' behaviour. A standpoint of 'I'm OK, you're not OK' is that of the cynic, complainer and general malcontent. The assertive standpoint is one of 'I'm OK, you're OK, but there are a few things that need pointing out.' Assertive behaviour should leave a situation clearer and better. It may arouse emotions and bring matters into the open, but it need not offend.

When to use assertive behaviour

If assertiveness could be used everywhere and at any time, the world would be a clearer and less frustrating place. As it is, some of us can be assertive with people we know well but not with strangers; with partners but not parents. Or we may be assertive on stage but quite shy off it. Assertiveness is most useful in situations where we need to put a point across to others. This should be done in a form which is clear, reasonable and true. The way we communicate should be open, direct and as pleasant as possible in the circumstances. Criticism should be fair and compliments sincere. We should be able to receive as well as give in a positive way. We can also use assertiveness when we want to convey our true feelings and our actual needs, wishes and desires. It promotes understanding with everyone we deal with – fellow professionals, agents, teachers, companies, friends and partners.

Common feelings can be divided into their four basic origins – happiness, sadness, fear and anger. To this could be added desire. Other feelings are essentially subsets of these:

- **happiness**: elation, enthusiasm, satisfaction, fun
- **sadness**: nostalgia, depression, homesickness, melancholy
- **anger**: frustration, irritability, fury, rage, seething
- **fear**: anxiety, phobia, foreboding, unease
- **desire**: greed, jealousy, envy, lust, ambition, longing, yearning

We are conditioned by our parents and the atmosphere in which we grew up to believe that some of these basic emotions are 'OK' to express, and others simply are not. Some families put on a happy face and brush sadness, fear and anger under the carpet. Others express irritability and envy but rarely happiness. A father may show only happiness or anger, while the mother shows sadness and fear. The child may choose one or the other as a role model. The result of all this is that our vocabulary of emotional expression is frequently incomplete. We may need to learn to recognise the full extent of our own feelings, and then find ways of speaking them out loud.

Performing artists express all the known emotions. As such they have the complete vocabulary of feelings within the sounds they create. But like musicians or dancers this may not mean that they can express such feelings in words. A more profound implication is that unless there is a true empathy for the whole range of emotions, they may not be actually realised in the interpretation of a piece. Those who find certain emotions difficult – such as anger – may ignore or suppress them in performance. Acknowledging anger and bringing it out into the open makes it possible to deal with. The anger is expressed and can die away, rather than lingering on as unresolved bad feelings and bitterness.

This applies not only to parts, but to the whole interaction between performers. If a colleague is frequently late for rehearsals, this wastes valuable time and angers those who have to wait. Assertiveness is about learning to say, 'I'm angry about this – it keeps happening. What do you suggest we do about it?' If the answer is 'Go jump in a lake', the reply is 'I'm still angry about this – I'd like some kind of solution.' If there is no suggestion of a solution, the feeling is 'I'm still not satisfied with this. If we can't resolve it now, we will have to come back to it later.' In this instance the anger can be conveyed verbally, without necessarily raising your voice. The anger is used like a barometer to read out your emotional state and wait for a reaction. If there is no reaction, the barometer 'reading' remains the same.

Sadness is another emotion that some find difficult to express verbally. In music it is one of the most expressive emotions, whether in ballads, blues or in the work of Tchaikovsky and Rachmaninov. Again, sadness may be blocked in performance if there is unresolved sadness in personal life such as from a bereavement. Both actors and musicians sometimes need to work through these deeper feelings in therapy to free up their expression on stage. Conversely, certain composers or parts may be upsetting enough to trigger emotions that are hard to handle and need to be talked through with someone sympathetic. In worst-case scenarios, actors and singers can lose their voices and freeze on stage, which is a red alert to deal with deeper or blocked feelings.

When assertiveness fails

Even if you are able to communicate what you want clearly, you may be met by a negative response. What then?

- If you are met by a show of superior bargaining force, you will be unable to get what you want. Such power techniques may work, but in the long run they lose respect and friends.
- If you are in actual physical danger, the 'fight or flight' response will over-ride the desire to negotiate verbally.
- If you are dealing with someone with highly developed manipulative techniques, you may find assertiveness and negotiating skills help you some of the way, but that ultimately you will end up playing sophisticated games for which you may or may not have a taste.
- You will find that some people in life simply do not give you the care and consideration you would like. This may be unfair and hurtful at times, but it is their problem, not yours. Difficult people may have problems of their own which show up as rigid or negative behaviour. You can change yourself and be more positive and adapting, but you cannot change the rest of the world, which will remain basically imperfect.

Despite many efforts you may have put in, there is little point in trying to please those people who do not understand you. Other people have their own ideals, sensitivities and lifestyles. This may not change, but assertiveness makes your own standpoint clear to others and to yourself. It also makes it easier to live by your own values rather than those of others. You may come to the awareness that your own happiness, fulfilment and dignity mean more to you than getting what you want all the time. You may win some and lose some, but if you stand by your words and actions you will be judged for what you are rather than what you get.

Negotiating skills

Many performers are self-employed, and as such find themselves in potential or actual negotiating situations a lot more often than they may realise. To start with, each gig offers a chance to negotiate items such as the fee; method and time of payment; expenses for travel, food or overnight stay; equipment available. Then there is the manager, the agent, the company, the bank and so forth, each representing a source of negotiation and sometimes a written contract. And then there are all the day-to-day situations, such as buying and selling bits of equipment, where a better deal on several items can add up to a lot of money.

Most performers have no formal training in negotiating skills, and may not even be aware of them at all. As such they are notoriously easy to 'rip off', which is the commonest complaint in business. Since they may be attempting to negotiate with company executives who have full legal back-up, or with shops, managers and agents who have better than average business skills, it is hardly surprising that the distribution of negotiating ability is somewhat one-sided. Here, then are some basic principles.

Who is buying and who is selling?

This sounds simple, but may be harder to assess accurately than it seems. Take, for instance, that experience we all go through in the most impressionable years of our lives – school. To the young child, it feels like going to a factory – you clock-in and clock-out at regular times; a record is kept of your work; you are given a periodical report; you have to work regularly with time off for meals; and in time you may be promoted by the 'manager' to the 'executive' position of prefect. It all feels as if the school is employing you to do work.

But who actually pays for education? Parents pay for state education through taxes, and for private education directly, and in time the student takes over through fees and loans. So 'being employed' is an illusion – you are buying your education, and employing the school to provide it. The same applies to banks, agents, managers, hospitals and all the bodies that we employ to give us services. We are the purchasers in each case, and the long-term effects of being constantly told what to do in school prepares us badly for seeing realistically who is employing whom in daily life, and for insisting on value-for-money service from the institutions we use. When it comes to taking out a bank account, it is easy to see the bank manager as the 'manager' of our finances, and to obey his commands and terms. But it is the holder of the account who pays the bank and should be able to negotiate terms. Those who have successfully obtained a reduction in interest rates or bank charges will testify that this is achievable. In fact, it is quite normal negotiating practice.

Another familiar illusion is the agent. Many performers are over-awed by the apparent power agents have to make or break their careers via their contacts in the business. But again, it is the performer who employs the agent. In theory this means talking to a variety of agents and taking on the one with the best terms and connections and a number of already successful acts. In reality it feels as if the agent is interviewing the performer to determine whether he or she will take them on or not, and then imposing terms. Terms can be very different, depending on whether they apply to gross or net. Gross is a lot better – percentages of net come after all sorts of deductions, some reasonable and some unreasonable.

The first basic step in successful negotiation is, therefore, to work out who is buying and who is selling, and then assume the correct attitude when negotiating.

When do you use negotiation?

There are many potential opportunities for negotiating – all those occasions when you do not want to give in to someone else's terms without modifying them to suit yourself. These include the following situations.

- Negotiating can be about making a deal. Whether you are buying or selling, you are after the best price and terms.
- Negotiating can also be about entering into a contract. You want to get the terms right, and make sure you will not be compromised later on. This can be a written contract, as with a recording company; it may also be a more 'explicit' explanation of something you are involved in, for example what your student rights are when you pay for a music-college education.
- Negotiating in its wider sense can be about getting terms that suit you for whatever you are doing. For example, if a fellow performer regularly delays rehearsals by turning up late, you will want to negotiate a verbal 'contract' that gives you some assurance that your time will not continue to be wasted in this way.
- Negotiating is something you do all the time with parents and people you live with. Whenever you say 'If... then...' you are probably negotiating something. Children learn to negotiate more pocket money in return for doing homework or helping with the housework. Parents

with newborn children negotiate constantly about who is going to look after the baby while the other sleeps or works.

In all these examples, you are seeking terms that suit both parties, and you are negotiating how much you are going to give away to get what you want. This tells us that negotiating is a process of exchange. In trading one thing for another the terms need not be equal or even entirely fair, but they should be perceived as acceptable by both parties. The reason for this is that negotiating is a voluntary activity, where either side can decline to participate or walk out. So the decision made will be a reflection of the wishes of both parties, either of whom can change the terms if they want to. Where there is no room for manoeuvre, then you are not negotiating.

Making a deal – the essential components of negotiating

Let us take the example of buying a guitar from a music shop. You want it even though you think the price is a bit high. You ask the salesman for a reduction, but he says the price is fixed. You can challenge this, and if the salesman has no authority to lower the price you can ask to see the manager, who does. Or you can 'repackage' the deal, and ask for a case or some sets of strings to be included in the price. By doing this you are happier with the deal because you think the price is nearer what you wanted to pay. The shop manager should still be making a profit, so both negotiating sides have come to a voluntary decision, the terms of which are acceptable.

People like to haggle a bit so they feel the work they have put in has given them a better deal. Consequently, they are happier with what they have bought or sold. It is only worth negotiating with the person who has the authority to make decisions. If you cannot change the price, change the package.

The first essential step in carrying out a successful negotiation is to ask a number of 'what if...' questions. This has distinct advantages over an immediate 'opening offer': it helps give you some background for the deal, including a feel of what the likely highest and lowest prices are or what could be included in the package, without revealing your expectations or committing yourself to an early offer. It gives you some idea of the authority of the person you are dealing with, and what they can and cannot do.

The next essential step is to come prepared with a list of good reasons for a discount. You will need solid arguments to beat down the price, since the seller usually (but not always) knows more about the goods than the buyer. If you are selling, prepare a list of special features of the goods you are selling, including sound reasons why it is worth more than cheaper alternatives. Believe in the value of what you are selling and stick to it, discounting the competition. When you are selling you are practising the opposite of what you are doing when you are buying – standing your ground against the buyer and increasing the perceived value of the goods.

The overall strategy for negotiation is to find a route to completion. Wherever you see a way out of the negotiation, steer the opposite party towards it. This is particularly important, since the alternative is dead-lock. Ask 'open' questions that keep the conversation going, such as 'How would you feel about...', rather than 'closed' ones that bring it to a possible stop with a yes/no answer, such as 'Is that the best you can do?' The longer you keep the negotiation going without suggesting an ultimatum, the more successful it is likely to be. The success of the nego-tiation depends on your opposite partner voluntarily accepting your terms as a way of completing the negotiation, and this can be done effectively in a series of positive steps in which you go over each term and part of the package.

Entering into a contract

The most important thing to remember is to get the terms right at the start. It is much harder to turn back and renegotiate later, and ground given away is unlikely to be regained for nothing.

Verbal agreements

Many agreements, such as between teacher and pupil, are predomi-nantly verbal. Take the example of starting a year in a performing arts school. You will have more protection against possible events if you know whether you get a refund if you miss time through illness, if you can change your teacher should you not get on well, and whether you can change in mid-term or between terms, and what solid guarantees you will be given about getting actual professional experience such as orchestral experience with the college orchestras. It also helps to know what the attitude is to performances or other work you may want to do during the year, and whether the college has any right or thinks they have any right to impose sanctions against you appearing in public without permission from them. It is further useful if the college has a specialist counsellor and will pay for specialised medical treatment, counselling or careers advice if you need it.

There are many cases of students who do not get on with teachers, or teachers that have such heavy professional commitments that they fail to turn up for long periods, and it is particularly difficult to announce, 'I want another teacher' in mid-term. Since the student is the one employ-ing the teacher, this should in theory be an easy matter, but in reality the request is liable to be met with answers like 'You can't change mid-term' or 'We don't have the facilities to offer you an alternative.' For the stu-dent paying top money for a college education, such answers are not entirely satisfactory, and may be a clear case for negotiation.

The problem with teachers and colleges is the age-old law of supply and demand. Sometimes it is a buyer's market, and sometimes it is a seller's. If the service is very much in demand, then the seller can dictate terms. The owner of a well-stocked cabin in the middle of the North Pole could make the passengers from a crashed aeroplane do almost anything for warmth and food: the deal might not be equal, but the passengers would regard it as an 'acceptable' negotiation if it prevented them having to crawl through the ice and snow on a hungry stomach in search of civilisation.

Likewise, the teacher in demand can impose terms like 'You have to do this my way if you want to learn with me.' This may be the deal on offer, or a way of getting the particular tuition you are after, but it still needs to be considered in terms of the positive or negative effects that changes may have. Similarly, the agent in demand can act in ways which seem disinterested or illogical when he is the one that has the top contacts and knows it. In all these cases, your best protection is to ask all the questions you can at the start. If you are not happy with the terms, change them or look elsewhere.

Once you take on the services of someone you are going to be paying, the next essential step is to state clearly what you want. There is an old saying that 'lawyers are only as good as the instructions they are given'. There are numerous variations on this, such as 'accountants charge less for auditing clear sets of figures than for shoeboxes full of bills and papers'. When it comes to paying for lessons, your teacher should be instructed as to:

- the styles of work you particularly like and want to add to your repertoire
- your career ambitions
- the sort of technique that suits you, including factors such as your particular body build, look and size. Also, the aspects of technique with which you are already satisfied and the aspects that could benefit from change
- the auditions or competitions you want to enter, and how you want to prepare for them
- anything else you would like, such as a list of contacts in the business, periodic assessments of how your standards are improving and how you compare with others, or advice on buying and selling instruments and getting things repaired.

Your manager or agent should, likewise, be informed of your ambitions, your particular style, and all the ongoing changes in your situation. He or she should be contacted regularly and asked for an update on any progress in getting you where you want to be in the business. As with teachers, any cause of dissatisfaction should be the signal to renegotiate terms in favour of a clearer understanding of what is expected for the money you are paying.

Written contracts

Written contracts with a number of clauses are a lot more serious than verbal ones. Be warned – they are usually drawn up by people who know an awful lot more about their effects than you do. In the United States, where lawyers are numerous and widely used in business, contracts are often skillfully drawn up to allow for a favourable outcome in all eventualities. This is what is usually contained in the small print. Such contracts are drawn up by lawyers familiar with typical legal loopholes and possibilities of litigation, and not only put you at a disadvantage but may cost you a good deal of money or bind you to terms you do not need or want. You are better off doing the following.

* Getting your union – Equity or the Musicians Union to read and give its opinion of any contract drawn up by another party.
* Getting your own specialised legal advice on what clauses may cause trouble, and insisting on changes. Here again, the union should help you with a list of recommended lawyers.
* Suggesting a contract of your own. This could be based on a standard contract drawn up by the union.
* Taking out legal services insurance (sometimes offered as part of a package deal with instrument insurance or the like), so you are insured against the possibility of having to use lawyers.

Threats, complaints and revenge fantasies

Using any of these tactics when negotiating is a mistake. They put the opposite party on the defensive, and are more likely to lead to a counterattack or a stand-off position where any prospect of agreement is aborted. If you have to make a threat as a last resort, be sure it is one that can be carried out, and not a 'sour grapes' one in which you are losing out yourself. For example, if you threaten to leave the band you are in, make sure you have an alternative in mind and can survive without the income. Otherwise carry on negotiating until total breakdown is unavoidable, while preparing 'plan B'.

Be careful about grievances, especially personal ones. Getting your own back is a common human emotion, and one way of releasing pent-up anger. But be careful that your grievance is not blown up out of realistic proportions by all sorts of psychological factors. You may be a person who rankles at the very thought of authority or being told what to do. You may hate businessmen or cold, efficient people. If you are already prone to react to certain people or sets of circumstances, you may ruin a good deal simply because you cannot sit on your grievance and put your own interests first.

Be careful about complaints for the same reason. What you want out of a complaint is for the goods or service to be changed to your satisfaction. By being firm but pleasant and offering creative solutions you are likely to achieve this. By starting with 'Now look here...' tactics, you are more likely to be brushed off with 'There's nothing we can do. If you want to pursue the matter, that's up to you.' A solution is always better than a fit of temper and a series of sarcastic remarks. And your own proposal for a solution is likely to suit you better than someone else's.

The 'human factor' in negotiating is a whole study in itself. Unless you are particularly adept at reading other people's minds and emotions, it is better to make negotiating a neutral matter, and keep feelings out of it. Skilful negotiators are manipulative, and can act out a whole range of human emotions. The difference with this is that they do so to win, whereas fits of temper when you want something are almost always a way to lose.

The final word about bad feelings, stored-up frustrations and revenge fantasies is that they take up a lot of your mental time. The same amount of time could be much more productively spent planning positive things to make your situation better. It is much better to be independent and keep a clear head, so you can plan your future actions to suit yourself and not just to frustrate 'them'. Let bygones be bygones, and see each new day as a new opportunity.

Tips and traps when negotiating

- Do not accept your opposite party's first offer when buying or selling. This is not negotiating; it is just giving in.
- Be pleasant, treat your negotiating partner with respect, and avoid getting on his nerves. This allows you both to enjoy the negotiating process and feel happy with its outcome.
- One of the best negotiating tactics for buyers is 'I really want it, but I just don't have that much money.' This can be usefully accompanied by doleful accounts of hard times, many children, the recession, etc. As long as 'I really want it' is convincing, the salesman continues to be interested. His response should be 'How much can you afford, then?', leading to a reasonable deal.
- Stick to the business in hand when negotiating. If you allow the other party to change the subject or waste time with unnecessary small talk you may become irritable and start losing ground mentally. If, however, you feel that small talk is creating a good feeling and enhancing the chance of a good deal, use it as long as it seems to lead to the main point.
- Negotiate on your territory if possible. Home games usually have better results than away ones.
- Come in strong with your first offer, but make it credible. Offer a low but defensible price if buying, or a high but defensible price when

selling. Then move as little as possible from the price, or move in small increments.

- Use the old technique of a 'mandate'. When buying say, 'My partner will allow me to go up to X price on this, but not beyond. If we cannot agree on that, I'll have to go back and talk it over'. Your mandate may or may not exist. Be prepared for the possibility that the same trick will be played on you. If it is, flatter the negotiating power of the opposite party by implying that he is not a mere stooge for his 'mandate'.
- Do not be pressurised by other people's time scales, whether they are too fast or too slow for you. Allow time for the negotiating process, and do not be afraid to slow down a speedy operator to a pace you feel comfortable with: he may simply be trying to lever you into an agreement with which you are less than happy.
- Do not be afraid to say no.
- Do not be put off by all the props used to project power and wealth. Flashy clothes and offices and 'I'm so busy' tactics such as keeping you waiting or taking telephone calls in front of you are all designed to imply that if you do not want the deal there are hundreds who do. Much of this may be total bluff. Salvador Dali was not the only one to say, 'When I fell on hard times I doubled the waiters' tips.' Stick to your ground, and state your terms clearly.
- Do not assume that a salesman has to make a profit over and above cost price. If a business has debts which are costing a great deal in interest, it may need money in the bank more than goods on the shelves. A lot of firms go out of business simply because of cash-flow problems.
- When selling, do not try to create goodwill – by throwing in this or that, for example – with the idea that a little generosity promotes fellowship. The intended attraction of 'something for nothing' can just as easily be taken as a sign that there may be more easy concessions to be had, and your position may start crumbling.
- When advertising, do not use ONO (or near offer): it invites the other party to come in way below your price, making the price in itself useless.
- Do not use 'No Offers' in advertising either: it takes the fun out of making a deal, and sounds hostile.
- Some people are simply mean. They may prefer to walk away saying, 'The price is too high' rather than accept a reasonable deal. Mean people can be spotted with a little practice – do not give them more time than you need to if a deal is unlikely.
- Do not put your foot in it by offering opinions and making idle comments that might offend. If you do not know your opposite party, do not make small talk like 'Elvis Presley was such a jerk, wasn't he?' You may be dealing with a lifetime member of the Elvis fan-club.

- Do not get caught out by goods you do not really want because they are thrown in at a reduced price, or by items on special offer. You will end up with a cupboard full of stuff you never use. Go for quality and a minimum of good things you really need. Good quality items last longer and have better resale prices.

Remember that all the skills you acquire in negotiating are just as likely to be used against you. With a little practice you will begin to see them coming, and when you have developed the ability to identify and resist them, this will add enormously to your confidence.

CHAPTER 10

Creativity

Exercise:

Take a sheet of paper. Write at the top the words: 'The first time I met Henry'. Look at it for a moment. Then continue with whatever thoughts or feelings come into your head until you are satisfied, or have filled in the page. Then stop. When you are finished (and please, not before!), read on for an analysis of what you have done.

Analysis

This simple exercise is about what could be called 'the window of choice' when you start to create. You may start with a narrow window of 'assumptions', or you may decide that you want a wide-open viewpoint with as few initial assumptions as possible. The fewer assumptions you make, the wider your choice will be. An immortal scene from the *Pink Panther* illustrates this, when Inspector Clouseau goes up to a man with a dog:

> Clouseau: *'Does your dog bite?'*
> Man with dog: *'No.'*
> Clouseau: (attempts to pet dog and gets bitten – recoils surprised and hurt)
> *'I thought you said your dog does not bite!'*
> Man with dog: *'That is not my dog.'*

We can identify with this joke because most of us would 'automatically' have made the same assumption. So when you write, 'The first time I met Henry', you have a similar set of 'automatic' responses, usually:

- 'I' refers to yourself
- 'Henry' is a man
- since you have been given a title, what follows must be a story of some kind
- because the title contains the word 'met', this story is about an actual meeting
- Henry is therefore a man whom you met for the first time, and the story describes the meeting, what happened, your feelings and reactions and his.

If you were to restrict yourself to these initial assumptions, you would be behaving in the same way as the man in the joke. By exploring alternatives we start to see the role played by originality in creativity. Among the possible alternatives could be any of the following.

- 'I' is a person of the opposite sex, a historic person (e.g. Henry VIII), an animal, an alien, etc.
- 'Henry' is a woman, an animal, an alien, a historic person (e.g. Henry VIII), an organisation called H.E.N.R.Y., etc.
- 'The first time I met Henry' is a book which has symbolic importance in a wholly different story.
- Instead of a story you could write a poem, make a sketch, write a film treatment, add lyrics and music, or make a paper dart with it and throw it out of the window.

If you were to do this exercise again having seen the possible alternatives, you would probably be tempted to do something different. During the minute or so that you have been reading this, your assumptions have embraced a much wider 'window of choice'.

You might, however, decide that you would prefer to write a story about a meeting with Henry, because that is what you would do best. Originality does not replace talent, but ways of creating other than those you habitually use may eventually combine both.

The joke about the dog makes us react because it works against our expectations. In the same way, the innovators in the arts made us react because they did things that at the time were unexpected. This is true for everyone from Shakespeare to Brecht, Nijinsky to Béjart, Beethoven to Stravinsky, Charlie Parker to Frank Zappa. Even ABBA started out by winning the Eurovision song contest with a song called 'Waterloo' – and how many names of famous historic battles have won a popular song contest?

The creative personality

The arts distinguishes between 'performing' and 'creative' forms. But if we were to assume that performing artists were very different from creative artists we would be wrong. All the personality indicators we have show that creativity is very high in performers (*see* Chapter 1), and of course a large number of performers were and are also creators – actors write and make movies, musicians write music and songs, and dancers choreograph and create new ballets. So if performers are potential or actual creatives, it is worth them knowing something about creativity and the creative process. It may reveal hidden talent, it may make money, and for actors it may represent a fruitful second option while waiting for work.

Creative people have certain common character traits that predispose them towards creative activity. Foremost among these are:

Intelligence. This is one of the factors that directly affects the quality of the creative process and the products it generates. It is not the same as creativity, but a certain level of reasoning ability makes a difference between the profound and the superficial. As Dante Gabriel Rossetti said: 'Conception, my boy, fundamental brainwork, is what makes the difference in all art.' Psychologists have suggested a sort of 'basic threshold' of about IQ 120, below which output suffers, but above which output varies not with intelligence but with personality.

Sensitivity. This provides the subtle appreciation of incoming sensory information and the ability to pick up veiled levels of meaning and nuance.

Imagination. This is the very essence of creativity. Imagination generates the huge quantity of ideas which are the food for the whole creative process and make the difference between richness and poverty of conception.

Competitiveness. This is the motor or dynamo that initiates creativity and keeps it in motion.

Critical detachment. Psychologists often hold that introversion is an essential part of the creative process. Inner emotional energy, the creative search for meaning and beauty and the process of critical detachment are clearly factors that contribute to the process of creating, whether it be composing in private or improvising in public on the bandstand. It is a quality that may be present in otherwise sociable people.

Radicalism. This makes the difference between accepting traditional solutions to problems and constantly seeking new or better ones.

Non-conformity. This embodies freedom from obligation to the social norms, and allows for the creation of work that challenges existing ways and standards.

Self-sufficiency. This is the ability to work alone. Self-sufficient people also have independence of judgement and action, which is part of the quality of originality.

Of the above attributes, performers in general show ample intelligence, sensitivity, imagination and high competitiveness. Although they are capable of applying critical detachment to their work, they tend to show much more warmth in social situations. While conceptually independent, performers are also team-spirited and value friendship and colleagues more than isolated creatives like writers and artists. They retain their own radical approach to problem-solving, and are non-conformist both individually and as a group.

The creative process

Factors in the creative process

Besides character traits, there are some factors which typify the creative process itself.

Contingencies. Creativity cannot come out of a void. It has to start with some stimulus or environment that provokes thoughts and feelings. Added to this must be some way of taking down the flow of the creative imagination, such as a pen and paper, computer or recording medium.

Symbolism. Imagination makes leaps into the unknown, linking all sorts of thoughts and feelings without apparent logic, just as the unconscious does in dreams. Freud described the unconscious as having no sense of time, linking apparently incongruous ideas not chronologically but by their hidden connections. Likewise the imagination creates symbols out of unusual links. The quality of 'sweetness' may link 'my love' to 'a red rose', giving the lyric 'My love is like a red, red rose'. Music may similarly evoke strong unconscious links with familiar emotions and perceptions, symbolising feelings, moods, actions, landscapes, even people. What it symbolises is often shared by large numbers of listeners. This is shown in the popular titles that have been given to pieces of music, such as 'Appassionata', 'Winter Wind' and 'Moonlight'.

Completion. It is important to distinguish between spontaneity and originality, and the ability to achieve a finished creative product. Free-flowing ideas are what performing is about, but writers and composers have no choice but to complete works so that they can be transcribed and performed.

Original choices. If we got a computer to supply a random series of notes it would be original but not necessarily creative because no process of 'choosing' has taken place. Originality of choice is essential. Without it we would get the same sounds again and again; with it we get all the advances in harmony, melody, rhythm and sound quality that distinguish the pioneers in music. Originality is 'unusual but adaptive' – it is rebellious but has an inner logic to its choices. Thinking implies hypotheses, and if there are no consistent patterns or orderly links between input and output, the process is random 'unthinking'. This is what usually separates the genius from the madman.

Flexibility and fluency. Flexibility is determined by the degree to which ideas are free to jump about and find new forms. Fluency is the strength of the flow of different ideas. Together with originality, flexibility and fluency are considered to be the vital elements in what psychologist J.P. Guilford calls 'divergent' thinking.

Complexity. During the creative process many ideas jostle for place in the final product. Juggling all these parallel thoughts requires a capacity for complex thinking. Typically, while one idea is actually conscious and being dealt with in a 'step-by-step' way, several others are bubbling just under the surface, ready to emerge into consciousness at any moment in the process. These 'unthinking' ideas are often much faster than the conscious process, and can combine easily into the shape of the creative thought-pattern.

Integration. The first processes in creativity are often unstructured and chaotic. This 'need for disorder' is the primary process which deals with immature forms. The 'need for order' is the secondary process, and the third process is the integration of both, creating a new 'order out of chaos'.

Humour, ambiguity and absurdity. One part of creativity is closely linked to humour – that of making an apparently absurd association that contains some unusual or startling hidden link. This happens when you are set to react to one thing (A), and find yourself reacting to another (B) because (A) and (B) are both similar and different. A good example is the feminist saying, 'A woman without a man is like a fish without a bicycle.' This is the opposite of the 'logical', which seeks the clearest link between like things, and represents the 'false logic' behind comedy.

Another element of humour is ambiguity, in which the solution is left open to the imagination rather than logically stated. Often there are two or more possible interpretations. This common factor of new associations links humour with creativity, and we receive a jolt of surprise when we can combine different ideas with surprising quickness and on different levels of meaning. Because it is so obvious and predictable, logic alone lacks this novel or humorous effect.

Steps in the creative process

Many models have been proposed using different steps, but one of the most widely accepted is the four-step theory. During all four stages, unstable or unsatisfactory situations are continually being turned into situations that offer solutions. Gaps are filled, and more harmonious relationships are formed between ideas. This requires grouping, structuring, and dividing wholes into parts which are worked on and recombined into wholes which better fit the overall concept.

Preparation. This includes choosing material and forms to work with, and 'orienting' oneself to the desired goal. It involves trial and error, re-evaluation of ideas, and it calls upon the total past creative experiences available.

Incubation. After the preliminary gathering of ideas, problems are turned over in the mind without trying to 'force' solutions. This can take anything from minutes to years, as material is elaborated and organised internally.

Inspiration. Material suddenly springs into an organised concept or form. Ideas come easily and spontaneously.

Completion. Solutions are produced and ideas put into practice. These solutions can then be generalised and applied to other problems.

Types of creativity

Not all of us may be creative in the same ways. Creativity may take different forms, such as:

- **Expressive creativity**, where the emphasis is on the quality of expression, not the 'product'.
- **Productive creativity**, where the emphasis is on the quality or quantity of the 'product'.
- **Inventive creativity**, where new uses are made of old elements, and common experiences are transformed into something quite different.
- **Innovative creativity**, where completely new ideas or principles are developed.

Artificial intelligence (AI) research has led to further definitions, as described in *This Virtual Life* (Evans, 2001):

Creativity, for the purposes of designing a model, is defined as the ability to generate novel ideas and artefacts that have value. A distinction is made between two types of novelty:

- P-creativity – ideas novel to the mind of the person, the basic form of creativity
- H-creativity – ideas novel to history as a whole, though not necessarily of great human importance. These by definition start off as P-creative.

Since the process is in its infancy, it is not likely to match great examples of creativity such as the works of Shakespeare or Bach. Consequently, models of AI typically address the question of P-creativity. It has occurred, however, that H-creative ideas have emerged, and even been awarded patents, e.g. designing a three-dimensional logic gate on a silicon chip. For the purposes of AI, there are three types of creativity considered –

- *Combinational* – novel combinations of familiar material, e.g. poetic imagery, jokes (the JAPE joke generator came up with 'what do you get when you cross a sheep with a kangaroo – a woolly jumper').
- *Exploratory* – novel versions within a familiar conceptual frame e.g. jazz, science, art.
- *Transformational* – new conceptual invention, e.g. 12 tone music, Kekule's ring molecule.

Sometimes it is hard to distinguish exploratory from transformational, and often exploratory creativity follows within the new dimension created by a transformational leap like that of Kekule. But truly transformational creativity creates whole new structures. The effect of new structures can be shock and amazement – an 'impossibilistic' surprise felt by the creator as well as the observer. The problem is that new structures may be so surprising that they are unintelligible or pass unnoticed because we lack the parameters to see them. A further step into the future would be computers that could make real H-creative advances. This opens up a whole new dimension to human understanding. If artificial intelligence were to come up with a paradigm for existence so different from ours that it was unrecognisable, then it would not only have to invent something that was a step further than our comprehension, it would have to have 'powers of persuasion' strong enough to show humans why such initially alien models were valuable to us, or indeed made sense at all!

Creatives in the education system

A study by Getzels and Jackson in 1962 compared highly creative students and students of high intelligence but low creativity. The results showed that the creative students:

- showed a good sense of humour
- chose more unusual vocations
- went for satisfaction rather than success and goal-achievement
- were less well-liked by teachers
- could obtain lower grades because of tendencies to independent ideas and stances rather than conformity and group-work.

The study also found that the conventional school system can fail to identify creative people and use their potential – as creative people know from their own experiences. Creatives, as described by Piers in 1968, have a richness of positive traits that are largely accepted, such as flexibility, tolerance of ambiguity, sense of humour, intuition, ability to deal with complex ideas, self-acceptance, self-confidence, strong motivation and involvement in what is happening. They also have rebellious and stubborn traits that can result in conflict, such as independence of judgement, persistence, curiosity, dissatisfaction with things as they are, autonomy and self-sufficiency.

The poor record of some schools in developing creativity is witnessed in punishment for rule-breaking, pressures to eliminate fantasy and curiosity, and suppression of unconventional attitudes and novel attempts at problem-solving. More emphasis is placed on stereotyped role-play, conventional sex-roles and goal-achievement. If the environment of the creative individual is not flexible, stimulating and accepting, such rebelliousness can easily lead to a self-perceived alienation from the system, resulting in, at worst, confusion, fear and timidity.

Such is far from the case in the specialist performing academies, which have been specially geared to the needs of developing talent since the first 'Fame School' of all – Lawlor's Professional School in Hollywood: 'Lawlor's looked like the prop department's idea of a school. School hours only took up half the day, since interviews were rarely held in the morning hours. There were about ten rooms scattered around a main hall, and most of them were equipped with wall mirrors, practise bars and pianos. By one o'clock the classrooms had been cleared for action. For the rest of the afternoon and evening everyone was practising juggling, tap routines, ballet, opera, blues, piano, violin, diction and contortions. Even the school telephone was an extension of the casting agencies.' (Cary, 1978)

Many of the most creative performers – actors, dancers and musicians – grew up in stimulating and accepting environments. Some were poor, some were affluent. One of the surprising common factors of these households, revealed in a Canadian study, was that the family argued continually. In fact, this was the factor that seemed to fit more homes than anything else. Children who get used to discussing issues and expressing themselves from an early age, and take the initiative in answering back, clearly develop their minds well, and in addition it has been shown that 'difficult' parents make a number of children more resourceful at problem-solving and manipulation. So it is not just a question of sympathy and guidance – stimulation may be just as important, as it is to babies in early years.

The original and the establishment

Few great artists were not ahead of their time. They were true to their own ways of expression rather than what they 'ought' to have done at the time, or what had gone before. The irony is that once this freshness of approach had got past its initial critics and an uncomprehending public, people gradually started to like and value its novelty. During the inevitable course of history, the iconoclasts became the establishment, and their way of doing things became the accepted way. Nothing was further from their minds at the moment of creation than how they *ought* to create what they did, and the same willingness to listen to one's inner voice guarantees the same freshness. Even if talent and acceptance emerge gradually, the right path leads to the right goals.

To imitate is easier for a beginner who as yet has no original voice. This is not artistic freedom; it is freedom from care. It may also be freedom from poverty, since many people like what they know. To leave the cosiness of tradition is to 'leave home'. And to leave home means to accept the need to look after yourself in fair weather and foul until such time as you can stand on your own two feet. The sacrifice of the cosy is a price many creative artists have thought worth making. Others have not wanted to make it or, like Stravinsky, reverted to the traditional in later life when they had other insights and artistic priorities.

Creating music and lyrics

Britain has a strong tradition of songwriting. Unlike other countries, including the United States (particularly Los Angeles, the songwriting capital of the world), songwriters in Britain generally write for their own use in bands rather than on commission for other singers. This makes it harder for 'songwriters' to exist in their own right.

The reasons for this are partly creative – the British are historically a creative and inventive people and tend to 'have a go at writing'. But there are sound financial reasons for writing your own material. A member of a band who pens a song on the band's record stands to gain a considerable amount of money in royalties if the record sells well. In fact, the royalties from records can easily come to more than the band would ever get touring or doing gigs. So band members need considerable inducements or threats to let go of their chance to write the band's material. Inducements include the opportunity to cover a hit and make quick money, while threats can come from the record company or producer to record a particular song or else.

Making money from the music industry in one form or another is one of the goals of a large number of teenagers and young adults. There are a number of different ways of doing this.

- Hearing music in their head and writing it down straight to manuscript.

- Writing with a piano, guitar, etc., to directly hear the notes as they write to manuscript.
- Writing at a polyphonic multi-timbral keyboard to 'hear' different instruments as they write.
- Playing or sampling into a keyboard connected to a computer and recording it as a MIDI file.
- Recording music as above and printing it out on manuscript from computer software.

The advantages of recording into a computer are the same as writing text on a word-processor – one has complete control over it, and it is easy to make changes or take the computer file directly into a studio and add further tracks. Composers differ in how they approach a new work. The first question is what to start with.

- The overall structure?
- The exact instrumentation?
- A rough plan?
- Some actual fragments that need putting together?

All such methods should be considered before finding ways that suit your writing personality. Some of us are planners and some are spontaneous and intuitive. We may want to follow our personality style closely – plan if we are planners or see how it turns out if we tend to improvise. On the other hand, we may want to explore deliberately the consequences of doing it 'the other way'. Improvisers may improve their work with more planning, planners may be able to explore more possibilities if they allow themselves to try things out rather than start with a complete structure or instrumentation.

Musicians frequently go through progressive stages of confidence and completion on their way to mastering the medium. They may start composing in a rough and sketchy way, then progress to better and fuller ways of putting music together, and there may be distinct moments of transition when confidence is felt to move on to another stage. Sometimes necessity forces the musician to write, if the band needs new material fast. The musician may start with the feeling he or she can write music but not words, and will try to find others to write the lyrics, with more or less success. Then something happens to create the idea of writing the lyrics as well. A friend or partner may give confidence-boosting support, there may not be a suitable lyric writer available; some ideas on an old piece of paper may suggest a song. Whatever the stimulus, the result is a complete song. If this looks fairly good, he may then try more. Creative people are creative by nature, and it is not so difficult to change from one medium to another.

Self-expression starts with knowledge of the self. In creative writing classes the first instruction given to any potential writer is 'write about what comes naturally to you'. A postman writes about life as a postman; a soldier writes about war. It is possible for a postman to write about war and a soldier to write about life as a postman, but this is probably not the best way to find one's identity as a creative artist. Our first stages of self-expression may be fairly clichéd, as when we imitate the style of middle-of-the-road chart material:

> I don't like foursomes, they talk too loud,
> I don't like threesomes, 'cos three's a crowd.
> I don't like onesomes, or mirrors on the wall,
> But there's one number that's got it all:
>
> And that's two, ooh ooh ooh,
> Just two, ooh ooh ooh,
> It's two, ooh ooh ooh,
> Just two, baby, me and you... me and you.
>
> © Andrew Evans, 1983

Even this type of writing, which is unashamedly 'popular' in style and intent, can become much more individual while retaining a catchy 'hook':

> You wear the latest image from your head down to your toes,
> You're turning all the heads around in every place you go.
> You've tested all the pieces so you know they all will fit,
> You're the ultimatest, up-to-datest identikit.
>
> Image image image, image day and night,
> Image image image, the image must be right.
> Image image image, it's the only thing you know,
> Image image image, you're the star of your own show.
>
> © Andrew Evans, 1983

It is nevertheless the 'personal' songs that have the most overall impact and are valued for their words as well as their music. Such songs reveal much more of the inner emotions and seek to identify particular human traits that resonate with the experiences and thoughts of many of us:

> Don't think that I'm indifferent,
> Don't think that I don't care.
> Although we've never spoken,
> I've always known you're there.

I see your face before me,
I hear each word you say.
It's only when you're near me,
I have to turn away.

And I love you so,
Though you're so far away.
And it's all so strange,
Not a word to say.

How then to continue? If you want help with rhymes, use a rhyming dictionary – the end justifies the means. Expand your capabilities – you do not know what you can do until you do it. When you are writing songs, try singing them – many songwriters have ended up singing their own work, and usually better than other artists for whom they originally wrote. If you need a songwriting instrument and do not play one, learn the basics of keyboard or guitar; guitar is easier to learn, but keyboard is much more practical for recording via MIDI. Use other musicians to help you when you need it. If you are having difficulty with a rhythmic feel, get a drummer to help you establish the basic rhythm. If you need more sophisticated chords but cannot find them yourself, get a keyboard player or musician with a good knowledge of chords to show you some alternatives until you locate what 'sounds' right. If you like to work directly with sounds, get someone familiar with MIDI to show you samples and get the ones you need down on tape or into your computer software.

There is a learning process involved in all these stages. In terms of songs – both music and words – you may have to write ten to get one good one, or thirty to get a 'set' you can perform live. So do not attempt to judge the quality of your work until you have a broad selection of good, bad and indifferent efforts. Quantity not quality is the first essential. Do as much as you can, either finished or fragments, because:

- it gives you a good idea of your personal style and how it is developing
- it helps you distinguish good from average from bad
- it gives you a whole library of ideas you can later incorporate into other songs
- it keeps you writing regularly and gets you used to 'being' a songwriter.

Above all, the transition to professionalism consists of turning out work that needs no excuses. If you find yourself saying, 'I'm sorry about all the crossings-out; I hope you can read it', or 'I've got the song somewhere on this tape – it may be on the other side – just ignore the phone ringing in the middle and imagine the bass line which I haven't got round to doing yet...', then you are wasting other people's time and creating the distinct impression that you are not very serious. Your work should be visually attractive and filed in an organised way. Lyrics should be typed or printed wherever possible – you may need to show your lyrics to people who could further your career. Keep your compositions in a loose-leaf file. If using a word-processor, store printouts in the same way. Finished work is necessary for any proper musical use.

When and where to write

There are generally two sorts of songs: inspirational ones and perspirational ones. The inspired ones can come in five minutes: they seem to be 'already worked out' and little effort is needed to get them together. This is because they have followed the classic creative process – idea–incubation–realisation. Your mind has done the work for you while you were unaware of it. Sometimes this happens during sleep and, if it does, get some paper the moment you wake and write it down instantly. This also applies to inspiration in general – whether you are in traffic, with friends, or shopping in a supermarket, make an instant note of any sudden inspiration. Beg or borrow something to write with and note down as much as you can: words, chords and melody line (e.g. CCDBCD).

These 'instant' songs are often very elegantly put together and have a natural flow and meaning – your own brain is capable of amazing feats of artistry if left to its own unconscious devices. If such songs are incomplete, the problem is finishing them, because it is difficult to match this inspirational quality and the added bits can appear monotonously contrived. If this happens, come back to it and by then your inner processes may have moved forward to a better solution.

Worked-on songs come into being through perspiration, patience and a certain amount of 'craft' – familiarity with the writing process and how to make things happen. The ideas may come more slowly and may be less inherently artistic, but after knocking ideas into shape a good product can gradually emerge.

Writing at an instrument has the advantage that you can try out different alternatives directly, and quickly keep or discard ideas. This sort of 'fooling around', waiting for ideas to come, can be quite useful, but does have the disadvantage that you may be skirting around the real 'essence' of a song, only changing the mechanics. A more natural spirit of creation can be achieved by allowing your imagination to do the visualising. Get away from your instruments, if possible, into a more conducive environment. This varies with individuals. Some like an empty hotel room, some a park or the countryside, some a train, some a busy café. Others like rhythmic stimulation, such as walking. The time of day is also helpful – some write best at night, some in the early morning, some in the afternoon.

Never underestimate your brain – it never sleeps. It carries on rearranging, modifying and restructuring material during both sleep and waking hours. It works on material when you are doing any number of other things. Rather than getting your conscious mind to labour on when no inspiration is coming, pass the whole thing over to your inner mental processes, and come back to it later. If the song being germinated hits a sympathetic chord somewhere inside you, it will grow and spark off other ideas quite naturally.

Copyright

In Britain, copyright comes into being from the moment a song is written down or recorded. Protecting copyright can be done as follows.

- Mark demos, scores, song sheets, etc. with the copyright sign © together with the year the song was written and the name(s) of the writer(s) of the lyrics and music.
- Deposit all such marked material in a bank or with a solicitor, or send them back to yourself by registered post, keeping them unopened with the posting slip.
- Get copyright signed to a publisher, who protects it and collects any money that becomes due to you.
- Join the Performing Rights Society (or the equivalent in another country) – they can supply details of eligibility.

The money you make out of copyright comes mainly from recordings and radio/television play. Sheet music is becoming steadily less lucrative, but a publishing deal can help generate new work if publishers promote songs. Smaller companies may be more dedicated than larger ones when it comes to promotional purposes, even if they have less overall influence and access to foreign markets – it depends how much interest the majors have in you. A larger company may also loan money for demos, recouping it later. But if little promotion results from a deal, the writer is 30–40 per cent better off owning his own publishing rights, and many start their own companies to do this. Pressure may be put on artists to sign to a record company's own publishers, but the artist is free to negotiate, and may prefer two separate deals giving two chances of promotion.

CHAPTER 11

Counselling and Healthcare for Performers

The performer in the UK is fortunate in having access to some of the best specialist help available anywhere. Britain was one of the first countries to embrace the idea that performing artists had a unique profile and set of problems, and thus a different kind of healthcare programme could and should be provided to meet their needs. This was helped by two other factors – the practical one being the support of all the unions and organisations involved. The Musicians Union has given generously since the start, and support from Equity has steadily increased. The Equity Trust Fund helped from the start, and so, notably, did the Musicians Benevolent Fund and the Royal Society of Musicians. The Dancers Resettlement Trust and Fund, now called the Dancers Career Development trust, provided generous and skilled support for dancers with the main companies and also some of the independents. We have good unions in the UK and they didn't need much persuading that the health and emotional welfare of their members was a priority: on the contrary they took the initiative in many ways.

The other key factor was the enthusiasm of the doctors, psychologists, counsellors and physical therapists themselves. The pioneers were all active in the arts and had good first-hand knowledge of the life of the performer – in the British Performing Arts Medical Trust (BPAMT), Dr Ian James was a violinist and Dr Garfield Davies a singer; in the International Society for the Study of Tensions in Performance, Carola Grindea was a notable pianist and teacher; in Arts Psychology Consultants, Andrew Evans was a professional bassist, Catherine Butler a professional oboist, Angelica MacArthur a professional dancer and Martin Lloyd-Elliott a fashion photographer. Dr Glenn Wilson, who organised the two first big international conferences in the UK at the Institute of Psychiatry, was a professional singer.

The combination of energy and innovation from such naturally creative personalities, and intimate and extensive knowledge of the profession, moved research and practice along at a rapid rate. Other enthusiasts joined in and cross-fertilised long discussions at conferences and in various committees, much new work was published in the journals of the above organisations, and textbooks were written by Garfield Davies, Andrew Evans, Glenn Wilson, Carola Grindea, Dr Ian Winspur and Dr Kit Wynn-Parry amongst others. Directories of specialist practitioners were compiled, and this new network spanned the whole of the UK within ten years.

Since the late 1980s, when all this mushroomed into being, innovation and constant activity has inevitably given way to a more long-term administrative approach, and all the above organisations have slimmed down into viable economic units. BPAMT leads the medical side of healthcare, ISSTIP continues with regular clinics and postural help at the London College of Music and is starting a course there to train other practitioners, and Arts Psychology Consultants continues to see a wide range of performers and creatives to give psychological help.

Psychologists like Martin Lloyd-Elliott, Andrew Evans and Glenn Wilson were increasingly in demand by the media in the 1990s because of their work with celebrities, and are now familiar TV 'talking heads' on fame documentaries and chat shows. They broadcast regularly, are often quoted in magazines, have written books and lectured on a range of media subjects like fame, escapism and body language, are involved in selecting contestants for shows like *The Race* and *The Big Trip*, and act as consultants for the new style *Big Brother*-type shows. The importance given to celebrities in modern culture has meant a lot of new media work for psychologists and the need to study the effects of fame – particularly overnight fame – on performers, though it has not had much impact on the medical and postural specialists.

The profile of performers making use of the healthcare facilities of the above organisations reveals some interesting information, and some of the data from the early 1990s is given below.

London arts clinics, 1990-1994

It is interesting to compare the data from the three main arts clinics seeing performers in London – The British Performing Arts Medicine Trust (BPAMT), Arts Psychology Consultants (APC), and the International Society for the Study of Tensions in Performance (ISSTIP) clinic at the London College of Music. The ISSTIP clinic is run by piano teacher and posture specialist Carola Grindea, who has developed the Grindea Technique to help musicians and other performers liberate their body of negative tensions in practising and performance. This clinic offers a multi-practitioner approach. Andrew Evans is the psychological advisor and Dr C.B. Wynn-Parry is the medical consultant and attends once a month.

	ISSTIP	BPAMT	APC
Number	363	478	199
Male %	37	35.5	50
Female %	63	64.5	50
Average age	26	31	n/a
Years of data	5 (90–4)	1 (94)	5 (90–4)

Using the categories established by the Arts Council, the percentages for each section of the arts are:

	ISSTIP	BPAMT	APC
Music	96.4	80	79
Dance	1.7	7	5
Drama	.3	9	7.5
Media/Art/Lit	1.6	4	8.5

The breakdown by profession shows an ISSTIP sample composed almost entirely of musicians. The choice of a music college setting appears to bias the numbers considerably towards musicians, though both BPAMT and Arts Psychology Consultants show a similar bias. On the face of it musicians seem more willing to seek direct help from performance arts organisations, while dancers and actors are currently more private in this respect. Within music, the breakdown of type of music was:

	ISSTIP	BPAMT	APC
Classical %	98	n/a	79
Pop %	2	n/a	21

In the setting of a classical music college, ISSTIP again shows a considerable bias to classical musicians which is not mirrored in the Arts Psychology Consultants split of 79 to 21 per cent, nor in the pool of London musicians in general. It has to be admitted, though, that performance anxiety is particularly rife in the classical population. As for the employed status of our general sample, this was:

	ISSTIP	BPAMT	APC
Professional %	36	79	66.8
Semi-pro %	.6	6	3
Amateur %	3.8	2	4.5
Students %	51.2	13	25.7
Teachers %	8.4	n/a	n/a

In view of the college setting, ISSTIP clinics see a proportionately larger number of students and teachers than BPAMT or APC. Even so, the fact that 36 per cent of ISSTIP clients are professional musicians does show that the clinic is known and used by a much wider clientele than would normally be internal to the London College of Music.

Within the music clients, there was a split as follows regarding chosen instrument:

	ISSTIP	BPAMT	APC
Strings %	29.0	18.1	23.0
Wind %	7.9	8.4	11.5
Brass %	2.9	7.2	6.7
Percussion %	0.9	8.4	7.4
Keyboard instruments %	36.0	19.3	8.9
Plucked instruments %	7.0	25.3	10.3
Voice %	15.0	13.3	27.0
Conductors %	0.9	n/a	3.7
Composers %	0.3	n/a	1.5

The most obvious feature of this is that the ISSTIP clinics have an unexpectedly high percentage of keyboard players, probably a bias due to the fact that Carola Grindea is particularly well known in keyboard circles. Carola is the initial point of contact for all those who attend. In 51.5 per cent of cases, she has dealt directly with the presenting problem, the treatment being postural adjustment, control of the player-instrument interaction, and breathing control. This leaves 42.7 per cent of cases which were seen by a medical specialist, usually Dr Kit Wynn-Parry, and a further 5.8 per cent of cases which were seen by other practitioners, mainly specialised arts psychologists and typically for performance anxiety, motivation problems and general personal issues. The data breakdown is as follows:

	ISSTIP	BPAMT	APC
Medicine %	42.7	79	n/a
Psychology %	5.8	13	100
Posture/Physio %	51.5	8	n/a

Inevitably, the nature of any organisation will determine the primary service offered to those who use it. The primary focus in the ISSTIP clinics is on posture control, breathing and music ergonomics, with a secondary emphasis on medical interventions and a tertiary emphasis on psychological methods. This would be exactly the other way around in Arts Psychology Consultants, who understandably deal with the psychological issues of performers and counsel them on their careers. BPAMT being a medical trust run by doctors would favour medical intervention of all kinds. Clearly a large number of musicians are using all these clinics – students, working professionals and teachers alike. They seem to get what the clinics are most equipped to offer, whether this exactly suited the problem not being clearly specified by the data. The client profile is certainly largely congruent with the profile of the clinic itself.

What help is available?

The whole range of help available may be a little bewildering at first sight, so here are some basic definitions of who is who.

The psychologist

Psychology is the study of human behaviour in all its forms, and its theory is made up of a large number of accurate and reliable 'studies' of varied aspects of human life. All psychologists do a three-year degree course followed by further study in their speciality. Occupational psychologists deal with careers, psychometric tests and people at work; clinical psychologists deal with mental health and brain function; and counselling psychologists use various therapy methods, including cognitive or behavioural approaches.

The counsellor

Counselling describes individual or group work which aims to create a good working environment for solving problems and increasing the positive self-worth of clients. Sessions usually last for fifty minutes and take place weekly, but counselling does not have to be long term. As well as general counsellors, there are specialised ones. They might concentrate on counselling students, for example, or on people who need specific help with their careers or in dealing with stress.

The psychotherapist and psychoanalyst

Psychotherapy covers longer term work done in greater depth, working with childhood memories, dreams, the unconscious, and the 'patient's' subjective perception of the therapist, called 'transference'. Sessions take place at least once a week, sometimes twice or more, and therapists expect a long-term commitment. General psychotherapists draw on the whole available theory from Freud to the present day, while those that train and specialise in the classical methods, such as those of Freud and Jung, call themselves psychoanalysts or 'analysts' for short.

The psychiatrist

The psychiatrist is a doctor who goes on to specialise in mental health. As a doctor he is authorised to prescribe drugs, and typically is attached to a hospital unit where he looks after patients with more serious mental problems, some needing ongoing medication.

The postural specialist or physical therapist

Posture work is typically done by teachers of the Alexander and Feldenkreis Techniques. Both are excellent for musicians and have a long history of positive results. Physiotherapy also deals with posture and ergonomics and has an important role in correcting misuse of the body. Osteopaths and chiropractors aim to heal the body using similar techniques like manipulation, and give good results with performers. Massage is another useful type of therapy.

The medical specialist
Certain medical specialists are particularly important to musicians. Ear, nose and throat (ENT) specialists cover hearing and the use of the voice; orthopaedic specialists deal with problems with bones and joints and the treatment of injuries; and occupational-health specialists are concerned with health issues related to people's jobs.

The complementary medicine practitioner
Complementary medicine is a developing field to which the musician is often attracted for its relaxed and informal treatment methods and its 'spiritual' belief system. Some methods, such as acupuncture and homeopathy, have a long tradition, while others are part of a rapidly expanding culture of alternative methodologies. The effectiveness of such methods may include wider issues than absolute scientific proof.

The creative therapist
Music therapy, art therapy, dance and movement therapy, drama therapy and psychodrama are often called the 'creative therapies', and are sometimes referred to as the 'expressive therapies'. They use the conventional art forms to elicit creative and expressive results in their subjects, and can be remarkably effective for actors, dancers and musicians. Some methods use the art form alone; others combine it with a therapeutic 'talking through' of issues and problems. Since they access non-verbal feelings and emotions, they can be both subtle and powerful in their effect. Therapists in this field are arts professionals with an intensive training in their particular therapy form.

Therapy methods

Several different types of counselling can be of help to performers. Career counselling helps when there is change in career, as with dancers at transition and actors and musicians following burnout, unemployment or injury. Personal and couples counselling helps with general issues. With specific performance issues like stage fright, motivation, peak performance or technical problems such as embouchure and bow shake, it clearly helps to talk to a specialist who is familiar with these issues and has seen a number of similar cases. In many cases this will be a psychologist or counsellor with a performing background, and fortunately there are a small but increasing number of these.

Counsellors perceive problems differently. When asked how he dealt with stage fright, a well-known sex therapist replied that he looked to improve sexual confidence, at which point the stage fright spontaneously improved. Similar statements have been made by doctors treating general health and counsellors treating the whole person – the idea is that when the person is better the problem is seen in a better perspective, and so spontaneously improves. In some cases of specific performance problems this is true, but in some it is not true. Studies have been undertaken to see if Alexander Technique helps performance anxiety, for instance, but the gains are hard to substantiate. The same is true of hypnotherapy.

In cases where a specific approach to the problem as well as the person is needed, such as performance anxiety, it helps to have a therapist who has the knowledge to deal directly with the issue presented by the performer. A method such as that outlined in this book goes directly to the problem and has helped in the vast majority of cases. Since such a method has already been worked out and refined over fifteen years with over 100 cases of performers, it clearly ought to be capable of achieving results and should also be faster than a generalised approach, needing only a short number of sessions in many cases. When it comes to dealing with problems like RSI and the dystonias, which have crucial effects on performers' careers, it is necessary to have as much accurate and up-to-date knowledge as possible, and this means attending conferences, reading research papers and talking to sufferers and specialists alike.

Above all there should be sympathy and understanding for the life and aims of the performer. This seems obvious but is not totally the case. Alcoholics have been advised to avoid the stress of surviving in an insecure profession where there can be a lot of competition and social drinking. Creative people with rich fantasy lives have been advised that their 'art' is the problem and that the therapeutic solution is to give it up. The idea that art is essentially a type of 'sublimation' of real life emotions is put forward by Ernest Jones: 'When one considers the material used in the five arts – paint, clay, stone, words and sounds – any psychologist must conclude that the passionate interest in bringing an orderliness out of chaos must signify at the same time an extraordinary sublimation of the most primitive infantile enjoyments and the most extreme denial of them.' This is a view that a large number of specialist counsellors would strongly disagree with, seeing the performing arts as a profound expression of the essence of humanity.

The performer's language

At its most alien, the language of the business can be full of jargon and technical terms. Dance has its technical language, much of it in French. The theatre is full of superstitions, sayings and technical language. Music probably has the most jargon of all – not only familiar terms such as 'gig' (job), 'dep' (substitute) and 'band' (orchestra), but more specialised terms like 'toys' (percussion), 'kit' (drum kit) and 'axe' (guitar). In addition, there is the rich slang like 'out to lunch' (weird), or 'cooking' (playing well), and a variety of sardonic understatements like 'he doesn't care, does he?' (he's just done something totally outrageous) or 'this is what we will find... we will find this...' (resignation at having to suffer another totally outrageous incident).

A musician talking freely to a colleague may say, 'I mainly do toys, and at the moment I'm depping for this guy on kit and so it's back to paradiddles again.' A violinist may say, 'I'm happy in the seconds but I was put in the firsts the other night and I freaked out on second desk.' A horn player may say, 'As you know, horns play 1–3 2–4 and I knew that on second horn my chances of a trial were pretty limited when they were auditioning for a new number one.' A number of musicians start in counselling with exactly this level of technical information about the problem within the first minutes of sitting down.

It may be difficult for any counsellor to know the full range of 'music speak', partly because it varies within jazz, rock and the classical world. Then there is all the dance language, much of it in French, such as, 'Why do I always put my back out when I do a *grand jeté en tournant?*' And then the theatre and film jargon. The more the performer can talk freely, however, the easier it may be to access particular problems. A therapist can talk for a whole session with an actor about how to deal with agents, for instance. To avoid frequent interventions, it is an advantage to know not only what such technical talk is about, but also the actual performing realities it is based on.

The performer as a counselling client

The performer in therapy starts with one important advantage – he or she is likely to be creative by nature and a good problem-solver. This means being able to play an active part in getting better and gaining insight into problems. Many performers are almost 'ideal' clients in counselling, and can make substantial progress quickly. In terms of profession, the performer may be mainly a 'performer' or mainly a 'creator'. The 'creative performers' are typically rock and jazz performers whose improvisations are 'the sound of surprise', as music critic Whitney Balliett put it. All share the need to eliminate conflicting inner motivations and to neutralise feelings that people are hostile to their work or expect too much of them. Since most people in the business are self-employed, self-dependent and self-absorbed in terms of the work they do, they are also liable to be very sensitive to any loss of their capacity to function properly. They may blame themselves and become depressed when they feel their capacities are being threatened or taken away.

Counselling students

In the life of the student there may be particular anxieties over teachers, exams and auditions, money, performing in front of others and career choices. Some very useful data comes from a 1990 study of one term's counselling at a leading UK music college by Andrew Evans, and contains data on the sixteen students seen individually.

Total subjects: 16 (8 male, 8 female)
Average age: 25
Country of origin: 8 UK, 8 non-UK
Type of course: Advanced 8, Performers 5, Graduate 2, Intermediate 1
Year at college: First 11, Second 1, Third 3, Fourth 1
Instrument: Voice 7, Strings 5, Conducting 2, Wind 1, Piano 1
Average sessions: 3 per student

Presenting symptoms:

Performance problems including stage fright	4
Medical performance problems needing referral	4
Careers analysis and motivational counselling	4
Academic problems with course, etc	2
Personal counselling	1
General problems	1
TOTAL:	16

The average age of twenty-five is older than average for the college as a whole, and one half of those seen were from outside the UK, more than expected from the general student ratio. There was also an above-expected proportion of first years, and also advanced students. A recurring profile is of a certain type of student – a foreign student, older than the typical student, doing an Advanced course and who has just arrived at college. Older and foreign students are typical 'counselling' categories in the student population, and this is borne out in the data. Counselling was typically around performance problems such as motivation, adjustment to course and course tutor, stage fright when performing or auditioning, and career counselling for a future professional career.

The data shows that while they have some degree of typical personal problems during their time at college, performing arts students are already very competitive, worried about their course, tutor and progress, and liable to the same performing anxieties and career issues as their older brethren in the profession. Some, indeed, are already earning good money from performing. So a specialist counsellor is really needed to deal with these concerns, which can be as technical in nature as with performers as a whole. Ideally, there should be a complete team approach to student care for performers.

A team approach for performance students

When a team of healthcare practitioners is used, it is possible to make significant gains by enabling such practitioners to operate within their particular area of expertise. In the case of any student population, a number of issues recur: accommodation difficulties, growing up, loneliness, encounters with the opposite sex, academic expectations, and so forth. For these problems, a general counsellor or therapist experienced with students is particularly effective. Equally, for the usual range of student medical problems a student medical service is required, whether on- or off-campus. A basic service would thus include:

- a student counsellor
- access to a General Practice.

In this case, the practitioners would rely on referring out any specialised problems. A more client-centered approach would include specialists. A team with a more specialised range of abilities would thus include:

- a counsellor specialising in performers
- a doctor attached to the college, with acquired knowledge of performers' problems.

A comprehensive team would include:

- a psychologist specialising in performers
- a doctor specially trained in dealing with performers
- further specialists as required, e.g. Alexander Technique.

In all these cases there will be a need for referring certain students to specialists. These include singers with problems of the ear, nose and throat, and performers with muscular/skeletal problems, tendonitis, repetitive strain injury, etc. The more specialised the regular college practitioners, the more likely they are to have already established a network of referrals to appropriate specialists, whom they may be familiar with through attending conferences or through personal contact and recommendation.

Ideally there should be a further range of programmed services to help the student to understand and cope with life and work in the profession. This would offer some or all of the following.

A careers advice service

Attending a performing arts college is an important transitional stage in the life of any performer. It may be the last period in which the full range of support services of a teaching body is available. After this students are, at worst, left to sink or swim in the profession. A number have later, in counselling, related how they learned about the profession through trial and error, with the result that decisions were taken which were subsequently regretted.

A range of 'open forum' talks to students

The attitude of students to a counselling service depends on how that service is perceived. Students who perceive a counsellor as a person who only deals with personal anxiety may deprive themselves of other equally important functions. Sport psychologists are now commonplace in athletics and sport, and are an accepted resource for healthy competitive people who want to enhance their range of skills and mental attitudes. Such help should be available in the same way to performers seeking to improve the quality of performance through such techniques as Alexander, Inner Game and peak performance, and who want to avoid stressors, maximise their motivation, make good career choices and learn how to prepare effectively and avoid burnout later in life.

Training for staff in the psychology and problem-range of musicians

As professionals themselves, members of the academic staff have an insight into the life of a performer, and many have a very good insight indeed. What the psychologist can add to this insight is an understanding of the psychology which underlies it. In addition, the counsellor who has gone through training in listening and counselling skills can offer techniques of dealing with situations where a counselling approach is required. These may be quite different from teaching skills.

Teamwork in clinic settings

We have already mentioned some key team members who get involved in medical, postural and psychological issues. Whether the problem is one of assessment, treatment or rehabilitation – or that of simultaneously treating a physical problem and a general case of performance anxiety – there is an obvious need to compare notes on a shared patient simply to optimise the treatment and share in any extra insights that one or other has obtained. Probably even more important than this is to offer the patient a coherent, believable and co-ordinated treatment plan. It is the patient who is by far the most confused, frustrated and not least out of pocket in being passed around willy nilly from one specialist to the next, and the suffering of the patient should be alleviated as much as possible by clear advice as to who is involved, why they are involved, what can and can't be done, what time-scale to expect, and simply how to convert free-floating anxiety and medico-speak overload into a credible recovery plan. If this can include actual practice plans, examinations at regular periods, ongoing psychological support and explanations of what is happening in plain language, so much the better.

I have been very impressed by the work of Dr Richard Norris in the USA in exhaustively analysing the ergonomics of performance and designing recovery programmes that are optimised down to the smallest significant detail. His thoroughness and care is a model for us all, and his book is included in the references.

The concept of the performance psychologist

By using the term 'performance psychologist' it may be possible to introduce performers to the idea that they have at their disposal the sort of resource that sportspeople call a 'sport psychologist'. If this serves to enlighten them to the realisation that a psychologist is not just a 'concerned therapist' who dwells on problems, but a friendly, accessible and expert resource that promotes added efficiency, then hopefully more of our performers will take advantage of the progress in expert treatment that has been steadily growing over the last decade into a whole new area of professional help that they can be proud of using.

Just as the sport psychologist needs to have some social role with clients and also do some degree of coaching, so the performance psychologist needs to go to concerts and shows to assess how progress is working in practice. Certain issues like stage fright also benefit from a coaching approach, where clients are taught to understand their mental and emotional responses to adrenalin. This inevitably takes the psychologist outside such therapy sacred cows as not socialising with the client and not being directive.

Performance specialists have found that in practice this is not as serious an issue as it is made out to be, and that performers are flexible enough to respond well. The flexible hours of the performer, in addition, require the psychologist to respond with open-ended planning of sessions. A dancer, for instance, usually gets her schedule on Friday and only then can plan session times. Sessions for busy actors and studio musicians may need to be changed at short notice as work or rehearsals come in. Performers on tour may have two sessions in one week followed by two months off. Clearly they are not interested in paying for sessions during such a tour. Again, this upsets some sacred cows of classical psychotherapy, but modern counsellors usually adapt easily.

The future of 'arts and health'

There is a traditional link between healthcare and the arts – many performers do charity work and some later become counsellors. Doctors love the theatre and are frequently amateur musicians. In many countries in Europe, Australia, Canada and the United States they have started important multi-disciplinary networks for medicine and the performing arts. Conferences bring together specialists of all kinds, and information is exchanged between doctors, teachers, psychologists, counsellors, posture specialists, union officials and performers themselves. Academic courses are starting up and we are moving towards the first series of certificates and diplomas in this specialist field. Clinics are being set up in Britain and abroad that use a team approach, and close co-operation between practitioners is rapidly increasing the pool of available knowledge and the ability to refer performers within the arts and health networks.

In addition, funding for treatment comes from leading bodies like the Musicians Union, the Musicians Benevolent Fund, the Equity Trust Fund and the Royal Society of Musicians of Great Britain, all of whom are particularly committed to the health of the performers. The United States has a larger network, with clinics on both the East and West coasts, some attached to institutes of the performing arts. Both countries have enormously important performing arts industries, so an adequate health network to deal with their healthcare issues is entirely appropriate.

A healthier future for performers

Although the performing arts has seen a number of wounding financial cutbacks in recent years which have left many with less work, performers themselves are showing some changes in attitude that are entirely positive. There was a period in both the cinema and in jazz and rock history where it was not only acceptable to drink and take drugs to the point of being a physical wreck, it was considered to be 'paying one's dues' and living up to the image of hard-living dead heroes. This has changed considerably for the better, not only with a saner younger generation, but with a healthier generation of older stars who have put earlier excesses behind them and who, like Sir Anthony Hopkins, are more than ready to talk to younger generations about their past lives and previous excesses and how they have transcended them. The 'tired and emotional' luvvie has become the mineral water-sipping friendly and alert career performer.

Performers are not only paying more attention to their health, they are also talking more frankly about issues that concern them and reading more self-help books. They are finding stage fright unacceptable in an age when it can be successfully dealt with, and are taking active steps to reduce stress. The huge increase in media interest in celebrity performers and new faces has raised the status of the performer considerably in the public eye, and because of the Internet and 'indie culture' there is also more widespread public acceptance and enthusiasm for 'minority music' such as jazz and World music. Performers are no longer required to become teenage misfits as they were in the pioneering 1950s and 1960s, though the rebel still exists in the form of the rocker and street-wise rapper. Nowadays jazz is something you can learn in music college, and the stars of yesterday are the professors of today.

The performer's life may never be as widely accepted as that of the establishment professions, such as medicine and law, but within it actors, dancers and musicians have hopefully become a happier breed. It would be good to imagine that the richness the performing arts has brought into the lives of so many people may one day be reflected in the respect and affection given to those who have made a lifetime commitment to creating and performing it.

Appendix

Personality data for performers

Number and percentages of subjects

	All Performers	Dance	Drama	Music (Class.)	Music (Popular)	(Music Total)	Unemp. Performers)
Subjects:	298	56	56	98	88	186	98
Percentages:	100	19	19	33	29	62	33

MBTI preferences

	Perf.	Dan.	Dra.	Mcla.	Mpop.	Mtot.	Unemp.
Introvert %	57	61	53	59	54	57	53
Extravert %	43	39	47	41	46	43	47
Intuitive %	79	69	83	87	75	82	73
Sensing %	21	31	17	13	25	18	27
Feeling %	60	61	57	60	60	60	60
Thinking %	40	39	43	40	40	40	40
Perceiving %	59	35	77	55	71	62	79
Judging %	41	65	23	45	29	38	21

Scores:

	Perf.	Dan.	Dra.	Mcla.	Mpop.	Mtot.	Unemp.
Introvert	6	6	4	8	4	6	3
Intuitive	6	8	20	19	18	18	17
Feeling	4	6	6	5	2	3	3
Perceiving	6	6	4	8	4	6	3

16PF first order factors

	Perf.	Dan.	Dra.	Mcla.	Mpop.	Mtot.	Unemp.
A Warmth	4.9	4.9	5.2	4.5	5.0	4.7	5.1
B Reasoning ability	7.5	7.5	7.2	8.0	7.3	7.7	7.0
C Mood stability	5.0	5.5	5.2	4.6	4.9	4.8	5.0
E Competitiveness	7.1	6.7	7.2	7.1	7.3	7.2	7.0
F Impulsivity	6.7	6.6	7.1	6.3	7.2	6.7	7.2
G Conscientiousness	4.6	5.5	3.7	5.1	4.1	4.6	3.8
H Boldness	6.3	6.7	6.4	6.1	6.3	6.2	6.1
I Sensitivity	7.6	7.1	7.0	7.8	8.1	7.9	7.8
L Suspiciousness	6.2	5.8	6.2	6.3	6.3	6.3	6.5
M Imagination	6.6	6.7	6.2	6.7	6.5	6.6	6.4
N Shrewdness	3.7	4.0	3.7	3.5	3.7	3.6	3.8

	Perf.	Dan.	Dra.	Mcla.	Mpop.	Mtot.	Unemp.
O Worry	5.7	5.3	6.0	5.7	5.7	5.7	5.6
Q1 Radicalness	6.3	5.7	6.5	6.0	6.9	6.4	6.7
Q2 Self-sufficiency	5.6	5.6	5.2	6.1	5.2	5.7	5.3
Q3 Self-control	4.2	5.1	3.1	4.5	4.1	4.3	3.9
Q4 Stress	6.0	5.8	6.0	6.2	6.0	6.1	5.7

16PF second order factors

	Perf.	Dan.	Dra.	Mcla.	Mpop.	Mtot.	Unemp.
Extraversion	6.0	6.1	6.4	5.4	6.3	5.8	6.2
Anxiety	6.3	5.7	6.6	6.4	6.5	6.4	6.4
Tough poise	4.5	4.8	5.1	4.5	4.0	4.3	4.3
Independence	7.2	6.8	7.3	7.1	7.5	7.3	7.3
Control	4.2	5.3	3.0	4.7	3.8	4.3	3.5
Neuroticism	5.7	5.4	5.7	6.0	5.7	5.8	5.7
Leadership	5.0	5.8	4.5	5.0	4.8	4.9	4.7
Creativity	7.6	7.4	7.0	8.3	7.5	7.9	7.2

Belbin team roles (from 16PF)

	Perf.	Dan.	Dra.	Mcla.	Mpop.	Mtot.	Unemp.
Plant	7.6	7.4	7.0	8.3	7.5	7.9	7.2
Resourcer	5.6	5.9	5.5	5.2	5.7	5.4	5.5
Shaper	6.9	6.1	7.6	6.8	7.1	7.0	7.0
Monitor	4.8	5.1	4.5	5.0	4.5	4.8	4.6
Completer	6.2	6.3	5.6	6.6	5.9	6.3	5.6
Chair	4.5	5.4	3.9	4.6	4.3	4.5	3.9
Team Worker	4.4	4.9	4.5	3.9	4.5	4.2	4.6
Company Worker	2.8	3.9	2.3	2.9	2.2	2.6	2.2

Holland occupational preference scores and mentions in top 3

	Perf.	Dan.	Dra.	Mcla.	Mpop.	Mtot.	Unemp.
Artistic	25	22	26	25	26	26	28
Social	20	20	21	20	19	19	20
Enterprising	16	16	16	16	16	16	15
Investigative	13	12	10	14	14	14	14
Realistic	9	8	9	9	13	11	13
Conventional	10	13	9	9	9	9	8
Artistic %	31	31	32	30	32	31	32
Social %	29	30	31	28	26	27	27
Enterprising %	20	20	21	19	19	19	19
Investigative %	11	6	7	16	12	14	12
Realistic %	5	2	6	3	10	7	9
Conventional %	5	12	4	3	1	2	1

References and Recommended Reading

Chapter 1 – The Performer's Personality

Buck, *Psychology for Musicians* (Oxford)

Evans, A., *The Secrets of Musical Confidence* (HarperCollins, UK, 1994). Please note that this book is presently only available from Arts Psychology Consultants, 29 Argyll Mansions, Hammersmith Rd, London W14 8QQ, at price £8 including postage and packing.

McClelland, D., *Hollywood on Hollywood – Tinsel Town Talks* (Winchester MA USA, 1985)

Myers, I.B. and Myers, P.B., *Gifts Differing* (Consulting Psychologists Press, Palo Alto, 1980)

Shuter-Dyson, R. and Gabriel, C., *The Psychology of Musical Ability* (Methuen, London, 1981)

Sloboda, J., *The Musical Mind* (Clarendon, UK, 1986)

Sloboda, J., 'Musical Excellence – how does it develop?' In Howe, M.J.A. (Ed.), *Encouraging the Development of Exceptional Skills and Talent* (British Psychological Society, Leicester, 1990)

Wills, G. and Cooper, C., *Pressure Sensitive* (Sage Books, UK, 1988)

Chapter 2 – Motivation

Berne, E., *Games People Play* (Penguin, 1968)

Berne, E., *What Do You Say After You Say Hello?* (Corgi, 1989)

Bull, Stephen J., *Sport Psychology* (The Crowood Press, UK 1991)

Gibson, I., *The Shameful Life of Salvador Dali* (Faber, London, 1996)

Lane, Y., *The Psychology of the Actor* (Secker and Warburg, London, 1959)

Winspur, I. and Wynn-Parry, B. *The Musician's Hand, A Clinical Guide* (Martin Dunitz, London, 1998)

Chapter 3 – Self-image, Identity and Confidence

Berne, E., *What Do You Say After You Say Hello?* (Corgi, 1989)

Bettelheim, B., *The Uses of Enchantment* (Penguin, 1988)

James, M. and Jongeward, D., *Born to Win* (Signet, 1978)

Chapter 4 – Preparation, Performance and Public Speaking

Bates, B.C., *The Way of the Actor* (Century Hutchinson, London, 1986)

Hamilton, L.H., *The Person Behind the Mask: A guide to Performing Arts Psychology* (Ablex, 1998)

Lane, Y., *The Psychology of the Actor* (Secker and Warburg, London, 1959)

Wilson, G.D., *Psychology for Performing Artists: Butterflies and Bouquets* (Jessica Kingsley, London, 1994)

Chapter 5 – Peak Performance and 'the Zone'

Blackstone, J. and Josipovic, Z., *Zen for Beginners* (Writers and Readers, NY, 1986)

Green, B., *The Inner Game of Music* (Pan, 1986)

Havas, K., *Stage Fright* (Bosworth, 1986)

Chapter 6 – Managing Your Adrenalin

Fresnel, E., Eltaz, E., Bourgault R., '*Voix et trac – stress anxiete de performance*', *Medecin des Arts*, **18**:3–6, 1996

Fresnel, E., *Le Trac* (Editions Solal, Marseilles, 1999)

Muller, D.K. and Kupersmuti, J.R., 'Louiseville-Pach psychiatric problems of performing artists', *Medical Problems of Performing Artists*, **5**:19–22, 1990

Schultz, W., 'Analysis of a symphony orchestra. Sociological and sociophysical aspects'. In Pipatee, M. (Ed.), *Stress and Music* (Wilhelm Braumuller, Vienna, 1981)

Winspur, I. and Wynn-Parry, B., *The Musician's Hand, A Clinical Guide* (Martin Dunitz, London 1998)

Chapter 7 – Overcoming Performance Anxiety

Dawkins, R., *The Selfish Gene* (OUP, Oxford, 1989)

James, M. and Jongeward, D., *Born to Win* (Signet, 1978)

Wilson, Dr G.D., *Psychology and Performing Arts* (Swets and Zeitlinger, Amsterdam, 1991)

Chapter 8 – Stress, Burnout and Unemployment

Burns, D.D., *Feeling Good* (Wholecare, US, 1999)

Wills, G. and Cooper, C., *Pressure Sensitive* (Sage Books, UK, 1988)

Chapter 9 – Career Management

Boller, P.F. Jr and Davis, R.L., *Hollywood Anecdotes* (Macmillan, London, 1987)

Cary, D.S., *Hollywood's Children – An Inside Account of the Child Star Era* (Southern Methodist University Press, Dallas, US, 1978)

Davies, R. (Ed.), *The Kenneth Williams Diaries* (Harper Collins, London, 1993)

Evans, A., *This Virtual Life – Escapism and Simulation in our Media World* (Fusion Paperbacks, London, 2001)

Evans, A. and Wilson, Dr G., *Fame, the Psychology of Stardom* (Vision Paperbacks, London, 1998)

Herman, G., *Rock 'n' Roll Babylon* (Plexus, London, 1982)

Reprinted from Holmes T.H. and Rahe R.H., 'The Social Readjustment Rating Scale', *Journal of Psychosomatic Research*, 11:213–18, 1967, with permission from Elsevier Science

Kennedy, G., *Everything is Negotiable* (Business Books, UK, 1990)

Lindenfield, G., *Assert Yourself* (Thorsons, London, 1986)

Norris, R., *The Musician's Survival Manual; a Guide to Preventing and Treating Injuries in Instrumentalists*, The International Conference of Symphony and Opera Musicians (ICSOM)

Winspur, I. and Wynn-Parry, B., *The Musician's Hand, A Clinical Guide* (Martin Dunitz, London, 1998)

Chapter 10 – Creativity

Arieti, S., *Creativity, the Magic Synthesis* (Basic Books, NY, 1976)

Cary, D.S., *Hollywood's Children – An Inside Account of the Child Star Era* (Southern Methodist University Press, Dallas, US, 1978)

Evans, A., *This Virtual Life – Escapism and Simulation in our Media World* (Fusion Paperbacks, London, 2001)

Ghiselin, B., *The Creative Process* (Mentor, 1958)

Storr, A., *The Dynamics Of Creation* (Penguin, UK, 1983)

Storr, A., *Solitude* (Fontana, UK, 1989)

Chapter 11 – Counselling and Healthcare for Performers

Evans, A., 'Counselling in the Arts', *CAWD Journal* 6/90

Evans, A., *The Secrets of Musical Confidence* (HarperCollins, UK, 1994). Please note that this book is presently only available from Arts Psychology Consultants, 29 Argyll Mansions, Hammersmith Rd, London W14 8QQ, at price £8 including postage and packing.

Norris, R., *The Musician's Survival Manual; a Guide to Preventing and Treating Injuries in Instrumentalists*, The International Conference of Symphony and Opera Musicians (ICSOM)

Organisations helpful to performers

Arts Psychology Consultants
29 Argyll Mansions, Hammersmith Rd, London W14 8QQ
Tel: 020-7602-2707
Website: www.artsandmedia.com
E-mail: andy@artsandmedia.com

British Actors Equity Association
Tel: 020-7379-6000
Website: http://www.equity.org.uk/

The Actors Centre
Tel: 020-7240-3940
Website: http://www.actorscentre.co.uk/

Actorclub (John Cunningham)
Tel: 020-7267-2759
Website: http://www.actorclub.co.uk/

The Equity Trust Fund, Suite 222, Africa House, 64-78 Kingsway, London WC2B 6BD Tel: 020-7404-6041
E-mail: keith@equitytrustfund.freeserve.co.uk

Dancers Career Development
Suite 222, Africa House, 64–78 Kingsway, London WC2B 6BG
Tel: 020-7404-6141
E-mail: linda@thedcd.org.uk, www.thedcd.org.uk

International Organisation for the Transition of Professional Dancers
President: Paul Bronkhorst
IOTPD, c/o Kunsten Cultuur Pensionen
En Verzekering, Postbus 85806, 2508 CM Den Haag, The Netherlands
Website: www.transition-iotpd.org

The British Musicians Union
Tel. 020-7582-5566
Website: http://www.musiciansunion.org.uk/

BPAMT
Helpline 020-7240-4500 or 0845 602 0235
Website: http://www.bpamt.co.uk/

The Royal Society of Musicians, 10 Stratford Place, London W1C 1BA
Tel: 020-7629-6137

The Incorporated Society of Musicians
Tel: 020-7629-4413
Website: http://www.ism.org/

The Musicians Benevolent Fund
Tel: 020-7636-4481
Website: http://www.mbf.org.uk/

ISSTIP
Tel: 020-7373-7307
Website: http://www.musiciansgallery.com/start/health/isstip.htm

Dr. Garfield Davies
Voice Dept, The London Clinic, 149 Harley Street, London W1G 6DE
Email: dgarfielddavies@aol.com

Dystonia organisations:
Website: http://www.stic.net/users/brett/, http://www.dystonia-foundation.org/, http://www.dystonia.org.uk/dystoniasocietyh.html, http://www.dystonia-bb.org (The Musicians with Dystonia bulletin board)

Psychologists at Law (Personal Injury cases):
Website: www.psychlaw.org

Acknowledgements

MBTI and Myers–Briggs Type Indicator are registered trademarks of Consulting Psychologists Press Inc. (CPP)

16PF is copyright © 1972, 1979, 1986, 1991 by the Institute for Personality and Ability Testing Inc., PO Box 1188, Champaign, Illinois 61824-1188, USA. All rights reserved. Reproduced with permission, '16PF' is a trademark belonging to IPAT. The UK editions of the 16PF4 Questionnaire and the 16PF5 Questionnaire are published by ASE (IPAT's UK licensee), Chiswick High Road, London W4 5TF a division of nferNelson.

The Self Directed Search is published by PAR (Psychological Assessment Resources Inc.), PO Box 98, Odessa, Florida 33556

Data references

Arts Psychology Consultants: Andy Evans, 29 Argyll Mansions, Hammersmith Rd, London W14 8QQ, Tel: 020-7602-2707
BPAMT Tel: 020-7240-4500
ISSTIP: Carola Grindea, 28 Emperor's Gate, London SW7 4HS, Tel. 020-7373-7307

Dancers in Transition
Paper presented by Andrew Evans at the IOTPD Lausanne Symposium on the Transition of Dancers, 1995

Unemployment in the arts
Paper presented by Andrew Evans at the International Conference of Psychology and the Performing Arts, Institute of Psychiatry, 1990

The ISSTIP clinics
Paper presented by Andrew Evans at the ISSTIP Conference, 1997

Contact the author

Andy Evans
Arts Psychology Consultants,
29 Argyll Mansions
Hammersmith Rd, London W14 8QQ
Tel. 020-7602-2707
Website: www.artsandmedia.com
E-mail: andy@artsandmedia.com

Index